The Poetics of Intimacy
and the Problem
of Sexual Abstinence

PETER LANG
New York · Washington, D.C./Baltimore · Boston · Bern
Frankfurt am Main · Berlin · Brussels · Vienna · Oxford

Michael J. Hartwig

The Poetics of Intimacy and the Problem of Sexual Abstinence

PETER LANG
New York · Washington, D.C./Baltimore · Boston · Bern
Frankfurt am Main · Berlin · Brussels · Vienna · Oxford

Library of Congress Cataloging-in-Publication Data

Hartwig, Michael J.
The poetics of intimacy and the problem
of sexual abstinence / Michael J. Hartwig.
p. cm.
Includes bibliographical references and index.
1. Sexual abstinence–Religious aspects–Christianity. 2. Intimacy (Psychology)–Religious
aspects–Christianity. 3. Christian ethics. 4. Sexual ethics. I. Title.
BT708.H37 241'.66–dc21 99-053062
ISBN 978-0-8204-4885-5 (hardcover)
ISBN 978-1-4331-0781-8 (paperback)

Die Deutsche Bibliothek-CIP-Einheitsaufnahme

Hartwig, Michael J.:
The poetics of intimacy and the problem
of sexual abstinence / Michael J. Hartwig.
–New York; Washington, D.C./Baltimore; Boston; Bern;
Frankfurt am Main; Berlin; Brussels; Vienna; Oxford: Lang.
ISBN 978-0-8204-4885-5 (hardcover)
ISBN 978-1-4331-0781-8 (paperback)

Cover art by Michael J. Hartwig
Cover design by Lisa Dillon

The paper in this book meets the guidelines for permanence and durability
of the Committee on Production Guidelines for Book Longevity
of the Council of Library Resources.

© 2000, 2009 Peter Lang Publishing, Inc., New York
29 Broadway, 18th floor, New York, NY 10006
www.peterlang.com

Printed in the United States of America

Dedicated To

Donald F. Baker

Life Companion ☙ Friend
Gay Activist ☙ Educator
Child of God
Poet of Love

❖ Acknowledgments

I would like to acknowledge several individuals instrumental to the successful completion of this manuscript.

Thanks to my mother, Patricia Elaine Hartwig for her proofreading and constructive suggestions for style, wording and grammar. Thanks to her and my father, H. Rudolf Hartwig, for their support throughout the project and their lessons in poetic love.

Thanks to the many students who, through class discussions, papers and conversations, have helped me refine and develop much of this material.

Thanks to my former colleagues at Albertus Magnus College, particularly Jeremiah Coffey and Sean O'Connell, for their feedback, stimulating conversations about this material, and collegial support.

Thanks to my life companion, Donald F. Baker, for his patience, his constructive feedback, for lively discussions about the concepts found herein, and for the lessons in love that our relationship has provided.

❖ Table of Contents

❖ Preface

> "... *everyone becomes a poet whom Love touches.*"
> Plato—*Symposium*

Recent official Christian denominational teachings about human sexuality have been increasingly positive, describing sexuality as an integral part of one's identity and well-being. This stands in stark contrast to earlier views which often presented sexuality as an irrational, beastly, and defiling urge requiring a well-constituted virtue of chastity to keep it and all associated pleasures within the confines of marriage and its reproductive purposes. Contemporary pastors, educators, and ethicists speak about the graces of the body, the importance of sexuality in sustaining love between spouses, the critical stages of psychosexual development and their roles in personal identity formation, the importance of emotions and touch, and how fear of and aversion to sexuality hinder healthy interpersonal life.

Accompanying this shift in appreciation of sexuality, marriage is no longer regarded as an institution centered primarily around household management and reproductive purposes but a covenant of love and intimacy, a relationship within which partners create a safe place to become vulnerable and self-disclosive, sharing power in mutual affection and support.

The diminished vilification of sexuality and the shift in our understanding of marriage create a new set of problems for Christian sexual morality. First of all, how do people prepare for committed relationships of covenantal sexual love? Is the virtue of chastity, understood primarily as control of sexual desire and pleasure, sufficient? If not, how do young adults learn how to be appropriately vulnerable,[1] to embody intimacy in graceful ways, to share power with another, to decide whether a particular relationship warrants commitment, and how to sustain affection through the various seasons and moods of relational life? Does sexual abstinence prepare young adults for these kinds of virtues?

Second, traditional Christian sexual morality does not permit the divorced to remarry. But given our appreciation of the graces of committed sexual love, is this a reasonable and loving expectation, particularly considering current divorce rates and life expectancies? Many denominations have answered with a resounding "no," but the Roman Catholic Church still prohibits divorce and remarriage. Does such a policy, effectively mandating long-term or lifelong sexual abstinence for large numbers of adults, enable and support these individuals in their spiritual journeys or seriously jeopardize their well-being by depriving them access to the vital resources and graces of marriage?

Third, given current evidence of the successes of committed sexual relationships among gay men and lesbians, is it reasonable or loving to deprive them of the graces and resources of committed sexual relationships by mandating lifelong sexual abstinence? Mandating lifelong sexual abstinence for gay men and lesbians increases the risks of self-destructive behavior, promiscuity, disassociative personality patterns, and unnecessary alienation from their families, the Christian community, and society.

Finally, should those who traditionally fail to qualify for marriage, the disabled and mentally ill, also be deprived of the graces of sexual companionship? How does long-term or lifelong abstinence increase the suffering of the disabled and mentally ill? Does sexual intimacy provide important resources for overcoming or learning to live gracefully with one's disabilities?

There is little consideration given within contemporary Christian moral reflection to the harms caused by long-term and lifelong sexual abstinence. In my pastoral and educational work, countless individuals have shared with me their agony over the disparity between their actual sexual lives and the moral expectations of the Church. Whether it be single adults, the divorced, gay men and lesbians, or the disabled, many claim that sexual intimacy is a vital grace and resource for personal well-being and spiritual growth and that its absence would constitute a profound impoverishment. I want to give serious consideration to their claims and make more explicit the kinds of harms and risks associated with long-term and lifelong sexual abstinence.

I want to do so within the context of a conversation about sexual virtue. What abilities and dispositions are needed to initiate and sustain graceful covenantal sexual life? What does it mean to flourish and excel as a sexual person? How is sexual flourishing related to the spiritual life, particularly a deepening and authentic relationship with God?

I will describe sexual flourishing as a poetics of intimacy, a term introduced by James Sears.[2] Sexuality is about intimacy. Intimacy is poetic because human beings have access to their own nature and subjectivity poetically (or metaphorically). Relationships, be they interpersonal, social, or spiritual, are also poetic since the parties involved are poetic or metaphorical subjects. The poetics of intimacy has personal, interpersonal, social, and spiritual dimensions. Graceful intimacy in one area requires a rich poetics of intimacy in the others.

I will consider how long-term and lifelong sexual abstinence often undermines the process by which we learn how to be intimate gracefully and poetically. I will consider how traditional Christian sexual morality, based on an essentialistic and dualistic model of human nature and sexuality, is not only inadequate for enabling and supporting sexual virtue in Western postindustrial societies but harmful precisely because it does not adequately anticipate the kinds of harms associated with sexual abstinence. I will show how addressing this problem is consistent with other principles and values of Christian morality and need not be regarded as impious or unfaithful to the tradition.

Notes

---

[1] Karen Lebacqz, "Appropriate Vulnerability," *Sexuality and the Sacred*, ed. James Nelson and Sandra P. Longfellow (Louisville, KY: Westminster/John Knox Press, 1994) 256-261.

[2] As will be noted later, I was first introduced to this term in an essay by James T. Sears, "Dilemmas and Possibilities of Sexuality Education," *Sexuality and the Curriculum*, ed. James T. Sears (New York: Teachers College Press, 1992).

❖ Chapter One

Is Traditional Sexual Morality Harmful?

Problems with Long-Term and Lifelong Sexual Abstinence

The Roman Catholic Church and many other Christian denominations continue to insist that certain groups of people practice long-term or lifelong sexual abstinence. In the Roman Catholic tradition, the divorced who have left bad marriages but cannot obtain an annulment are expected to practice sexual abstinence for the rest of their lives. In most mainstream Christian churches, gay men and lesbians are expected to practice lifelong sexual abstinence. Although attitudes about single adult sexuality have changed substantially, the official expectation of most Christian churches is that unmarried adults remain sexually abstinent. People with mental and physical disabilities are sometimes not permitted to marry and are thus expected to practice lifelong sexual abstinence.

Official moral rules about sexual abstinence are not followed by many otherwise practicing Christians. Most single adults and gay men and lesbians engage in sexual intimacy.[1] Many divorced Christians remarry. Anecdotal evidence from those working in the field of services for people with mental and physical disabilities suggests that a good number engage in sexual intimacy from time to time. People in these groups often note that they find traditional Christian sexual morality not just inconvenient or difficult; it seems unjust and counterproductive to personal well-being.

I want to ask: Is long-term and lifelong sexual abstinence harmful to personal and/or social well-being and, if so, what implication does this have for traditional Christian sexual morality? When I mentioned to some friends and associates that I was writing a book on the **immorality** of sexual abstinence, that is, on the harm caused by sexual abstinence, they became agitated. "It's one thing," they suggested, "to say that sexual intimacy is important for people's flourishing and well-being. But to say that sexual abstinence is immoral or harmful is going too far."

I admit that my thesis is counter intuitive in the light of some contemporary trends. First, the documented danger of contracting a sexually transmitted disease or HIV has led many educators, legislators, parents and ministers to advocate a return to abstinence-only sexual morality for all people outside heterosexual marriage. Given the dangers, this seems like good advice. But abstinence-only education programs do not decrease the incidence of teenage sexuality and, without information about safe and/or safer sex practices, the abstinence-only strategy increases risks to teenagers.[2] Some studies have actually shown that teaching strategies for protecting oneself from sexually transmitted disease decreases the incidence of teenage sex.[3]

Second, there are strong cultural biases which shame women (and men) into marriage. Young adult women who are not in a committed sexual relationship or not actively seeking one are often regarded as either strange, incomplete, or pitiable. Well-intentioned coupled friends frequently offer unsolicited advice on how to find a partner and/or even try to set up meetings and dates for their single friends. There is still strong pressure put on women to stay in unsatisfying or unhealthy relationships since it is assumed that being in a relationship is better than not being in one. There have been a number of movements launched in popular culture to remove the stigma associated with being single. If I argue that sexual abstinence is immoral, am I not buttressing former cultural biases against singlehood? Am I not reinforcing the shame associated with singlehood? Moreover, there are those who have chosen to remain single after the death of a spouse or after separation from a failed marriage. Some young adults abstain from sex for moral reasons, and there are those who have chosen celibacy as a form of religious life. Does my thesis imply that these people are "immoral" or sinful?

And finally, some would argue that contemporary postindustrialized societies are obsessed with sex. Some of them would argue that long-term and lifelong sexual abstinence are important countercultural signs, moderating social preoccupation with sex. Some would argue that civilization is, to some extent, predicated on the control of sexual libido. Therefore, my thesis could be viewed as a capitulation to the social preoccupation with sex and, ultimately, not helpful to personal and social well-being.

A short response to these concerns is in order here; a more elaborate one will be presented later in the body of the text. I will argue that **one** of the reasons why long-term or lifelong sexual abstinence is problematic is because it usually undermines the development of our capacity to love with greater depth and integrity. Here, my concern is not so much with sex itself but with what sexually intimate relationships have the capacity to enable. It is true that sexually intimate relationships are not the only way that people develop their capacity to love with greater depth and integrity. However, as I hope to show, other types of relationships, particularly friendships and business associations, do not normally include the kind of depth and intimacy that challenge us to root out the deepest fears we have about our loveableness or our capacity to love. We have all constructed different levels of self-protection, facades we project for acceptance and security. Intimate relationships have the capacity to move us beyond those fears and mystifications; most of our other relationships permit us to sustain them.

It is true that some people are able to root out their deepest fears about being loveable and find ways to love profoundly, authentically, and with greater integrity even apart from sexually intimate relationships. But doing so requires special circumstances, unique personal gifts/resources, and auxiliary supports which most people do not have. We should not assume that these resources are universally present; therefore, I want to argue that when institutions **impose** long-term or lifelong sexual abstinence on individuals the assumption should be that this will deprive them of the usual context and resources with which they will grow to love with greater authenticity and depth, the usual context for interpersonal mutuality (the actual exchange of interpersonal love), the usual context for important physical touch and intimacy, and the usual context for intimate association and its concomitant goods (both personal and socioeconomic).

This argument should not be construed to suggest that those who are not in a sexually intimate relationship are immoral. As I will elaborate at the end of this introductory chapter, there are many ways that intimacy is served through periodic sexual abstinence. Moreover, some individuals may come to the conclusion that they are in circumstances, possess personal gifts/resources, or have access to auxiliary goods which will assure substantial progress in the capacity to love with greater depth and integrity without being involved in sexually intimate relationships.

What I am concerned with is the manner in which the moral ideal of sexual abstinence outside of marriage is used in ways that deprive individuals of resources essential to their personal and spiritual well-being. Several recent events have convinced me that the continuance of traditional Christian sexual moral rules (requiring sexual abstinence for the divorced, gay men and lesbians, single adults, and persons with mental and physical disabilities) is causing significant harm. The existence of these norms is being used in divisive and hurtful ways.

In the 208th general assembly of the Presbyterian Church of America (summer 1996), the "fidelity and chastity" clause, requiring officers of the Church (and implicitly all others) to maintain fidelity in marriage and chastity in singleness and all other relationships, was a deliberate attempt to exclude gay men and lesbians from ministry in the Church. It sent a chilling wave of intolerance and moralistic judgment throughout the Church, not just to ministers but to many single adults who were implicitly condemned by the teaching. In 1997, a small contingent of the United Church of Christ attempted to pass a similar resolution. Although it was defeated, it illustrates the manner in which traditional sexual norms requiring sexual abstinence can be used in divisive and disempowering ways.

The Episcopal Church has been struggling with this issue for several years. If everyone outside valid heterosexual marriage is expected to practice sexual abstinence, then gay men and lesbians in committed sexual relationships are not suitable candidates for ordination (at least so the argument goes). But many successful priests are gay and lesbian and have been living in committed sexual relationships for years. There is a significant contingent of the denomination that does not want to validate openly gay and lesbian ministers in the Church. They consider this a gross compromise of their moral tradition. They cling tenaciously to the moral ideal of abstinence outside marriage and define marriage as a covenant of love between one man and one woman. The traditional moral rule about sexual abstinence, then, is the foundation stone for institutional exclusion of gay men and lesbians from ministry in the Church. It also connotes a second class ecclesial status to gay men and lesbians. Those who have been in loving and committed relationships for decades are shamed into thinking that their relationships are counterfeit and not sacred.

The Roman Catholic situation is even more complex. Perhaps the most painful issue for Roman Catholics has been the prohibition of remarriage after divorce. Countless otherwise devout Catholics, after the failure of their marriages, must either remain sexually abstinent or suffer institutional shame and alienation if they remarry civilly.

The National Conference of Catholic Bishops recently issued a pastoral document, "Always Our Children,"[4] which emphasized the importance of loving gay and lesbian children. While the Bishops confirmed much of the findings of contemporary research about the character of sexual orientation and its inalterability, they reiterated traditional teaching that the only genuinely moral option for gay men and lesbians is lifelong sexual abstinence. Only those gay men and lesbians who are "chaste" may provide leadership or ministry in the Church.

One suspects that the institutionalization of celibacy in the Roman Catholic priesthood creates a presumption in favor of the reasonableness and holiness of sexual abstinence. So when the institutional Roman Catholic Church (led by celibates) reiterates its position that the divorced, gay men and lesbians, and those with mental and physical disabilities must live the rest of their lives in sexual abstinence, it apparently does not recognize the harm caused.

For example, a young devout Catholic woman married when she was twenty-five. She and her husband had enjoyed a conventional courtship and early marriage. They had successful jobs and gave birth to two girls. After about five years, her husband became increasingly irritable and violent. They went through counseling, but he did not stop his behavior. They divorced and then sought an annulment. While Church officials were sympathetic with the young woman's plight, they could not find reasons to annul the marriage. When she began dating again, her local pastor suggested that he was not at liberty to permit her to marry nor to give her communion should she decide to marry civilly. In effect, the Church expected her to practice lifelong sexual abstinence.

Another similar recent case involved the dismissal of a divorced and remarried female teacher from a parochial school. She was considered one of the best teachers in the school, an active member of the parish, a generous and talented individual. She had married a man who was divorced and could not obtain an annulment. According to archdiocesan policies the pastor was required to ask for her resignation. Parish members were heartbroken at the loss of her ministry, and the alienation she felt from her faith community was devastating. Few in the parish could understand why her remarriage was problematic. This caused extraordinary professional and emotional harm to the woman, and it represented an enormous loss of ministry for the parish.

A gay male couple in the South had been attending a Baptist Church for several years when several members of the congregation approached the pastor. They felt it was inconsistent with their Biblical faith to permit the couple to participate without some admission of the sinfulness of their relationship. The pastor agreed that the only morally permissible way for gay people to live out their lives was in perpetual celibacy. The couple was asked to sign a statement to that effect. They refused and were asked to leave the congregation. What few realized in this case was that a teenage member of the congregation was struggling with his sexual identity. Convinced that he was gay, the teen struggled with how he could live out his life as a devout Christian. The action of the congregation convinced him that it was incompatible with his Christian faith to be gay. He pleaded with God to change his orientation, he attempted several relationships with girlfriends and, in the end, despairing and disillusioned, he took his life.

This parallels the famous case of Bobby Griffith. Bobby's mother, Mary, a devout member of a conservative Presbyterian congregation, launched an impassioned campaign to heal Bobby of his homosexuality. Bobby struggled with accepting himself as a gay man, but his mother's religious message was too strong. Unable to overcome feelings of disillusionment and self-hate, he killed himself. Mary came to realize that she and her brand of Christian morality are what killed Bobby. She has become a leader of PFLAG (Parents, Families and Friends of Lesbians and Gays), speaking out in behalf of lesbian and gay youth.[5]

At a recent religious academic conference, one of the panelists noted that the Catholic Church did not consider sexual orientation a matter of sin. According to him, it is more or less accepted as true that people have little choice about sexual orientation. But, he insisted, the Church is not at liberty to change the natural law or the traditions of the Church with respect to the morality of same gender sexual activity. When asked what gay men and lesbians should do, he responded that, as difficult as it might seem, God expects them to practice sexual abstinence.

Recently, at a Presbyterian congregation, a religious education minister was fired because it became known that she spent the night on occasion with a male friend she was dating. They had been going together for about a year but had not yet made formal plans to marry. The pastor felt her behavior was inconsistent with the congregation's recent decision to expect all unmarried adults to practice chastity. He simultaneously announced that couples seeking marriage in the Church could not be living together during the six months prior to their ceremony.

Many individuals who are divorced, gay or lesbian, or single adults continue to engage in relationships that include sexual intimacy. Many of these individuals feel deeply conflicted about their behavior. Otherwise devoutly religious, they often conduct their relationships clandestinely and/or feel deep shame or guilt for what they do. For the divorced and remarried, it is more difficult to avoid institutional problems with the Catholic Church, so many leave the Church feeling deeply betrayed. Gay men and lesbians who attempt to form more stable and psychologically healthy relationships invariably become less hidden and, therefore, encounter many of the shaming mechanisms of their families, churches, and civic organizations. Many sexually active single adults leave the Church out of the shame and hypocrisy they feel for their behavior. They often return when they marry but then face additional shame for not being practicing Christians while seeking a "Church" wedding.

The profound disillusionment, pain, and shame that the divorced, gay men and lesbians, and sexually active single adults experience is increasingly met with statements by tradition-preserving Church officials that they are not at liberty to make changes in divinely instituted moral norms. This seems to imply that, even if these norms caused harm or serious hardship, they could not be changed because they are divinely instituted. This suggests that moral law is arbitrary and not necessarily related to human well-being. Consequently, God is implicitly portrayed as making moral laws either by whim or in accord with some abstract rational order.

This is not the picture of God portrayed by Jewish and Christian Scriptures: "Now, Israel, hear the statutes and decrees which I am teaching you to observe, that you may live, and may enter in and take possession of the land which the Lord, the God of your fathers, is giving you. . . . Observe them carefully, for thus will you give evidence of your wisdom and intelligence to the nations, who will hear of all these statutes and say, 'This great nation is truly a wise and intelligent people.' For what great nation is there that has gods so close to it as the Lord, our God, is to us whenever we call upon him? Or what great nation has statutes and decrees that are as just as this whole law which I am setting before you today?" (Deuteronomy 4: 1, 6–8) Another passage in The Book of Deuteronomy emphasizes the intent of the moral law to enable life and well-being: "Be careful, therefore, to do as the Lord, your God, has commanded you, not turning aside to the right or to the left, but following exactly the way prescribed for you by the Lord, your God, that you may live and prosper and may have long life in the land which you are to occupy." (Deuteronomy 5: 32–33). The moral law of the Jewish people was supposed to reflect a wisdom and insight about the conditions and practices within which human beings would flourish.

In Christian Scriptures, Jesus is not presented as an arbitrary moral lawgiver but as one concerned with the well-being and life of those he has called. John presents Jesus as the good shepherd who knows his sheep and they him. John reports Jesus saying, "I have come that they might have life and have it more abundantly." (John 10:10) The prologue of John's Gospel emphasizes that the coming of Jesus was for empowerment. "In the beginning was the Word; the Word was in God's presence, and the Word was God. He was present to God in the beginning. Through him all things came into being and apart from him nothing came to be. Whatever came to be in him, found life, life for the light of all people. . . . To his own he came . . . any who did accept him he empowered to become children of God. . . . The Word became flesh and made his dwelling among us, and we have seen his glory: the glory of an only Son coming from the Father, filled with enduring love." (John 1: 1–4, 11–12, 14)

Within the Jewish and Christian moral traditions, moral norms are ultimately intended to enable human well-being, human flourishing. That is not to say that every just moral norm will be experienced as liberating and empowering. Under the influence of selfishness and conflicted interests, morality does not always look like it is in one's best interest. It is important not to reject moral norms simply because they are inconvenient or difficult.

However, norms which are not empowering or ennobling should not be honored. Morality ideally enables human excellence. When moral norms undermine the attainment of that excellence, they need to be questioned. When moral norms deprive us of resources vital to our flourishing and well-being, they need to be examined. While the questioning of traditional morality seems impious, it seems even more impious to sustain a set of moral norms that depict God as a sadist!

Normally, when people are intentionally deprived of resources vital to their flourishing and well-being, such deprivation is considered unjust and immoral. For example, when children are deprived of an adequate education, basic health care, food, and security they are crippled for life. This is increasingly regarded as criminal and unjust. Likewise, when through discrimination (ethnic, religious, gender, nationality, handicap or other reasons) adults are deprived access to work, housing, food, health services, and other basic goods, this is viewed increasingly as unjust and inhumane, a violation of their basic rights as human beings. When human beings do not have access to work, housing, food, health services and other basic goods, it is more difficult to sustain their lives with dignity.

I want to argue that sexual intimacy is one of the vital resources for personal well-being. Its absence constitutes an impoverishment that is unjust and immoral, particularly when mandated! Marvin Ellison describes sexuality as "our embodied capacity for intimate connection." And, with Carter Heyward who speaks of sexual desire as our "embodied longing for mutuality,"[6] he argues that sexual desire is an embodied longing for "physical, emotional, and spiritual embrace of others, the world, and God, the sacred Source of life."[7]

Mandated long-term and lifelong sexual abstinence is personally, socially, and spiritually alienating if sexuality is our embodied capacity for intimate connection with ourselves, with others, and with God. Paradoxically, occasions for imposed long-term and lifelong sexual abstinence are increasing. Contemporary postindustrialized cultures present new problems for traditional Christian sexual morality.

Although postindustrial cultures are not necessarily psychologically, spiritually, or morally healthy, they are the context and horizon within which people must live out their sexuality. Educational and economic needs usually make marriage impractical and ill-advised before one's late twenties. This increases the length of time in which many adults are single.

Likewise, models of marriage have changed. In earlier societies, marriage was largely a matter of passing on family patrimony, managing households, and having children. Many marriages were arranged for economic reasons. Although hoped for, romance and affection were not considered essential to a sound marriage. Power was not necessarily shared in these relationships. Women did not enjoy economic or cultural independence. Today, even relatively conservative Christians expect marriage to be consensual, grounded in affection or romantic love, and to include the sharing of power between husband and wife. Women have increased economic and cultural independence, permitting them to leave abusive and unsatisfying marriages. These advances are generally held to be just and good.

Preparing for a household-management-and-reproductively-centered marriage required the cultivation of certain dispositions or virtues, chief among them being self-control. Passing on family patrimony depended on carefully guarded legitimacy of offspring. Female sexual activity before or outside marriage constituted a major threat to establishing and maintaining patrimony. Cultural models of male excellence included rationality and self-control. So for both women and men, control of sexual passion was an overall strategy for right conduct. People married relatively young, and sexual self-control was expected prior to marriage. During marriage, sexual self-control was also important for keeping relations within marriage, for maintaining proper household order through managing passions, and for achieving a more spiritual and rational way of life.

As will be elaborated more extensively in future parts of this work, committed sexual relationships built upon mutual affection and sharing of power require cultivation of other dispositions and virtues, one among them being the capacity to become "appropriately vulnerable."[8] Sexual self-control may be important, but it must be coupled with the ability to become appropriately vulnerable and intimate with one's sexual companion. Sexual self-control alone will normally undermine the project of achieving interpersonal intimacy in marriage or other committed sexual relationships. This may require addressing the long process most contemporary adults go through in selecting a life sexual companion. If marriages are consensual and require some sense of a successful narrative of interpersonal intimacy before a lifelong commitment is made, sexual abstinence may not only be inappropriate as a premarital strategy but also a harmful and more risky preparation for successful sexual commitments.

In many respects, more expectations are placed on marriage today. This may account for an increase in the divorce rate,[9] which, in turn, makes the traditional Christian prohibition of remarriage after divorce more widespread and problematic than in earlier generations. Many Protestant churches have responded by interpreting a couple of New Testament passages to include the possibility of divorce and remarriage. The Roman Catholic Church has strictly enforced the concept of marital indissolubility but has liberalized grounds for annulment.

Both of these strategies have produced political fallout. For Biblically oriented Protestant churches who claim they cannot change moral injunctions against gay men and lesbians, their liberal divorce and remarriage policies appear hypocritical and heterosexist. For example, one of the texts used to defend the practice of remarriage in Protestant denominations is Paul's concern about the danger of burning with sexual desire to the point that it leads to sinful sexual union or personal disintegration. (1 Corinthians 7) Many wonder why it is considered important for heterosexuals, but not homosexuals, to enjoy sexual companionship.

While many divorced Roman Catholics have availed themselves of annulment procedures, they often do so resentfully. They suspect, whether correctly or not, that it invalidates whatever good existed in their failed marriages, particularly the original love and affection they may have had for each other. They are concerned about the implications of an annulment for the legitimacy of their children (technically not affected by annulments) and the fact that many of the parties who were said to have given "defective consent" are permitted to remarry without problem.

Many individuals, who are not able to obtain an annulment and attempt to live out the Church's demand for lifelong abstinence, suffer tremendously. Some are left with the burdens of child rearing without any of the assistance that would normally accompany coupled parenting. Some may have grown accustomed to companionship and sexual intimacy which, now absent, breed a dark and cold loneliness. This, in turn, undermines the immune system, making them more vulnerable to periodic illness.[10] Perhaps more serious is that the absence of sexual companionship, for many, represents the loss of the vital context for personal integration and growth.

A far more challenging issue has arisen with homosexuality and traditional Christian sexual morality. Many homosexual persons in earlier historical epochs would have entered heterosexual marriages and done the best they could. There is little evidence that people inclined to same gender sexual intimacy would have spent the rest of their lives in sexual abstinence. In fact, the concept of sexual orientation is a modern insight. Earlier theories about sexuality focused on behavior and assumed a universal heterosexual nature. Sexual conduct, rather than sexual nature, was diverse and represented perverted choices. It was thought that, with proper sexual conduct (heterosexual marriage), any same gender sexual inclinations could be overcome.

Today, we know this is not the case. Researchers increasingly consider sexual orientation neither a matter of conscious choice nor something alterable. It is increasingly difficult to find well informed Christian ministers recommending that gay men or lesbians enter into heterosexual relationships. This is unjust to the heterosexual partner and a futile strategy for overcoming one's homosexual orientation. Thus, the Church is faced with a relatively new problem. What are gay men and lesbians to do if heterosexual marriage is inappropriate and if changing one's orientation is unreasonable and unlikely? If one is constrained to find an answer within traditional norms, abstinence looks like the only answer.

But the imposition of abstinence on gay men and lesbians is harmful. It increases the propensity for casual and anonymous sexual encounters which are problematic for their increased risk of physical harm and for the potential (if they become habitual) of psychological immaturity. Casual anonymous sexual encounters encourage a degree of superficiality which, if habitual, can lead to a more general disassociative form of interacting with others. One becomes less capable of developing intimacy with others or with oneself, and this jeopardizes intimacy with God.

If the gay man or lesbian actually succeeds in remaining sexually abstinent, he or she does so at a great cost. One way of accomplishing this requires the sublimation of sexual energy into some other activity, loading it (the activity) with a degree of importance superseding its actual reality. One may then become obsessed with certain projects, giving them exaggerated weight. Or one must become obsessed with repressing one's feelings and emotions. Although earlier Stoic models of psychological health may have included this strategy, contemporary psychologists warn that this is personally alienating, severing an individual from important resources for decision-making and effective interaction with others.

It is important to note that for much of the history of Christianity long-term and lifelong abstinence was usually voluntary and practiced by a minority of individuals (widows, monks, nuns and priests). There were not large numbers of single adults (people married young), nor large numbers of divorced (divorce was rare and life expectancy shorter), nor self-acknowledged homosexual persons who did not marry. Although the Roman Catholic Church encouraged a good deal of periodic sexual abstinence in marriage,[11] there is little evidence that this was widely practiced or that it was regularly long-term or lifelong. The Church must take note of the fact that its traditional sexual morality, coupled with changing social profiles and practices, creates a new problem that affects an increasingly large number of individuals. In order to conform to traditional Christian sexual morality, large numbers of otherwise devout Christians are faced with the prospects of long-term or lifelong sexual abstinence. And, if this is harmful, the Church must come to grips with the fact that the intended effect of its moral code (enabling human excellence and well-being) is not successful given the current cultural context within which it must be practiced.

Social pressures during the 1960's and 1970's on traditional Christian sexual morality seemed capable of being handled with minor adjustments to the tradition. Protestants tacitly endorsed the use of contraceptives in marriage, made little fuss over sexually active single adults, and permitted remarriage after divorce as a concession to human frailty and God's mercy. Roman Catholics were forced to reconceptualize the relationship between conscience and Church teaching with regard to contraception and, although many left the Church over *Humanae Vitae*,[12] most married (and practicing) Catholics today use some form of artificial contraception. As mentioned earlier, Roman Catholics liberalized annulment procedures, permitting many to remarry within the Church. And like Protestants, Roman Catholics made little fuss over sexually active single adults.

Two issues, however, have precipitated new crises in most Christian churches. First, the AIDS epidemic of the early 1980's forced a more serious look at sexuality education. Churches could no longer sustain the illusion that their traditional ethic was being followed by simply ignoring the practice of adolescents and young adults. They had to acknowledge and incorporate sexual practices of teens and young adults into sexuality programs with the aim of preventing transmission of HIV. Some educators were disturbed by apparent inconsistencies between moral ideals and practice. How could they educate young people about prevention of HIV transmission without acknowledging that most young people were sexually active? Did such education tacitly encourage the practice of morally unacceptable behavior? If so, wouldn't teaching sexual abstinence be preferable within Christian contexts? This forced a reconsideration of whether the traditional sexual ethic prohibiting sexual intimacy between unmarried persons was still valid. The trend in many Christian circles has been to return to a more traditional formulation of sexual ethics by encouraging sexual abstinence until one is married. Little attention has been given, however, to the fact that the conditions within which traditional sexual morality was elaborated are no longer the case. Does long-term sexual abstinence adequately prepare young adults for the kinds of sexual/marital commitments they are expected to make?

Second, the emerging profile of gay and lesbian sexuality has profoundly challenged traditional Christian sexual ethics. Both the statistical number of people who are openly gay and lesbian and the scientific information about sexual orientation (derived from biological, psychological and sociological studies) have undermined former biases, stereotypes, and myths. Social and ecclesial vilification of gay men and lesbians as a group of people is no longer justifiable given the evidence at hand. Efforts of gay men and lesbians to live out their sexuality in enriching and responsible ways confront Christianity with a new dilemma. Sexual abstinence does not appear to be a reasonable option, and the enforcement of it by condemning same gender sexual intimacy only encourages the practice of more dangerous and personally impoverishing forms of behavior like clandestine, promiscuous, and risky sexual encounters. But the acceptance of responsible and enriching gay and lesbian sexual commitments forces the Church to consider such things as commitment ceremonies (gay marriage), ordaining gay and lesbian ministers who happen to be in openly gay and lesbian relationships, and reconceptualizing sexuality education so as to remove heterosexist bias. This, of course, would require more than minor adjustments to the moral tradition. It strikes at the heart of the sexist and heterosexist bias of Christian sexual morality.

The lesson of the Galileo affair sheds light on this situation. In the 17th century, Galileo was condemned for proposing information that would require profound paradigm shifts for the Church. Former models of seeing the earth and human beings as the center of the universe were having to be rethought. According to Pope John Paul II in a letter he wrote in 1992, the Church feared the consequences of having to "all at once overcome habits of thought and to devise a way of teaching" about the profound changes in world view implied in the discoveries of Copernicus and in the teachings of Galileo.[13] According to the Pope, the central error of theologians who condemned Galileo was the failure to distinguish the meaning of Scripture from the meaning given to it by interpreters. If there seems to be a contradiction between Scripture and the discoveries of "clear and certain reasoning," the interpreter of Scripture "does not understand it (Scripture) correctly."[14]

The Pope appealed to a long-standing principle of Christianity, the authority of reason. Since early Christianity gradually came to an understanding that Jesus was fully human and fully divine,[15] this meant that humanity (and human reason) would always be one of the authorities for authentic Christian belief and practice. Although Christian belief is always theological (grounded in God), it is also always grounded in anthropology (an understanding of human being).[16] The Church cannot propose as authoritative a teaching that is inconsistent with the best information at hand about humanity. Moreover, since the early Church gradually came to understand itself to be a universal rather than sectarian religion, it sought to defend its moral claims by appealing to natural law rather than sectarian authority.

Recently, the appeal to natural law as the ground of Christian morality has been challenged in many ways. Most notably, many scholars question the idea of an essential and universal human nature. Human beings are historical and cultural beings. Human excellence is grounded in particular historical and cultural contexts. While much of this critique is valid, one aspect of the original intuition of early Christian thinkers in appealing to natural law still seems relevant: it is inconsistent with a nonsectarian religion to be authoritarian. By appealing to some notion of natural law or human nature, ethicists argue that the authority of their claims rests in the human good as such, in some notion of human excellence or human flourishing and not merely with the authority of Scripture or institutional positions of authority.

In this earlier Catholic approach, moral teachings were proposed as if reasonable people reasoning reasonably would find them reasonable. Disagreement could occur, but it would be in the light of some fallacy of reasoning. That is why John Paul II was able to appeal to the notion that when there is an apparent contradiction between Scripture and clear and certain reasoning we must trust clear and certain reasoning and find new ways of understanding the Scripture in question. It would seem that the same principle applies to the Christian tradition in general. When there is an apparent contradiction between clear and certain reasoning and the teachings of the tradition, the interpreters of the tradition must find new ways of understanding the tradition. This was, according to the Pope, the central fallacy of the theologians who condemned Galileo: they could not conceptualize an alternative to the paradigm out of which they viewed the world. The geocentric universe was so ingrained in their way of thinking that any other view of the universe seemed "unreasonable."

Traditional Christian sexual morality is heterosexual-marital-and-reproductively-centered. That paradigm is so ingrained in the world view of most people that the idea of a reasonable paradigm centered around something else is almost inconceivable. But the information emerging from biology, psychology and sociology is forcing us to reconceptualize sexual anthropology. What led Copernicus to his insights were hypotheses (paradigms) which, when applied to various problems, offered more consistent and coherent solutions. In the area of sexual morality, the traditional paradigm requires so many "corrections" in order to meet current needs that it has become increasingly cumbersome and not persuasive. We need a model or paradigm of sexual excellence that provides more consistent and coherent solutions to the kinds of moral dilemmas contemporary people face in postindustrialized societies. We are bound to make the same mistakes of the 17th century unless we are willing to rethink moral paradigms in the light of new information.

My thesis is that long-term and lifelong sexual abstinence is harmful. Since traditional Christian sexual morality would require an increasingly large number of people to practice long-term and lifelong sexual abstinence in contemporary society, it is imperative that we explore alternative paradigms of sexual virtue that prevent this harm from occurring. The Church must develop a sexual ethic that affirms the importance of sexual intimacy for the overall maturation, flourishing, and excellence of human life and remove those norms which would unjustly deprive people of that vital resource.

Proposing that sexual intimacy is important for the overall maturation, flourishing, and excellence of human life is not a particularly novel assertion. Many contemporary Christian sexual ethicists have made that assertion. But tradition-preserving Christians and Church officials could retort that even if traditional norms are inadequate, out of date, or not persuasive, they cause no harm and may be better than alternatives. Until ecclesial and civil officials take note of the harm associated with sexual abstinence, the impetus to seek alternative ethical paradigms will be weak. It is important to outline here some of the reasons why sexual intimacy is so vital and its absence problematic.

Role of Sexuality in Overall Human Well-Being

It may come as a surprise to know that in the 13th century Thomas Aquinas, one of the great thinkers of the Christian tradition, asked whether sexual abstinence might not be immoral.[17] Aquinas assumed, with most of Western culture, that the (sole) purpose of sexuality was reproduction. Could anyone ever morally forego such an important human enterprise? Aquinas' answer was to suggest that for the sake of higher psychological (spiritual) goods, an individual could forsake sexuality. For Aquinas, what one was giving up was not the value of sexual intimacy in overall human well-being. What he had in mind was the renunciation of the good of raising a family. According to a noted Thomistic scholar, Servais Pinckaers, Aquinas was novel in that he understood natural inclinations to have a spiritual orientation. If one could forsake a natural good in order to achieve a spiritual one more perfectly, one had not compromised the inherent orientation of that natural good or one's own humanity.[18] And since Aquinas did not understand sexual intimacy to in any way enhance one's ability to love God, sexual abstinence was not only not harmful but actually perfecting.

Even for those who were not considering lifelong celibacy as a way of life, Aquinas considered sexual abstinence an important means for developing the virtue of chastity, sexual self-control. This involved restricting sexual pleasure to marital reproductive situations. Sexual abstinence was an important moral preparation for marriage and even had its place in marriage. Chastity restrained sexual desire and pleasure to their reasonable ends, procreation. By doing so, it enabled married people to understand their ultimate fulfillment to consist in God, not in sexual fulfillment or mutuality. In other words, sexual abstinence did not undermine the project of learning how to love. Sexual abstinence freed individuals to give themselves more wholeheartedly to the love of

God. Sexual abstinence limited the impact of irrational passions on the mind, thus liberating it for love of genuine goodness and truth: God.

The Jewish tradition had also considered the question of sexual abstinence. On two accounts, sexual abstinence was considered **immoral**. First, it violated God's first commandment to human beings, "be fruitful and multiply." (Genesis 1:28) This commandment was taken so seriously that in some texts Jewish men were encouraged to divorce barren wives for the sake of marrying those who could bear children. Unmarried mature Jewish men were considered a moral disgrace.

Second, sexual abstinence was considered immoral because, according to God, "it is not good for the man to be alone." (Genesis 2:18) Sexual companionship was considered an original blessing of God's creation and integral to personal well-being. The importance of sexual companionship even mitigated the concern for reproduction by allowing infertile couples to remain together for the sake of their union. There was little expressed concern in the Jewish tradition about developing virtues of sexual self-control, although sexual intimacy was restricted to marital contexts out of regard for the legitimacy of children and the proprietary interests of other men. Thus, prior to marriage, individuals were to abstain from sex.

Both the Jewish and Thomistic responses to the question of the morality of sexual abstinence were, in part, psychological. According to Thomas, sexual intimacy was not integral to human excellence or personal well-being. It was an ancillary good which, in fact, ought to be minimized or chastised for the sake of higher spiritual/psychological goods. Thus, long-term or lifelong sexual abstinence was not problematic and in most instances considered ideal or superior to sexual relationships. There was presumably no psychological or spiritual harm caused by abstaining from sexual intimacy. The Jewish response, on the other hand, suggested that personal well-being and human excellence were not possible apart from sexual companionship. Thus, long-term or lifelong sexual abstinence was not only ill-advised but, in most instances, considered immoral or significantly short of religious goodness.   Long-term absence of sexual intimacy was considered psychologically harmful. The two responses correspond to different understandings of human psychology and human nature.

Traditional Christian responses to the issue of sexual abstinence include those of the reformers, most notably Martin Luther and John Calvin. Reacting to corruption in the Roman Catholic clergy, both criticized the medieval institution of mandatory celibacy for clergy. They did so by appealing to God's creative design of sexual companionship. Human beings were created to be social, to enjoy mutuality. Particularly for John Calvin, that sociality was itself a sexual one. Human beings were created male and female.[19] Neither Luther nor Calvin would have wanted to assert that lifelong or long-term sexual abstinence was "immoral," but they did suggest that the imposition of mandatory celibacy on clergy ran counter to God's creative design, hinting at some sense of harm.

Both Luther and Calvin expressed concern about the harm caused to those who were prohibited from remarriage by the Roman Catholic Church. Calvin felt that only a select few, if any, were given the charism of celibacy by God. Marriage was an important remedy for sexual desire.[20] Luther did not favor divorce but was duly concerned about the plight of those who were not permitted to remarry. In *Babylonian Captivity of the Church*, he raised concerns about the "infinite perils of those who, without any fault of their own, are nowadays compelled to remain unmarried; that is, those whose wives or husbands have run away and deserted them."[21]

The difference between Jewish and traditional Roman Catholic responses to the issue of sexual abstinence highlights an underlying tension in contemporary sexual ethics debate. Traditional Western sexual morality is largely inherited from traditional Roman Catholic Christian sexual morality elaborated under the influence of Greek dualistic anthropologies. An anthropology is a theory of human nature. Dualistic ones argue that human beings are made up of sensual and spiritual parts (the body and the soul) and that these are essentially antagonistic. Accordingly, human excellence is achieved when the superior and more essentially human part, the spiritual/rational soul with its capacity for union with God, achieves preeminence and governs the inferior and animalistic part, the body with its sensuality/sexuality. Thus, sexual pleasure and sexual intimacy must be minimized in order for the superior spiritual and soulful part of human nature to flourish.

Traditional Western sexual ethics makes sense in the light of the psychology within which it was elaborated. Much of the tension over sexual ethics today occurs because ethical norms have not been adjusted to reflect contemporary shifts in psychology. The Reformation anticipated some of those shifts, most notably a less dualistic attitude toward sexuality, but was still deeply influenced by inherited sexist and heterosexist paradigms which led to viewing women as subordinate to men and homosexuality as a perversion of the created order. Modern psychology is much less dualistic. Sensuality and embodiment are not considered antagonistic to what is essentially human or even "rational."[22] Rather, sensuality and embodiment are integral to human wholeness. Like the Reformers, modern psychology is increasingly appreciative of the social character of human nature and recognizes the importance of intimacy for the overall maturation and flourishing of personal life.

The writings of Audre Lorde,[23] Carter Heyward[24] and James Nelson[25] have helped scholars appreciate how the denigration of sensuality and the body in theological, philosophical, and moral systems contributes to sexual violence. Nelson was one of the earlier Christian ethicist to highlight the costs of dualism, particularly to women who had been traditionally associated with the sensual, hence, inferior and dangerous aspects of human nature.[26] Heyward argues that the disassociation of oneself from the pleasures of one's own body leads to the view that other peoples' bodies may be violated without harming them. Conversely, reclaiming the sacredness of embodied pleasures should lead to a greater respect and justice toward the bodies of others. Appreciation for the pleasurableness of our own bodies and feelings grounds our ability to be compassionate, that is to "feel with" (compassio) others.[27] Erotic pleasure is one of the primary ways that we experience our connectedness to each other. Eros does not need to be beaten down by "reason," as if it were an inferior and irrational urge. Such a view suggests that we are essentially "reason" and that our bodies and sensuality are alien. Christine Gudorf argues that sexual pleasure is not an irresistible urge, essentially out of control. Rather it is a grace and blessing, a "premoral good."[28] Eros is an embodied grace that connects us to others.[29] When we appreciate it as a blessing, we are less inclined to disassociate it from interpersonal mutuality which it serves. Sexual immorality is not primarily a matter of an errant erotic sensuality but rather a symptom of dualistic thinking that severs eros from its personal and sacred ground!

There is increasing scientific evidence that absence of affectionate touch is associated with increased violence. Robert Hatfield's research has identified numerous studies which show a correlation between touch deprivation and neurological atrophy which, in turn, lead to increased violence towards others and self.[30]

Married adults are psychologically and physically healthier than nonmarried ones. The statistics supporting this fact should be equally applicable to other committed sexual relationships (gay and lesbian relationships as well as heterosexual relationships which are cohabitational but not formally constituted by a marriage ceremony). In an extensive summary of studies, Gove, Briggs-Style, and Hughes found that the married "have lower rates of treatment for mental illness . . .,"[31] that their "psychological well-being . . . is substantially better than that of the unmarried,"[32] and that the "married have substantially lower mortality rates than have the unmarried . . ."[33]

Gove and his associates considered the social selection theory, that is, the hypothesis that the reason the married enjoy better psychological and physical well-being is that healthier people tend to marry. But they did not find that this explained the statistical differences. They cite an extensive study conducted by Pearlin and Johnson which suggests that, while marriage does not prevent economic and social problems, it does provide resources for managing the stress of such external pressures.[34]

They also found that marriage provides an important consolidation and foundation for one's identity. Following the work of P. A. Thoits, they summarized that since the human self is social, one's sense of well-being is closely related to being "embedded in a system of regularized relationships in which personal ties are defined by reciprocal rights and obligations."[35] Moreover, one's sense of self-worth, loveableness and social worth depends on support from close relationships and on successfully sustaining significant relationships.[36] While one's sense of loveableness and social identity can be obtained through other types of relationships, it would appear that in marriage (and other committed sexual relationships) these are more secure and provide a deeper and more complete sense of well-being.

Intimacy refers to both the depth at which an individual is aware of him/herself and the depth at which he/she shares with others. One cannot be intimate with another unless one is comfortable and intimate with oneself. Modern psychology has provided resources for understanding why some people have difficulty becoming intimate with others. Often, unresolved conflicts are held repressed in the unconscious. This is a defense strategy that permits the individual to disassociate him/herself from painful memories or experiences. One of the tasks of adult life is to work through these repressed conflicts in order to love more completely and genuinely. Since most of these conflicts are interpersonal, significant adult relationships are the context in which individuals are constrained to address these repressed unconscious feelings, providing opportunities for maturation and integration. Sexually intimate relationships have the greatest capacity to provoke interior transformation and maturation.   Sexual intimacy does not guarantee growth and maturation, but it is increasingly thought that without it some of the most significant interior work is left undone.

For example, the awakening of adult sexuality during adolescence becomes the occasion for the recognition of one's capacity for profound interiority and mutuality. The relative superficiality of juvenile relationships and interiority gives way to new depth, feeling and desire. Furthermore, modern psychology has identified that self-awareness and self-disclosure accompany experiences of vulnerability. Embodiment and sensuality are primary dimensions where we become aware of our vulnerability, receive communication from others, and are self-disclosing to others. Intimacy with self and with others must be embodied and is usually rooted in some sense of emotional and physical vulnerability.

Karen Lebacqz refers to "appropriate vulnerability" as the context for genuine mutuality.[37] For Lebacqz, mutual self-disclosure does not occur without vulnerability. Two people cannot become close without self-disclosure. In other words, mutuality or love between two people is not very profound unless there is significant self-disclosure and self-transparency. This invariably involves a kind of emotional vulnerability. In the sharing of the deeper parts of myself the other has the capacity to wound me through insensitivity or indifference. Thus, we must learn how to be vulnerable and honor the vulnerability of our companions in order to share profound mutuality.

According to Lebacqz, not all vulnerability is appropriate. We must learn to recognize what level of vulnerability or self-disclosure is appropriate given a particular interpersonal exchange. Moreover, we must learn to recognize the kinds of exchanges that are likely to result in a respect of our vulnerability and those that will not. Normally, this means that trust and a history of respect in a relationship are crucial for further self-disclosure and vulnerability. Traditional prohibitions of sex before marriage implicitly suggested that vulnerability becomes "appropriate" only inside the commitment and trust of marriage.

There is some concern today about whether one can make an informed commitment to marriage without an established narrative of trust and appropriate vulnerability. Most couples who marry today have engaged in sexual intercourse prior to their commitment. This has been crudely described as a kind of test of sexual compatibility. But it is much more. It involves at least an intuitive sense that long-term interpersonal intimacy cannot be sustained unless one's partner knows how to become vulnerable, knows how to respect and honor one's own vulnerability, and can embody that in tender physical intimacy. Since even Christian authorities expect marriage to be more than a reproductive and household-management institution, they need to find institutional ways of affirming couples' sexual attempts to establish successful narratives of interpersonal mutuality prior to exchanging formal marriage vows.

Poetics of Sexual Intimacy

This is why I will argue that a more appropriate way to think about sexual morality is from the perspective of "a poetics of intimacy."[38] James T. Sears introduced this concept in an article on sexuality education. To my knowledge, no one has elaborated what such a poetics of intimacy might encompass. The shift to a poetic centered sexual morality is warranted for a number of reasons.

First, the traditional approach focuses on the containment and restriction of sexual desire. This has had the unintended effect of cultivating a distrust of sexuality that either leads to an alienation from one's sexual feelings, toxic shame and guilt about sexual feelings, or moments of sexual intimacy preceded by the need to anesthetize oneself with alcohol or drugs in order to mitigate one's sense of guilt or shame (thus leading to increased risk for untimely pregnancy, sexually transmitted disease, or sexual violence).

Second, the traditional approach has tended to emphasize the dangers associated with sexual intimacy and not the blessings. Consequently, it offers little if any instruction on how to develop positive, integrating, and flourishing forms of sexual life. It may rightly guard against harms but does little to empower or illumine.

Third, the traditional approach assumes that a limited set of norms or rules encompasses the range of sexual decisions that must be made. As we have come to appreciate in recent decades, sexuality is a complex reality involving biological, psychological, sociological and personal/individual dimensions. None of us begins in the same place, has the same sense of embodiment, or forms relationships with the same kinds of individuals. Our sexual stories are diverse and require personally unique authorship.

Fourth, contemporary Christian efforts to reform the theology of marriage have described marriage as a covenantal and mutual self-giving.[39] This shift has influenced marriage preparation programs in many different Christian denominations. Notable, however, are recent Papal and Vatican documents which continue to employ traditional concepts of self-mastery and self-control as prerequisites for authentic love. The implication is that self-mastery is possible and that it grounds the capacity for genuine sexual intimacy. But this fails to take into account more recent phenomenological discourse about social and interpersonal models of the self. One is not first an individual who gives him/herself to another individual. One is first and foremost relational, interpersonal, social.[40] We discover who we are in mutuality. Moreover, neither one's deepest interiority nor the life of an intimate relationship is subject to complete possession or total comprehension. We and our relationships are always deepening, growing, and changing. We are dialectical, transcendental and poetic subjects.

This is not to suggest that one is merely relational and not also individual or that one has no sense of a personal identity or self-possession. But it is to say that the self is characterized by a depth and richness that is only ultimately accessible in poetic or metaphoric rather than in conceptual and moralistic language.[41] Moral norms are important for establishing certain boundaries, perhaps to identify certain minimum standards of justice, but they are ultimately incapable of expressing the mystery of personal life. In a similar sense, religious language is poetic and metaphoric. The mystery of God cannot be adequately expressed in conceptual language. We need metaphors and stories which suggest various dimensions and facets of God's reality.[42]

Describing sexual virtue in terms of a poetics of intimacy begins with the claim that sexual excellence or sexual flourishing has to do with intimacy: intimacy with self, with others, and with God. Moreover, intimacy with self, with others, and with God develops and flourishes poetically. A poetic approach to sexual morality would involve encouraging people to acquire and practice the dispositions and graces of poetic intimacy. This ideally mediates between two extremes, the reduction of sexual intimacy to physical self-gratification (promiscuous and recreational sex) and the totalizing of sexual intimacy to household-management-and-reproductively-centered purposefulness in traditional sexual morality. The former obviously fails to appreciate the personal richness of the other, merely using him/her for one's own gratification. The latter subordinates and ties all forms of intimacy to one form, heterosexual-marital-and-reproductively-intentional. This fails to appreciate the plurality of sexual identity and the different contexts, moments, seasons, and dimensions of mutuality.

The poetics of intimacy refers to the different kinds of internal dispositions or attitudes (virtues) one must cultivate in order to initiate and sustain relationships of deep interpersonal intimacy. These internal dispositions must be richer than those envisioned by traditional sexual morality, focused as it was on the virtue of chastity. The poetics of intimacy includes an appreciation for the complexity of personal identity and interpersonal relationships, recognizing different types of relationships, different seasons of a relationship's life, and different challenges and opportunities couples face in the course of their love. Within the paradigm I hope to elaborate, sexuality is a resource for a rich poetics of intimacy. But not all sexual activity is supportive of a poetics of intimacy.

In an age where moralistic rhetoric is often interpreted as synonymous with rigid, reactionary and authoritarian forms of religious or social ideology, a poetic approach to sexual intimacy might be interpreted more as an invitation to responsibility than an imposition of it. Ideally, moral reflection and wisdom do not envision a restriction of human aspirations. Rather, morality is an invitation to personal growth and flourishing. A poetic approach to sexual life ideally would be an invitation to take up the opportunity to learn to love deeply and richly.

Traditional sexual moral language includes universal categories of right and wrong relationships, right and wrong expressions of sexual intimacy, and right and wrong ways to be men and women. We live in a much more pluralistic culture and, while that has its problems, we have come to appreciate the fact that many people flourish, enjoy well-being, and love genuinely and faithfully in different kinds of relationships, each with their own history and own pattern of intimacy. Goodness does not come in one form. It is personally and culturally varied.[43]

A poetics of intimacy would include an appreciation for the personal uniqueness of moral goodness without succumbing to relativism. Edward Vacek's thoughtful essay on love suggests that there are common dynamics that count for love, but the concrete lived story of any particular love is unique to those involved.[44] Vacek argues that there are different subjects, kinds and objects of love and that each of these makes a difference in the particular experience of love.[45] It is precisely because of this "triadic" structure of love that it cannot be merely relativistic or egocentric. When I make the other merely a projection of my desires, I cease to love. When I seek union with the other in such a way that I cease to be a unique subject, there is no self that remains to love the other. If we are not attentive to the kind of love in which we participate, we often impose onto it a form which stifles. Vacek emphasizes the importance of love being a "unity-in-difference." No matter how deep the sharing and intimacy between two lovers, no matter how deeply each desires to have and hold the other, they cannot sustain love without sustaining both the unity and the autonomy (difference) of each other. Without those differences, subject and object cease to be, and the ground of love ceases.[46]

A poetics of intimacy must be attentive and illuminating of the social resources and patterns of meaning and love within which we live. We come to know and experience ourselves not only in relationships but in the matrix of language, rituals, myths, institutions, and other socially constituting dynamics. Some of these hinder the development of a rich poetic form of loving because they manufacture and produce mass forms of the self. What we find sexually appealing in others sometimes changes when fashion, media or advertising trends change. Loving genuinely involves a delicate balance between resisting socially manufactured forms of love and intimacy and admitting that we are deeply shaped, for better and for worse, by the social patterns of meaning within which we are invariably situated. Thus, issues of social justice are part of a poetics of intimacy.

Physical Intimacy/Sexual Intimacy

An important question for our study is whether interpersonal intimacy is possible without physical intimacy. Can we participate in relationships of significant vulnerability and mutuality without physical intimacy? If so, then it would appear that sexual abstinence does not undermine the achievement of one of the prime markers of human flourishing. If not, then sexual abstinence would constitute a serious harm to personal well-being and, unless warranted by more serious concerns, be immoral (particularly when mandated).

The body is one of the primary experiences we have of existential fragility. Our existence is threatened when our bodily integrity and well-being are threatened. Famine, disease, injury, violence and death are sources of profound existential anxiety. Thus, embodiment is one of the places where we feel vulnerable. Consequently, when we seek to assure others of our love and support, we do so by seeking to confirm their physical well-being. Feeding one another, caring for the sick, protecting those who have been injured, protecting each other from unjust attack, and mourning with those who have lost loved ones are all ways we seek to confirm each other in being and in love. Moreover, these acts of human solidarity customarily include embodied gestures.

Sensuality is also a prime experience of existential fragility. Sensuality refers to our capacity for sight, touch, smell, hearing and taste. In the area of touch, our bodies have the capacity for extraordinary sensation and stimulation, most notably through the stimulation of genital organs. Feelings of sexual attraction and arousal are frequently spontaneous. Most adults can remember times they have felt weak in the knees or an overwhelming rush of sensation throughout their body at the sight of an extraordinarily handsome or beautiful person. We experience deep and profound longing to be touched and held. We are aware of places on our body that are sensitive to touch. When they are stimulated they seem to make us more transparent. We lose a sense of self-control and desire union with the other.

Conversely, when seeking to avoid self-disclosure or intimacy with another, we avoid eye contact, speech and, most importantly, touch. When hoping for intimacy we look for signs in the other of tender touch and affection. In their absence, words of love or friendship ring hollow. Various physical signs of affection, then, are important ways that we communicate and come to know the love and tenderness of each other. It is difficult to see how profound mutuality could flourish in the absence of physical intimacy.

But we still have not answered our fundamental question. Is sexual intimacy necessary for profound interpersonal intimacy? Again, modern psychology may help us with this concern. Sigmund Freud's identification of the unconscious has profoundly shaped modern understandings of human nature even though many psychologists no longer entirely endorse Freud's account of particular neuroses. Repressed psychological trauma, particularly from early childhood, is an important challenge for maturation and psychological health. An individual's ability to act rationally and lovingly rather than compulsively and defensively depends, to a great extent, on the resolution of repressed conflicts. Most of these conflicts are interpersonal in nature and only become fully apparent in the self-transparency of profoundly intimate relationships. Intimate relationships not only provide the context for self-transparency, they also provide the mutuality where the healing of unconscious conflicts can occur. Thus, in the absence of sexually and emotionally intimate relationships, one often remains stuck in unconscious unresolved traumas or mystifications.[47] These, in turn, leave the individual less capable of genuine love.

This leads to an important question for sexual ethics. Under what conditions do people establish the level of self-transparency necessary for loving with integrity, for seeing oneself and others truthfully and not with the illusions of repressed unconscious conflicts? How and where do they learn to share deeply and profoundly? And granting the Christian belief that union with God is our ultimate human destiny, how do we learn to be intimate at the level capable of intimacy with God?

Traditional Christian anthropology assumed that intimacy with God was a spiritual and/or intellectual activity, one that required developing a detachment from the delights of the body, sensuality and sexuality. Loving one's fellow human being was arguably central to this process as noted earlier. But it was also assumed that love of neighbor usually involved matters of justice and/or charity, not necessarily intimacy. It was assumed that one could be intimate with God by withdrawing into one's interior inner self where God is.

There is much to be said for this notion that intimacy with God is immediate and readily accessible through a quieting of one's active complex daily life and entering into an interior divine presence. Even modern philosophy, under the influence of Hegel, would suggest that God is imminent and fully integral to human consciousness. Certainly the impetus for much of monastic life in Christianity derives from an ascetic contemplative awakening to God who is ever present. In the light of this religious psychology, sexual intimacy would not be necessary for the full flourishing of human nature. Thus, moral norms requiring long-term or lifelong sexual abstinence technically never would have been unjust or inhumane. They might be difficult but not impossible or contrary to one's well-being.

Many modern atheists, particularly under the influence of Freud and Feuerbach, have argued that God is merely an infantile projection of the human need for security and the expression of the highest possibilities of human consciousness itself, nothing more. Accordingly, withdrawal into an interior divine presence is really just a withdrawal into the self. Worship of God is really a worship of human possibilities. To the extent that self-transparency is limited by our own neuroses and self-idealizing, the spiritual life is frequently a self-delusional escape from the complex reality of genuine interpersonal and social existence.

Atheistic theses about the delusional character of belief in God are not without problems. Even if their account of much of religious belief is persuasive, it does not lead necessarily to the conclusion that God does not exist or that all spirituality is delusional. However, the insights of contemporary psychology and philosophy of religion should not be written off as insignificant. Most religious believers can probably appreciate how easy it is to fashion God in accord with what we want or need God to be for us! And religious hypocrisy is not difficult to locate or identify in various religious groups or individuals. This must have been part of Jesus' intent to link love of neighbor with love of God. Withdrawal into a neat interior religious life is not a substitute for the complex demands of justice and right relationship with one's fellow human beings. Persistent and gross discrepancies between one's alleged relationship with God and one's real relationship with fellow human beings suggest that the alleged "good" relationship with God is probably inauthentic and self-deceiving.

What is the connection between sexual intimacy and love of God? There may be two ways of answering this. One, sexuality is the phenomenon that awakens the capacity to love deeply and intimately. When intense sexual desire awakens at adolescence, the interiority of the young person deepens and yearns for intimate companionship. Use of metaphorical language about sexual desire to describe desire for God in *The Song of Songs* and in spiritual classics like John of the Cross' *The Living Flame of Love* suggests that awareness of one's sexual desire, emotional vulnerability, and the profound interiority that longs for companionship are grounds for understanding what intimacy and union with God could be like. Thus, one's awareness of one's own sexuality is foundational for experiencing the call to profound intimacy with God.

Two, if intimacy with God is analogous to sexual intimacy (as affirmed in Biblical and classical spiritual writings), then the various mystifications that hinder authentic human intimate love are likely to be operative in our approach to God. John Bradshaw coined the phrase "mystification" to refer to the ways that young children (and perhaps adults) are sometimes shamed into thinking that something about them is not acceptable or loveable. To compensate for their sense of rejection they develop false selves and defensive strategies to please parents or other security providing adults.[48]

As adults we perpetuate these strategies, attempting to be someone we are not in order to please or acting defensively to compensate for and/or protect some interior vulnerable part of ourselves. While many people challenge us to get over our various mystifications, it is the love and affection of our sexual companions who accept our emotional vulnerability, heal our sense of unloveableness and invite us to greater authenticity. While it is not theoretically impossible for us to experience a call to more authentic love in intimate dialogue with God, it is more likely that the call to authentic love occurs in interpersonal relationships, particularly in sexual covenantal mutual ones.

Carter Heyward talks about the process of struggling to share power with another in sexual mutual relationships.[49] This is one of the most difficult processes we have to go through in personal maturation. One of the marks of human excellence is the capacity to respect, celebrate and share in the personal power or autonomy of other human beings. We have typically called this "being loving and just." On the contrary, people who are overpowering, controlling, unable to empower others, and unable to become appropriately vulnerable in intimate relationships are not persons of excellence. It is true that all sorts of relationships challenge us to recognize the reality of each other and to establish relationships that are loving and just (where we share power with each other). But the most challenging arena for this transformation is in committed sexually intimate relationships. Professional and casual relationships have built-in boundaries that usually soften the kind of feedback and emotional vulnerability needed for profound interior transformation. Committed sexually intimate relationships do not have these same boundaries and, consequently, are enormously challenging relationships. Sexual intimacy is normally the context within which people achieve the level of self-transparency that makes profound emotional intimacy possible.

From a religious ethical perspective, the above conclusion is important. Within the Christian tradition, union with God has been considered the ultimate good of the human person. Various types of Christian spirituality indicate ways of achieving intimacy with God. But if the normal way that an individual loves integrally and not delusionally is by first going through the chrysalis of interpersonal mutuality and, if such mutuality is normally established in the transparency of a physically intimate relationship, then intimacy and union with God are likely to be more authentic for those who are in or have been in committed sexually intimate relationships than for those who have not.

For Western Christianity (particularly Roman Catholic), with its long history of spirituality being shaped within a sexually celibate tradition, this conclusion could be quite confounding. Does this render most of Western spirituality specious and delusional? To some extent, yes! We must consider the possibility that a tradition which emphasizes sexual abstinence as the superior way to spiritual maturity may be mistaken and may have elevated a delusional spirituality as normative and authentic. In traditional Christianity there is very little concern raised about the dangers and pitfalls associated with long-term sexual abstinence or lifelong celibacy. Some individuals may pull it off well, but the inherent tendencies of lifelong celibacy to foster spiritual delusion, psychological immaturity and individualistic self-absorption need to be taken seriously and made part of the calculus of sexual ethics.

In order to achieve intimacy with self, others, and God, one must develop an ever more genuine self-transparency. We cannot love ourselves, others, or God unless we are engaged in a genuine and authentic self-disclosure or self-gift. We are not naturally self-transparent but develop false images of ourselves in response to various conflictive situations. Much of Western philosophy, theology and psychology includes accounts of how human beings form false images of themselves and what kind of therapy is needed to regain greater integrity and authenticity.

It seems that sexual abstinence risks increasing delusional images of the self precisely by accentuating disassociative and abstract images of the self. The sexual celibate is tempted to hold on to an image of the self that is free from the unsettledness, spontaneity, and erotic passion that calls the self outside of itself into real relationship with real persons in the world.[50] In identifying with a spiritual, transcendent, and rational image of the self, the individual does not have to deal with aspects of the self that are disclosed in intimate conflict with others. The other with whom one shares physical intimacy has the capacity to mirror back to the self aspects of the self that he/she is unwilling to face.

Curiously, in former ages, heterosexual marriage may have contributed to these same problems. Models of marriage built on institutional reproductive goods and not on interpersonal mutuality may also have contributed to psychological immaturity, spiritual delusion and self-absorption. Marriage partners were not necessarily expected or encouraged to learn how to share emotional power with each other or create the conditions where profound emotional intimacy could grow and develop. Some couples, notwithstanding, fell in love and established a life narrative of sexual and emotional intimacy with each other. Others established this intimacy with individuals outside the institutional marital relationship. Men often sought emotionally engaging relationships with friends, colleagues or even mistresses. Women shared a good deal of emotional intimacy with each other in various kinds of household, familial or social relationships.

Christian morality needs to acknowledge the importance of sexual intimacy for the psychological and spiritual maturation and well-being of people and then foster the kinds of relationships wherein that will occur. If the Church continues to honor consecrated celibacy, it needs to do so in such a way that celibates do not become alienated from the humanizing and maturing dynamics of sexual intimacy. Perhaps the Church could rethink what is meant by celibacy. It should not be conceived of as a life-style that avoids embodied forms of intimate love nor avoids the kinds of relationships that require learning how to share power with others. I suspect that warm, loving, compassionate and psychologically well-integrated celibates are those who have learned how to form close friendships, express affection in embodied ways and have lived in households or communities that require a good deal of negotiation and sharing of interpersonal power.

Implications for Single Adults

What does the foregoing analysis suggest about those who are not involved in sexually intimate relationships? Are we to conclude that they are immoral? Is the widow who has not remarried or the single female adult who is not currently sexually involved to be considered immoral?

First, we should distinguish between lifelong, long-term and periodic sexual abstinence. The kinds of harms associated with sexual abstinence derive from long-term and lifelong but not periodic abstinence. To suggest that sexual companionship is integral to personal maturation and flourishing does not mean that one must be engaging in sexual intimacy at all times in order to flourish. There are good reasons to avoid sexual intimacy, most particularly in situations where one's emotional and/or physical vulnerability are not likely to be honored or respected[51] or where refraining from physical sexual intimacy is a sign of respect and compassion for the physical and/or emotional needs of one's sexual partner. Periodic sexual abstinence is a valuable and important strategy for protecting one another's physical and emotional vulnerability.

Psychological or personal harm occurs in situations of long-term or lifelong sexual abstinence. Sometimes, however, individuals are abstinent by default, not by choice. Though consciously searching for an intimate companion they may have been unsuccessful. The search for sexual companionship is itself evidence of the importance that individuals attribute to it for their well-being. They often experience the lack of sexual companionship to be an impoverishment. But it would be tragic to shame such individuals. The thesis of this book is primarily directed at those **moral norms** of the Christian tradition (and secular society) which do not take into account harms associated with **mandated** long-term and lifelong sexual abstinence. Does this imply that those who practice long-term or lifelong sexual abstinence by choice are impoverished or harmed?

Some single adults are single by choice. As will be elaborated later in this work, there are different motivations for such a choice. It would seem that the choice to remain single in order to avoid the unsettledness and challenges of mutuality would involve a more serious avoidance of the vocation to intimacy. It would be difficult to see how this could be reconciled with the ideals of a reformed model of Christian moral excellence grounded in covenantal mutual love.

Some individuals may abstain from sexual intimacy out of profound emotional fear and trauma associated with sex. This is not uncommon for people who have been physically, emotionally or sexually abused. These individuals may have a good deal of difficulty allowing themselves to become emotionally or physically vulnerable in sexually intimate relationships. The fear or trauma they experienced earlier in life is a real disabling phenomenon that cannot be summarily dismissed. It would be inappropriate to suggest that these individuals are immoral by not engaging in sexual intimacy. The absence of sexual intimacy in their lives may constitute an impoverishment, but they may not have developed the requisite internal dispositions that would enable them to enter and sustain flourishing and healthy sexual relationships. For these individuals sexual intimacy might very well involve situations where their emotional vulnerability would not be adequately safeguarded.

Some individuals find themselves no longer part of former sexually intimate relationships by virtue of divorce, death of one's partner or the voluntary dissolution of a relationship. Sometimes people choose not to pursue sexually intimate relationships either for a long period of time or for the rest of their lives. This may not constitute a compromise of their personal flourishing for a number of reasons. In some instances, the former relationships were abusive or traumatic. These individuals need to develop other internal dispositions before they initiate healthy sexually intimate relationships in the future.

Others may need some time to process former sexual relationships. Sexual abstinence may be a way of preserving the solitude and interior space for this work. In essence, they are still being transformed by sexual intimacy but in a delayed and subsequent manner. It would seem that sexual intimacy for these people is not personally impoverishing.

Still others choose to remain single after leaving long relationships of codependency. There are some individuals who have so defined themselves in relationship to others that they need to recover a sense of their own intrinsic worth and identity. Singleness may be an important season in their own poetics of intimacy. In other words, in order to be a good poet of intimacy one must have an appropriate sense of one's own autonomy. Some individuals have been deprived of that through psychologically abusive and controlling relationships. Paradoxically, singleness in such a context serves intimacy!

Finally, there are those who choose to remain single not out of response to a codependent past nor out of need to process the lessons of an ending relationship but as a deliberate choice or preference for singleness. An important question that must be addressed is whether such long-term or lifelong singleness is harmful to personal well-being and, hence, an immoral choice.

Although traditional Christian sexual morality expected singles to remain sexually abstinent, the reasons given were largely to protect family patrimony or to restrain sexual desire and pleasure out of respect for dualistic models of moral psychology. Since these concerns are increasingly absent in contemporary Christian moral reflection, it is not at all clear that Christian morality should require sexual abstinence of singles. An individual who deliberately chooses to remain single may also have access to opportunities for significant sexual intimacy in enduring and mutual relationships. Therefore, someone who chooses to remain single need not suffer the impoverishing features of long-term or lifelong abstinence.

However, it would be difficult to endorse either a form of long-term singleness that thrived on promiscuous sexual encounters or one which was deprived of any significant interpersonal intimacy or mutuality. Both lack the kinds of relationships where the self flourishes and comes into an authentic autonomy.

In summary, the notion that long-term or lifelong sexual abstinence may be immoral is not primarily a matter of judging the moral character of those who are abstinent. Most of us are not in a position to appreciate the poetic context of an individual's choices about how to live out his/her vocation to intimacy.   Rather, the immorality of sexual abstinence refers to a prima facie judgment about harms associated with long-term lack of sexual companionship and to moral norms that require (otherwise morally competent) individuals to abstain from sexual intimacy for long periods of time. These moral norms are usually supported by theories of sexuality that fail to recognize sexual intimacy's importance in the maturation and flourishing of personal life and, thus, constitute a personally alienating and abusive moral system.

Implications for Adolescent Sexuality

A few remarks about sexuality education and adolescent sexuality are in order. Long-term sexual abstinence is impoverishing for adults. Young adolescents are not usually capable of the kind of emotional intimacy that would constitute an impoverishment in its absence. Some psychologists raise concern about the potential disassociative character of premature sexual intimacy among adolescents since the ability to integrate emotional and physical intimacy is not yet in place. Sexual addiction can develop under such circumstances. Thus, sexual intimacy among young adolescents could jeopardize personal maturation and integration and should be discouraged. But these concerns need to be offset by new insights into the psychologically neutral aspect of sexual experimentation and play among adolescents. Sex between a fourteen-year-old and a twenty-year-old involves significant disparities of power and risks exploitation and trauma for the fourteen-year-old. But sexual play or experimentation between two fourteen-year-olds may not carry with it this same risk.

The obvious challenge facing sexuality educators is that adolescents do engage in sexual intimacy and need information about how to protect themselves from sexually transmitted disease, HIV, untimely pregnancy, and physical and emotional trauma. The fear that more hygienic information about sexuality would increase sexual activity is not confirmed by the most recent statistics which show a decrease in sexual activity among teens who have had extensive education about contraceptives and safer sex.[52]

But if my thesis is correct, that long-term sexual abstinence among adults is impoverishing and not a good preparation for committed sexual relationships, then the discouragement of teen sexual intimacy needs to be accompanied with a positive portrayal of the blessings associated with sexual intimacy and an avoidance of the shaming of sexual intimacy before marriage or other committed relationships. This is obviously a difficult and delicate matter. How does one discourage premature sexual intimacy among those who intensely desire physical sexual intimacy and who often assume they are emotionally mature enough to form intimate relationships without shaming or vilifying sexual intimacy? Some studies suggest that adolescents who have a healthy mix of friendships and family relationships where they are validated and loved are less likely to turn to sex in a desperate attempt to get validation. When adolescents are sufficiently challenged with various educational, athletic and other expressive activities, they are less likely to turn to sex as a compensation for boredom or purposelessness.

I hope to show that a poetic approach to sexuality education and sexual virtue is a necessary complement and balance to a moral one. Rather than merely imposing moral restrictions, a poetic approach invites young people and adults to recognize the rich promise of sexuality and the conditions with which those possibilities are best realized. There is no substitute for the awkward and imperfect lessons that adolescents must learn in order to become responsible and graceful poets of sexual intimacy. An ethic that seeks to entirely eliminate the risks and imperfections of adolescents (through abstinence-only programs) seriously risks undermining the achievement of abilities that make adult sexuality satisfying and graceful. We must develop sexuality education programs that balance concern for the dangers of premature and irresponsible sexual intimacy with the dangers associated with sexual abstinence.

Notes

1   E. O. Laumann, J.H.Gagnon, R.T.Michael and S. Michaels, *The Social Organization of Sexuality: Sexual Practices in the United States* (Chicago: University of Chicago Press, 1994) pp. 88–89.

2   *SEICUS Report*, August/September 1994.

3   Rand Corporation Study reported in *Los Angeles Times* and *USA Today*, 1999.

4   National Conference of Catholic Bishops (Committee on Marriage and Family), "Always Our Children," *Origins*, vol. 27: no. 17, Oct. 9, 1997, pp. 285–291.

5   This powerful story is told in *Prayers for Bobby: A Mother's Coming To Terms With The Suicide Of Her Gay Son*, written by Leroy Aarons (San Francisco: HarperSanFrancisco, 1995).

6   Carter Heyward, *Touching Our Strength: The Erotic as the Power and the Love of God* (San Francisco: Harper and Row, 1989) pp. 3 and 95.

7   Marvin M. Ellison, *Erotic Justice: A Liberating Ethic of Sexuality* (Louiseville, KY: Westminster John Knox Press, 1996) pp. 2, 28–29.

8   Karen Lebacqz, "Appropriate Vulnerability," *Sexuality and the Sacred*, ed. James B. Nelson and Sandra P. Longfellow (Louisville: Westminster/John Knox Press, 1994) pp. 256–261.

9   Actually, recent studies suggest that the divorce rate may be decreasing slightly.

10 Ground breaking work in this area was undertaken by Ashley Montagu. *Touching: The Human Significance of the Skin* 3rd. ed. (New York: Harper and Row, 1986) note particularly chapters 5–7. Robert Hatfield has also synthesized a vast amount of recent research on touch deprivation in adults

and its harmful impact on their lives and in society: Robert Hatfied, "Touch and Human Sexuality," *Human Sexuality: An Encyclopedia*, V. Bullough, B. Bullough and A. Stein (Eds.) (New York: Garland Pub., 1994).

[11] Uta Ranke-Heinemann, *Eunuchs For The Kingdom of Heaven: Women, Sexuality, and the Catholic Church*, trans. Peter Heinegg (New York: Penguin Books, 1990) chapter 10.

[12] *Humanae Vitae*, Pope Paul VI, 1968. It banned the use of artificial contraception.

[13] Pope John Paul II, "Lessons from the Galileo Case," *Origins* (12 Nov. 1992) par. 7.

[14] Ibid., par. 9, attributed to Augustine.

[15] The Council of Chalcedon, 451 C.E., declared that Jesus was fully human and fully divine.

[16] Karl Rahner, *Foundations of Christian Faith: An Introduction to the Idea of Christianity*, trans. William V. Dych (New York: Seabury Press, 1978) Chapter One, particularly pp. 24–25.

[17] Thomas Aquinas, *Summa Theologica*, IIaIIae, q. 152 a. 2.

[18] Servais Pinckaers, *The Sources of Christian Ethics*, trans. by Sr. Mary Thomas Noble (Washington, D.C.: Catholic University of America Press, 1995) pp. 447–448.

[19] John Calvin, *Commentary on Genesis*.

[20] John Calvin, *Divine Institutes*, n. 42.

[21] Martin Luther, *Babylonian Captivity of the Church*.

[22] Several recent studies in neural function are providing evidence of the importance of sensuality and emotion for reason. They include: *Descartes' Error: Emotion, Reason and the Human Brain*, Antonio Demasio (New York: Grosset/Putnam, 1994) and *The Emotional Brain*, Joseph LeDoux (New York: Simon and Schuster, 1996).

[23] Audre Lorde, *Sister Outsider: Essays and Speeches* (Trumansburg, N.Y.: Crossing Press, 1984).

[24] Carter Heyward, Op. cit.

[25] James Nelson, *Embodiment* (Minneapolis: Augsburg, 1978).

[26] Ibid., pp. 58–68.

27 Another fruitful elaboration of this notion is found in several of Matthew Fox's works, notably, *A Spirituality Named Compassion* (Minneapolis: Winston Press, 1979).

28 Christine E. Gudorf, *Body, Sex and Pleasure* (Cleveland: Pilgrim Press, 1994) pp. 81–138.

29 Heyward, Op. cit., chapter six.

30 Hatfield, Op. cit, p.583 (citing J.W. Prescott, "Somatosensory affectional deprivation (SAD) theory of drug and alcohol abuse," *National Institute on Drug Abuse Research Monograph Series*, 1980, 30, 286–296, and J.W. Prescott, "Body pleasure and the origins of violence," in *Bulletin of the Atomic Scientists*, 1975, 11, 10–20.

31 Walter R. Gove, Carolyn Briggs Style, Michael Hughes, "The Effect of Marriage on the Well-Being of Adults," *Journal of Family Issues*: 11 (1) March, 1990, p. 5.

32 Ibid., p. 7.

33 Ibid., p. 7.

34 Ibid., p. 13, citing L. Pearlin and J. Johnson, "Marital status, life strains and depression," in *American Sociological Review*, 42, 704–715.

35 Ibid., p. 15.

36 Ibid., p. 15.

37 Karen Lebacqz, Op cit. pp. 256–261.

38 James T. Sears, "Dilemmas and Possibilities of Sexuality Education," *Sexuality and the Curriculum*, ed. James T. Sears (New York: Teachers College Press, 1992) p.14.

39 See *The Book of Common Prayer* (Episcopal rite of blessing marriages) and *Gaudium et Spes* (Vatican II's reform of the theology of marriage) as exemplary in this matter.

40 Martin Buber, *I and Thou*, trans. Walter Kaufman (New York: Charles Scribner's Sons, 1970).

41 Thomas R. Kopfensteiner, "The Metaphoric Structure of Normativity," *Theological Studies*, 58 (1997) 331–346.

42 Sallie McFague, *Metaphorical Theology: Models of God in Religious Language* (Philadelphia: Fortress Press, 1982).

43 James F. Keenan, "Proposing Cardinal Virtues," in *Theological Studies* 56 (1995) 712.

[44]   Edward Collins Vacek, *Love, Human and Divine: The Heart of Christian Ethics* (Washington, D.C., Georgetown Univ. Press, 1994) 42–47.

[45]   Ibid., p. 44.

[46]   Ibid., pp. 22–24.

[47]   John Bradshaw, *Creating Love: The Next Great Stage of Growth* (New York: Bantam Books, 1992) pp. 6–7.

[48]   John Bradshaw, Op. cit., p.6.

[49]   Carter Heyward, Op. cit., pp. 99–100.

[50]   Iris Murdoch, *The Sovereignty of the Good* (London: Routledge and Kegan Paul, 1970).

[51]   Lebaczq, Op.cit., pp. 259–260.

[52]   Mark Schuster, "Impact of a High School Condom Availability Program on Sexual Attitudes and Behaviors," Alan Guttmacher Institute, 1998.

❖ Chapter Two

Existential Insecurity and Addiction to Sexual Renunciation

Western Apprehension of Sexuality

It is fair to say that in the West sexuality has been regarded with suspicion. There are carefully elaborated norms for when and where sexual expression is appropriate, strict rituals for initiating and severing sexual relationships, resistance to formal sexuality education programs, strong cultural shaming mechanisms for those who deviate from established sexual norms, and fairly consistent models of virtue centered on sexual self-control and the minimization of sexual pleasure.

Many who read this book are bound to be concerned about the well-being of their children and loved ones. On the surface of things, sexuality is dangerous. Life threatening and disabling diseases are transmitted through sexual contact. Young people are vulnerable to emotional trauma associated with premature sexual intimacy. Young and old are vulnerable to sexual violence and the dangerous emotional instability of scorned lovers. Families and friends are torn apart by failed marriages and sexual infidelity. Conception of new life outside of stable family environments seems tragic for both the future child and for the adolescents or adults whose lives are often complicated by responsibilities they might not have anticipated. Sexual desire is a powerful emotion that seems to compromise our judgment at times. Wouldn't we all be better served by a more traditional model of sexual self-control and tighter boundaries of sexual intimacy? Isn't the thesis of this book misplaced given the problems generated by sexuality? Don't the dangers of sexuality warrant a more cautious and conservative response?

There are real dangers associated with sexuality. Those dangers warrant our attention and respect in the elaboration of a reasonable sexual ethic. However, the thesis of this book is that **some** of the dangers associated with sexuality lie with the absence of sexual intimacy and with the elaboration of dualistic anthropologies and dualistic models of the relationship between sexuality and human flourishing.

As already noted, a dualistic anthropology is a theory that understands human beings to be composed of a sensual/body part and a rational/spiritual part and that these parts are essentially antagonistic and/or hierarchically ordered. Dualistic anthropologies argue that what is essentially human is reason. The body and its sensuality (and sexuality) are inferior and/or unessential and in need of being ruled by the superior and essential dimension of human nature, reason. Accordingly, in order to achieve human perfection, one must grow increasingly detached from the body and its sensuality in order to identify more perfectly with the rational/spiritual selves that we are. Dualistic anthropology has been a fundamental tenet of much of Western philosophical, religious, and cultural history. Our theories about human nature have been shifting in the light of new information and models derived from psychology, biology, neurology, philosophy, and sociology. Dualistic anthropology is increasingly incompatible with current theories about human well-being. Since most of Western and Christian sexual morality was elaborated within a now outdated dualistic anthropology, it is no wonder that we are finding it less and less compelling as a model of sexual virtue and human excellence.

The objective of this chapter is to identify the reasons why dualistic anthropologies and dualistic sexual moralities made sense at one time or, at least, appeared to make sense. What is it about human existence that tempts us to problematicize sexuality? Do alternative strategies that avoid the dangers of dualism exist for dealing with these underlying anxieties?

Existential Insecurity

We cannot adequately address the problematization of sexuality without understanding a more fundamental level of anxiety associated with human subjectivity itself. In his great work, *The Phenomenology of Spirit*,[1] G.W.F. Hegel describes how human consciousness produces personal insecurity or anxiety. This so-called existential insecurity (an insecurity over our being and existence) is what tempts human beings into developing strategies of control and self-possession and accounts for some of the Western apprehension of sexuality and its addiction to dualistic anthropologies.

Modern philosophical models of consciousness and subjectivity were influenced by Hegel's description of how human beings think and act. Prior to Hegel, it was assumed that human consciousness was singular. One group of scholars believed that the human mind was essentially passive to the real objective world. Another group believed that the mind was more active, shaping the world through innate rational categories. Hegel sought to develop a theory of consciousness which affirmed the reality and interaction of both these models.

According to Hegel, when an individual focuses on an object or a motive for action, two dimensions of his/her subjectivity are engaged: an immediate awareness or consciousness of the object (a type of passive awareness) as well as a shaping or transcending consciousness. Objects are able to be identified thanks to the horizon or context against which they stand out. If you as a reader are looking at this book, it is recognized as such in part out of contrast with what it is not. The table or your hands or lap are a context or horizon against which the book stands out as a distinct object. The objectification and identification of the book as such could not occur without your being able to simultaneously focus on the object **and** contextualize it.

According to Hegel, since both of these aspects of consciousness (immediate awareness of objects and the contextualizing or transcending of them) are rooted in our own subjectivity, we become aware of ourselves precisely because we do not coincide completely with the objects of our thought. We become self-conscious precisely as more than or greater than any particular object with which we are engaged and/or greater than any particular action we anticipate or perform. In other words, if the mind was merely passive to reality, it would be filled with the reality of whatever it viewed and be unaware of itself as distinct from the object of thought. Similarly, if thought was merely a matter of projecting the mind, there would be no ability to distinguish the self from what the self is not.

Since we experience ourselves as both more than whatever we are engaged in or doing **and** as what we are engaged in and doing, there is a fundamental dissonance or lack of harmony at the heart of our own lives. We are what we are not and not what we are.[2] We sense a self within a self, an otherness in ourselves that, to some extent, is ourself. We are not at ease with this interior personal dissonance. We yearn to be ourselves. We want to cohere with ourselves, to possess ourselves with integrity, wholeness, and completeness. But we cannot.

As a consequence, Hegel said that human beings seek to find something that can bridge the gap they experience between themselves and themselves, some object that can so fully engage them that they would finally be complete and whole. But every attempt to do that only further deepens the dissonance since anything they desire and engage requires the accompanying transcending/contextualizing consciousness that leaves them fundamentally dissatisfied. Since this transcending/contextualizing consciousness finds no limit to its reach, human beings experience their own inwardness or self-consciousness as an infinite longing.[3]

Human subjectivity is characterized then by an infinite depth or longing that cannot coincide with itself, cannot complete itself, cannot possess itself. Every attempt to complete or perfect the self by doing something or having something requires the engagement of the very transcendental features of subjectivity that deepen and exacerbate this interior depth and infinite horizon. This, in turn, leads to a pervasive sense of ontological insecurity, an uneasiness or insecurity over our own being.

Human beings are those beings whose being is not secure, in full self-possession, complete, or whole. Human beings are those beings who experience themselves always at issue, in question, changing and developing.[4] There is, as it were, a kind of inevitable self-surpassing that is both elating because it is aggrandizing but also anxiety producing because the self is always in a state of disruption, unsettledness, and turmoil. Since this sense of unsettledness is set against an infinite horizon, it produces a sense of the possibility of one's total unraveling and disruption, hence an insecurity that is not minimal or superficial but profound and total. Human beings stand between the promise of greatness (the elation that comes with an awareness of infinite possibility) and the abyss of self-annihilation (the awareness that one's being is fragile and perpetually and irretrievably out of one's control).

The temptation, perhaps even an imperative, is to find a strategy, a relationship, a system, or some object that can compensate or overcome this fundamental subjective sense of insecurity. Indeed, the human attempt to resolve the pain and anxiety of ontological insecurity may be a central hermeneutical (interpretive key) insight for understanding all sorts of human endeavors and institutions, from religion to morality to economics to politics. What grounds our allegiance to the moral, religious, political, economic and cultural institutions of which we are a part? Is it this deep ontological insecurity? If so, it may both explain the ultimacy we want to attribute to them as well as the final inadequacy they manifest. And this tension between ultimacy and inadequacy may be the most wrenching realization of post-modern life. We are increasingly aware that our religious, moral, political and economic institutions are historical and cultural constructions. We have, in some sense, become aware of this out of their inability (inadequacy) to provide the kind of stability and order we had anticipated. But, we are also aware that a merely relativistic and contingent set of religious, moral, political and economic institutions does not elicit the kind of allegiance, nor provide the kind of coherence, we yearn for as reasoning creatures. Emmanuel Levinas highlighted this tension in his work, *Totality and Infinity*,[5] and anticipated some of the new models of truth that have been proposed by people like Iris Murdoch and Wendy Farley.[6] Levinas, Murdoch, and Farley point out that attempts to totalize or reify truth contradict the always transcendent aspect of it. The totalizing or objectification of truth is a form of idolatry. It should be seen for what it is, an addiction that attempts to compensate for existential/ontological insecurity.

Existential Insecurity and Sexuality

These insights are illuminating for understanding sexual morality. As Hegel noted, the inability of people to coincide with themselves leads to the search for self-completion in an "other." The thought runs something like this: "If I can't achieve possession of myself through my own efforts, perhaps the recognition and appreciation of my subjectivity by another subject would give me back myself in a way that I can't achieve on my own." Hegel suggests that we long for recognition of ourselves (love) in the consciousness of the other. We typically load our intimate relationships with enormous expectations. We long for fulfillment, for the realization of the infinite longing that we harbor deep within ourselves.

Intimate relationships, then, also have the potential to create enormous anxiety and suffering. If one stakes one's ontological security on the recognition and love of another, and the other betrays him/her or doesn't offer the level of recognition or love anticipated, then one's own incoherence and alienation from oneself is felt in a renewed and more intense form. Hegel's description of our longing for recognition and the desire for interpersonal intimacy help account for why sexually intimate relationships carry with them the danger of being emotionally devastating. We enter sexually intimate relationships with very high expectations. And there is always the danger, indeed the inclination, to make the other merely a projection of our own subjective needs. The famous Hegelian analysis of the master/slave relationship describes this dynamic.

According to Hegel, our ontological insecurity is inclined to demand total recognition and love from the other or total devotion to another. Either our own subjectivity must fill the consciousness of the other (domination) or our own subjectivity must be filled with the consciousness of the other (submission). This need for total recognition by another or total devotion to another accounts, in part, for the appeal of sexual abstinence.

How does this appeal of sexual abstinence develop? The reality of the person with whom I am in relationship is not exhausted in his/her being for me or recognition and love of me. First of all, there are things I will do that do not deserve recognition or affirmation by the other. Second, the other's own dignity and reality are more than a projection of my own desires or needs. The other deserves recognition and love from me as well and not merely when he/she does what I desire or want from him/her.

The reality of the other as distinct and different from me and I as distinct and different from him/her means three things. First, we cannot use each other to complete or possess ourselves. We simply cannot get the kind of recognition or self-completion from the other that we might idealize. Second, conflict and/or difference are part and parcel of any relationship. The other is not to be merely a projection of my own needs and desires nor am I to be merely a projection of the needs and desires of the other. Third, as another subject, the other adds a new level of unrest, disruption, and change in my life. Close relationships add new levels of ontological self-surpassing or unrest to our lives.

It should then come as no surprise that some moral, philosophical, and religious traditions have advocated either the suppression of erotic desire or the elimination of sexual relationships altogether. Erotic desire draws us into relationship with other real persons. It is an apparent source of unrest, disruption, and insecurity. It certainly reminds us that we are not self-possessed or self-completed. If sexual relations could be rationalized, reified, or institutionalized, we could take some of the disruptiveness away from them. Stoic efforts to describe marriage as an institution primarily centered in reproduction and household management are one form of this rationalization and institutionalization of sexual relationships. The ideal couple, according to Stoic thought, would become *"apatheia,"* without passion for each other. They would fulfill the purposes of marriage with a rational detachment.

Sexual abstinence is appealing because it purportedly eliminates the unsettledness or disruptiveness of sexual relationships. Much of the language associated with consecrated virginity in Christianity (freely chosen lives of sexual renunciation) refers to a kind of purity or singleness of heart. Peter Brown elucidates the importance of this theme in Judaism and Christianity of the first two centuries of the common era.[7] In many respects, Jewish and Christian spirituality involved not so much a battle between the flesh and the spirit but a battle for singleness and purity of heart. True peace would come when one's heart was no longer divided, when there was no more duplicity in the self. This meant not only an absence of duplicity with respect to one's fellow human being but an absence of duplicity with respect to God.

It is easy to see how sexual desire could be regarded as a threat to singleness of heart. Not only does it have the potential to pull an individual in various directions at the same time (competing desires) but it manifests the unsettledness and restlessness of the will. Moreover, it must have been obvious even to those who lived in a different social milieu that relations between spouses often brought with them emotional conflict. One could be much more focused, devoted, and committed if one did not have to attend to the subjectivity of other real persons. One could be more single-hearted if one did not have to share power with another person in intimacy. And under the intense persecution of Christians during the first three centuries of Christianity, those who did not have to think about loyalty to and/or loss of spouses or children could more unwaveringly sacrifice their lives for the cause! Uta Ranke-Heinemann cites the Roman Catholic Catechism (published after the Council of Trent) as an example of the view that sexual relationships disrupt the vocation to holiness: "that all would wish to strive after the virtue of continence, for believers can find nothing more blessed in this life than that their spirit, distracted by no worldly cares and after quieting and subduing every pleasure of the flesh, should rest solely in the zeal of godliness and in the contemplation of heavenly things."[8]

Is this singleness of heart a mark of human excellence or a strategy for dealing with ontological insecurity, a kind of idolatrous objectification and reification of God? Is the unmitigated commitment of an individual to a cause, to a religion, to a principle, to a god a sign of excellence and virtue or a substitute for living with the contingency, complexity, and unsettledness that invariably accompany transcendental subjectivity?

The answer to these questions is central to the thesis of this book! Both Roman Catholic exaltation of consecrated celibacy and the more general Christian notion that long-term or lifelong sexual abstinence is not harmful (for the divorced and for gay men and lesbians) assume that human excellence or human perfection is achieved through a single-hearted love of God. Single-hearted devotion to God is a way of giving focus and shape to human transcendental subjectivity. But is this focus or shape an authentic one? Does it correspond to the exigencies of our subjectivity? Does it correspond to the rich potential of relationship with God?

Relationship With or Rest in God?

It is true that human subjectivity gives rise to a profound interiority that longs to be filled, that longs to be engaged. This interiority (traditionally called the soul) is aptly described as infinitely profound. Nothing short of that which is itself infinite and inexhaustible could ever hope to engage its full richness. Thus, it is assumed, with Augustine's famous saying, "our hearts are restless until they rest in Thee," that our full realization can be had only in the Supreme Good who is God. But as a number of so-called process theologians have remarked, the idea of an actual infinite is self-contradictory.[9] The idea of infinity includes the notion of always more, always becoming, always extending.

When God is objectified and reified, God's always transcendent character ceases to be transcendent. God cannot really be an **object** of devotion in the sense of a finite determinate thing. God is an infinite horizon, an inexhaustible ground or subject of relationality and connectedness, incapable of being engaged (comprehended or possessed) with a single-hearted focus. The way to union with God must be relational, a relationship between transcendental subjects, not determinate objects.

The hope of finding rest or completion in God seems to be a misplaced hope. It is a hope that makes sense, given the frustration we experience over our own transcendental subjectivity, but it is a hope that both circumvents the reality of God and attempts to suppress the dynamic character of our own subjectivity. Relationship with God, like relationships with other subjects, is dynamic, unfolding, developing, even, one dare say, disruptive and unsettling. Moreover, if all of reality is comprehended by the being of God, then relationship with God includes relationship with other transcendental subjects. This means that relationship with God cannot escape the difficult process of learning how to be mutual with other human subjects, however disruptive, unsettled, and conflictual that might be. This seems to harken back to Jesus' admonitions that one cannot claim to love God without loving one's fellow human being. And loving one's fellow human being is not an abstract idealized notion but a notion that involves messy and complex interaction like the example of the Samaritan caring for the robbery victim, Jesus' caring for lepers, Jesus' relationship with the tax collector, or Jesus' interaction with women (given the ritual purity codes of Jewish life).

We must begin to regard singleness of heart for what it really is, a tempting form of self-completion that circumvents the demanding and conflicting contours of real interpersonal mutuality. This is not to say that focus, direction, commitment, perseverance, and devotion are unimportant; but, it is to say that they must be complemented with the kind of mutuality or love that invariably challenges us with disruptiveness, unsettledness, and conflicting obligations.

This is one of the reasons why long-term and lifelong sexual abstinence is impoverishing. It deprives us of the kinds of relationships where we both practice and learn how to be genuinely and profoundly mutual. Again, I want to reiterate that many types of relationships offer the opportunity for genuine mutuality; but, sexually intimate relationships offer the greatest potential and challenge for learning how to love mutually. Other types of relationships have built-in boundaries which appropriately limit the level of intimacy and self-transparency and transformation.

Addiction to Sexual Renunciation

The foregoing analysis should illustrate why sexual abstinence becomes addictive and can be used by addictive systems.[10] Addictive behavior uses substances or processes to cope with the disruptiveness and unsettledness of emotions. Since the addictive substance or process does not really provide the hoped for solution but only a temporary or superficial fix through the emotional satisfaction of the substance or process, the addict must keep going back. The grip of addiction stems both from the high or satisfaction it provides and from the ontological insecurity it purports to fix.

One would assume that there is a greater temptation to become addicted to sex rather than sexual abstinence. And, indeed, there are many who use sex to cope with their emotional lives. But, just as some individuals are addicted to work and to various obsessive compulsions to order and neatness, sexual abstinence has the propensity to become addictive because it purports to offer a reprieve from the emotional vagaries of sexual intimacy. It provides a kind of control against the emotional disruptiveness of mutuality. It provides an illusion of order and self-control against the seemingly chaotic and uncontrollable forces of sexual desire. And, as with most addictions, the more one becomes dependent on the substance or process to stave off the chaos of the feared emotion the more powerful and overwhelming those emotions appear. So those addicted to sexual abstinence begin to regard the dangers of sexual desire and sexual intimacy way out of proportion.

The obsessive and compulsive behavior of addiction is certainly evidenced by some of the statements made by celibate writers/authorities in Roman Catholicism. Uta Ranke-Heinemann chronicles this obsession and its eventual imposition on the laity in the form of increased expectation of periodic and long-term sexual abstinence. Augustine, for example, considered sexual desire evil and encouraged its minimalization. He called for sexual abstinence on "Sundays and feast days, in Lent, during the catechumenate (preparation period for Baptism), and, in general, at prayer time. Prayer pleases God better, he says, when it is spiritual, that is when a person is free from carnal desires.[11] Jerome wrote: "The apostle says, one cannot pray during the time that one has relations with one's wife. Thus, if prayer is made impossible by coitus, then this is certainly still more true for what is more than prayer, the reception of the body of Christ . . . I speak to the consciences of those who communicate on the same day that they have marital relations."[12] And Origen wrote: "He comes thoughtlessly into the sanctuary of the church who comes there after the conjugal act and its impurity, so as presumptuously to receive the Eucharistic bread. He dishonors and desecrates what is holy."[13]

Albert the Great believed that sensual pleasure "paralyzed the mind" and "enervated the spirit" such that one could not contemplate sacred things.[14] William of Auvergne (d. 1249), Bishop of Paris, encouraged married people to "flee all physical pleasure because pleasure hinders the soul's development." He even praised men who cultivated an "icy" disposition to their wives (as a sign of sexual virtue).[15] Aquinas also stressed how sexual pleasure suppresses and "completely checks the use of reason," that it "stifles reason" and "absorbs the mind."[16]

Michael Crosby cites a particularly shocking statement by Peter Damian in the eleventh century about the dangers of women for clerical purity:

> You vipers full of madness, parading the ardor of your ungovernable lust, through your lovers you mutilate Christ, who is the head of the clergy. . .You snatch away the unhappy men from their ministry of the sacred altar, in which they were engaged, that you may strangle them with the slimy glue of your passion . . . [17]

Crosby states that earlier attempts to enforce celibacy were grounded, in part, in maintaining ritual purity. Since that rationale is no longer part of the theology of sexuality or priesthood, "the core of the celibacy issue remains connected to the need to preserve clerical control."[18] Despite increases in Catholic population in the United States, the number of clergy continues to decrease. Many dioceses have had to close smaller parishes and staff larger ones with fewer priests. Some parishes do not have resident priests and must forego celebration of the Eucharist from time to time. Many have advocated opening up the priesthood to married men and women. The Vatican has responded by stating that those issues are closed and not open for discussion.The unwillingness to open up dialogue and discussion is a sign of compulsive control and institutional addiction to authority. The fact that these issues center around sexuality suggests that the addiction also includes an addiction to sexual control.

Although other Christian denominations do not mandate celibacy for ordained ministers, institutional control is associated with new efforts to enforce sexual abstinence on single adults and gay men and lesbians. As noted earlier, several mainstream Christian denominations have used traditional moral norms about sexual abstinence outside of heterosexual marriage in an attempt exclude openly gay and lesbian people from becoming ministers. When justification of these positions is offered, appeal is made to the authority of Scripture or the long-standing tradition of the Church. No effort is made to respond to contemporary evidence of the health and grace associated with committed sexual relationships among gay men or lesbians nor to the importance for single adults of establishing narratives of successful intimacy before making marriage commitments. In short, the appeal to the value of sexual abstinence, whether in the Roman Catholic Church or in other Christian denominations, is no longer made with regard to evidence from the social sciences about the psychological health of sexual intimacy or its absence but simply as a matter of institutional authority. It is as if a grown-up son or daughter is asking his/her parent why they may not do something and the parent says, "because I said so." The unwillingness or inability to move beyond authoritarianism is a sign of addictive or compulsive control and, when it centers on matters of sexuality, it is most probably a sign of addiction to control of sexuality.

Ontological Insecurity and Sexual Desire: New Approaches

If modern philosophical accounts of human subjectivity are correct in suggesting that human beings enjoy a dialectical and transcendental subjectivity, and if, as Walter Davis argues, this is not a fault, a fall from some primordial wholeness, but an original and fundamental condition of human nature, then attempts to overcome it through strategies of self-possession and self-completion are at best futile and at worst self-contradictory and harmful.[19] As Matthew Fox notes in *Original Blessing*, Christian theology has been preoccupied with the theme of human failure, "original sin," and our need for redemption at the expense of another equally valid theme of human history, our "original blessing."[20] The original blessings of creation were not obliterated by sin. These blessings should be a source of grace, growth, renewal, and life. But, if we view them as problematic, we alienate ourselves from them. Are unsettledness, disquietude, disruptiveness, and constant self-surpassing (transcendence) problems to be brought under control or are they aspects of the original blessing of human nature? Are our attempts to suppress the dialectical character of our subjectivity, in other words, our attempts to achieve a stable and secure self-mastery free from disruptiveness and change, the original sin? Human creativity, reason, and spirituality would be impossible without a dialectical subjectivity, without an infinite horizon within which all our projects occur.

Paradoxically, ontological insecurity, the experience that our being is always at stake, always in question, always in flux, always unsettled, always disruptive, is a blessing! It does not feel like a blessing because we also desire and need coherence, order, continuity and predictability. Human beings are caught in an existential state of both longing for self-possession and self-completion and experiencing that very longing as a result of a disruptive dialectical subjectivity. Stoic efforts to gain ultimate self-mastery and Christian emphasis on the Fall and our need for redemption are systems which have emphasized the longing for coherence at the expense of the blessing of unsettledness and change. As Fox rightly notes, we need to recover a creation-centered spirituality, a creation-centered approach to our being.

Since addiction to sexual control is symptomatic of our discomfort with existential insecurity, release from that addiction is only possible if we give up the fear of unsettledness, disruptiveness, creativity, spontaneity, and vulnerability. We have to learn to name those feelings as blessings, as feelings associated with the richness of our own nature. Most people fear that in doing so they will succumb to a Dionysian fury, overwhelmed by the irrationality of sexual desire or other appetites. They do not trust their bodies, they do not trust their emotions, they do not trust their sexuality, they do not trust the original blessings of their nature.

Carter Heyward and Christine Gudorf are two among several who have attempted to redeem the blessings associated with sexual desire and bodily pleasures. Heyward speaks of eros as our embodied yearning for mutuality. The longing for love or mutuality is not primarily or exclusively a cognitive or spiritual reality. It is one that is deeply grounded in our embodiment. As such, our various sexual urges are gifts that draw us into relationship with others. Heyward speaks of them as some of our most powerful experiences of God's grace calling us into relationship. Thus, eros is a strength, a grace, a blessing. The vilification of eros alienates us from the blessings of our body, from each other, and from God.[21]

Gudorf's notion that sexual pleasure is a premoral good parallels Fox's language of original blessing. She speaks about the basic goodness of sexual pleasure as one of the gifts of God's creation. She also focuses on the manner in which earlier Christian thinkers, particularly Augustine and Jerome, vilified sexual pleasure as irresistible. For example, Jerome believed that only those who had never experienced sexual pleasure could be free from "its dangerous tentacles."[22]

As Gudorf notes, and as many readers will in fact attest, sexual desire and sexual pleasure are not irresistible. In all sorts of situations people experience sexual desire and do not act on it. She notes that many lovers, particularly those who have been with each other for some time, will postpone sexual gratification either to enhance pleasure or to find a more suitable context for its enjoyment.

There may be a greater propensity for men to think of sexual desire and sexual pleasure as irresistible due to the spontaneity of erection. Gudorf notes several works by James Nelson on this subject.[23] Particularly during adolescence, but certainly not absent in adult life, men experience spontaneous erections. Perhaps it would be easier to deny the spontaneousness of sexual desire if it were primarily a matter of sexual thoughts; but, particularly for men, there is an embodied manifestation that is difficult to ignore. To whatever extent men and women are socialized to think that self-control and self-mastery are laudable goals, the spontaneity of sexual desire and sexual erection is bound to be disconcerting.

But the social or, in this case, ecclesial vilification of sexual desire and sexual spontaneity as undermining of the project of self-mastery and self-control severs us from one of the primary blessings of our nature. The result is dangerous.

As Gudorf notes, the feelings and emotions associated with our sexuality are important messages for helping us know the state we are in, how we are. She states:

> All of us need to hear the messages circulating in our bodies, to interpret them correctly, and to cooperate with them. Repression— denial of the body messages—is dangerous, even fatal. Denial of some specific body messages—of chronic pain, of tiredness, of changes in our body's rhythms—is frequently responsible, especially in men, for unnecessary deaths due to late discovery of conditions such as cancer and hypertension, which are treatable when discovered early. We need to listen to our body messages so that we act to meet our needs— whether they are for rest, for physical closeness, for release of muscle tension, for interpersonal intimacy, or many others.[24]

Alienation from our sexual feelings severs us from important messages about our relationships. It leaves us ill equipped to interpret what is going on so that we can make responsible decisions. Sexual desire is not a threat to responsibility as much as its repression is. We need to learn to trust the wisdom of our embodied yearnings and trust our ability to contextualize them appropriately.

One of the important features of human subjectivity is our ability to contextualize things. Things are not just what they are; they assume importance and value, to some extent, through the manner in which they are appropriated, associated, and contextualized by us. The ability to see things from varying perspectives enables enormous creativity on the part of human beings. Technology is a way of putting things together creatively. If we couldn't see new ways to contextualize and associate things, this would be impossible.

Likewise, human gestures and actions need contextualization. The gift from an associate can be an expression of affection or a bribe. An embrace can express friendship, solidarity, or sexual interest. The movement of war planes may be a military practice, a new defensive strategy, or an indication of hostility. Our successful interaction with each other requires the ability to understand the context of various actions. It requires the ability to appropriately contextualize what we wish to express. And this, in part, depends upon mutually recognizable signals and syntax.

Contextualization is a way of understanding. And with understanding we are enabled to act appropriately. If I understand another's embrace to be an expression of friendship, I do not have to fear sexual interest which might be inappropriate. If a nation understands its neighbor's military movements to be a military exercise, it does not have to react as if they represent an attack. When I understand that the scraping noise on the side of the house is a tree branch shaking in the wind, I am freed from the gripping fear I initially had that it was a burglar.

Similarly, if we contextualize sexual desire as irresistible, we are likely to fear it and seek its repression whenever it arises. If, on the other hand, we understand sexual desire to be an embodied yearning for mutuality,[25] we are enabled to act in ways that serve mutuality. As Thomas Moore notes in his recent book, *The Soul of Sex*,[26] "This eros we feel in sex and romance is also the broader magnetism that holds the universe together, the go-between spirit said to keep the planets in orbit and the seasons on track. What we seek in sex is not only bodily satisfaction, but a response to the soul's need for all that eros offers, for a world that holds together and a whole life that is creative and motivated by love."[27] Rather than seeking to control and repress sexual desire, we need to learn how to listen to its stirrings, asking rather how our soul is seeking to connect with life.

Let me illustrate with an example. Mike is a hard working financial manager. He has been married to Jean for seven years. They have two young children. Jean is an interior decorator working out of their home. Mike and Jean both put in long hours at work. Between their jobs, activities involving the children, and responsibilities for their aging parents they have not been very attentive to their relationship. They have sex about once a month.

Mike hired a new executive assistant who happens to be quite attractive. Susan is bright, has a very pleasant personality, and shares Mike's interest in music. Mike begins to notice that he has developed a strong attraction for Susan. He obsesses about her, spends more and more time with her discussing various recording artists, and is frequently aroused. One day, Susan brings a file into his office and casually puts her hand on his shoulder as they are looking at it together. Mike nearly loses control of himself. Startled by his feelings, he tells himself he must get control of his feelings or ruin his marriage. He decides he must begin to communicate a more professional and distant demeanor toward Susan. Susan does not understand Mike's shift in mood and begins to assume she is not doing her job adequately. This, in turn, undermines her customary self-confidence and begins to interfere with her relationship with Joan, her life partner.

Mike's sexual desire for Susan is not irresistible or dangerous. It is his body telling him that he is not attending to needs for emotional and sexual intimacy. Instead, he contextualizes it as an irrational aberrant urge leading him away from his commitment to Jean. If he were able to recognize it as his body's yearning for mutuality, he might be able to take it as a signal that his primary sexual relationship needs attention. In so doing he would gain the power to act appropriately, recognizing that Susan is not the threat, that his workaholism is! He might even begin to notice signs that Susan's friendliness is just that, and that she is involved with someone else. It is not Mike's sexual feelings that lead him to be out of control but rather their repression and lack of contextualization.

We need to begin to ask of our sexual desires what lessons we can learn from them, what soulful longings or movements need attention. This strategy automatically releases us from any sense of their irresistibility and gives us the ability to contextualize them and act in accord with other commitments and values. Some of our sexual desires might represent our delight in the physical beauty of others. Contextualizing them as such frees us to celebrate them for what they are and nothing more. We do not have to act on them. Sometimes our sexual desires represent the need for intimacy and touch. We may be in relationships where disagreements have cooled our closeness or where we have not been sufficiently affectionate.

Even when we are not in a committed sexual relationship and when sexual desire is predictably strong, we need not act on the desire. A group of my friends have recently recounted how in several instances they felt strong sexual desire for someone, but, when they began to get to know them, they became sexually less interested due to signs of emotional incompatibility. For them, sexuality was clearly a powerful force drawing them into relationships of intimate mutuality. But when sexual desire did not serve mutuality, it became automatically less compelling and powerful. It was not an irresistible force, it was a grace and teacher.

There may be two groups of people for whom sexual desire is more problematic: adolescents and celibates. As will be noted later in the book, adolescents are faced with an enormous challenge. The pubertal awakening of sexuality and its increased capacity and desire for emotional intimacy are two forces that are not naturally integrated. Andre Guindon notes that these two forces, the "tender" (capacity for intimacy) and the "sensual" (sexual urges) have to be brought into balance so that tenderness is sensual and sensuality is tender.[28]

Recent studies in touch deprivation suggest that adolescents are particularly susceptible to shifting patterns of touch. Accustomed to getting a good deal of touch from parents and peers as children, adolescents find their parents and their peers less comfortable with touch. There is speculation that, since adolescents are not normally capable of the kind of emotional intimacy associated with sexual intimacy, what they really crave in their sexual activity is the touch they so vitally need and are not getting in other contexts.[29]

Sensuality and tenderness being initially unintegrated, the adolescent is more prone to expressions of sensuality that lack a corresponding emotional intimacy or emotional intimacy that lacks warmth and touch. But even here there is a wisdom in sexuality. The adolescent learns that sexual urges bring him/her into intimate contact with another person, not just a body. In these encounters, both parties learn how to contextualize their feelings, gradually distinguishing between infatuation and genuine love. Both parties learn that physical expressions of affection require appropriate timing and sensitivity or they are misread and hurtful.

The mistrust of adolescent sexuality and its subsequent control severs young people from the very lessons that prepare them for successful adult relationships. Their lack of experience in learning how to distinguish infatuation from genuine mutuality leads them to form superficially romantic adult relationships that are not sustainable. Their lack of experience in learning how to give graceful and embodied expression to mutuality leads to adult relationships that are often devoid of satisfying sexual intimacy.

Again, let me emphasize that I do not think it is helpful to encourage young adolescents to become sexually active. Premature sexual intimacy for teenagers can be emotionally traumatic and physically dangerous. But the vilification of sexual desire and the attempt to control adolescent sexuality with strong shaming mechanisms and abstinence only programs do not serve the development of sexual virtue. Teenagers who have a healthy constellation of relationships with friends, parents, and other adult mentoring figures, and who are involved in a rich variety of activities, will not tend to use sex as compensation for boredom or as a desperate attempt to get affection or validation. Compulsive sex among teenagers is physically and psychologically dangerous, but it is a symptom of larger relational and life problems, not "the" problem. I believe that if teenagers are taught to contextualize their sexual feelings with a rich poetics of intimacy and are provided with models of sexual virtue, they will develop an acute sensitivity to the lessons and graces of sexuality.

Celibates, those who have deliberately chosen to live out their sexuality in long-term or lifelong sexual abstinence, are at risk of developing exaggerated fear and apprehension of sexual desire. When celibacy is chosen out of the belief that sex is ritually defiling or as an attempt to achieve a self-mastery or single-heartedness undisturbed by the disruptiveness of sexual desire, the primary work of the celibate is to contain sexual desire. This, of course, gives sexual desire a new and more potent power. The effort to contain sexual desire actually increases the celibate's attention to sexuality, and its vilification contextualizes it as danger rather than grace; hence, sexuality's importance and power are exaggerated.

When celibacy is chosen as an alternative way to achieve intimacy with others, then the containment of sexual desire is not its primary objective. Michael Crosby defines healthy celibacy as "the embrace of a divinely-offered gift inviting one to freely choose a life-commitment of abstention from genital intimacy which expresses itself in an alternate intimacy with God and others."[30] In such a context, sexual desire can still be contextualized as our embodied yearning for mutuality, for intimacy. The celibate can accept sexual desire as a gift and grace that draws him/her toward others and grounds mutually enriching connectedness. It is difficult to see how intimacy with others could be established, communicated and sustained, though, without affection, without the warm embrace of physical touch.

Returning to my earlier hypothesis, if the celibate, even Crosby's so-called intimate one, does not intimately share life with another to the extent that he/she is challenged to root out his/her inauthenticities, then to what purpose does it serve? How does it serve love of others and love of God? The monastic tradition envisions a sharing of life among monks or nuns that has the capacity to root out inauthenticities. Members of religious communities often come to know one another quite intimately and, by not pairing off into exclusive relationships, communal intimacy is cultivated and preserved. But, monastic life is a special context for which many are not suited and requires resources we can assume most people do not have.

Some contemporary married couples have discovered ways to sustain emotional and physical intimacy with each other while remaining open to emotional intimacy with others. Their experience may bring into question whether sexual abstinence is the only way that one can be open to intimacy with others and with God (in the way that religious celibates often describe as the motivation for their way of life). Married people are able to establish emotional intimacy with others while still honoring the sexual exclusivity of their relationship. Married people are also able to establish intimacy with God while still honoring intimacy with their partners. Mary Anne McPherson Oliver has described the legacy of bias against conjugal spirituality in Christianity and suggests that sexual union can embody profound mystical union with the other and with God.

> Sexual union begins as a function of two personalities, a single-hearted expression of relatedness and love, but on the edge of ecstasy lovers are totally transformed, becoming totally unlike themselves in any other setting. As Carla Needleman describes it, sexual passion, by displacing the recognizable self, leaves space for 'a force, organic and of compelling power, that acts through us and for a short period of time changes us into beings quite different from the way we are all the rest of the time . . .'[31]

One suspects that the belief that sexual abstinence can enable greater intimacy with others and with God is a legacy of Augustinian belief that sexual pleasure eclipses one's rational faculties. Since God is identified with truth, ecstatic pleasure could not possibly accompany union or intimacy with God. In Augustinian thought, marital love is considered an impediment to profound spirituality. This perspective is influenced by the idea that union with God involves a perfection and completion of human faculties. Since sexual intimacy involves an ongoing dis-ruptiveness, unsettledness, spontaneity, ecstasy, and vulnerability, it suggests to Augustine a still imperfect state of human existence and, therefore, does not represent moral or spiritual excellence.

While celibacy understood as an abstention from genital sexuality in order to establish intimacy with others and with God is less dangerous than celibacy understood as abstention from genital sexuality because it is defiling and disruptive, it is still a decision to use sexual abstinence as a means of achieving self-perfection, as a means of achieving union with God. It invariably identifies intimacy with God as something that is free from the kinds of impulses, unsettledness, conflicts, and challenges of sexual mutuality. It idealizes that relationship and risks severing the individual from the grace and lessons of sexual intimacy. The idealizing of our own perfection either through self-mastery or through union with a perfect self-possessed supreme being is a seductive temptation given the character of our dialectical subjectivity. But it is no less a seduction and does not deliver the promised perfection and excellence it purports.

Notes

[1]   G.W. F. Hegel, *The Phenomenology of Spirit*, trans. A. V. Miller (New York: Oxford Univ. Press, 1977).

[2]   Walter Davis, *Inwardness and Existence: Subjectivity In/And Hegel, Heidegger, Marx and Freud* (Madison: Univ. of Wisconsin Press, 1989) p. 21.

[3]   Soren Kierkegaard, cf. Walter Davis, Ibid., p. 131.

[4]   Martin Heidegger, *Being and Time*, trans. John Macquarrie and William Richardson (New York: 1962), Davis, Op. cit., pp. 107–109.

[5]   Emmanuel Levinas, *Totality and Infinity*, trans. by Alphonso Lingis (Pittsburgh: Duquesne Univ. Press, 1969).

[6]   Wendy Farley, *Eros for the Other: Retaining Truth in a Pluralistic World* (Penn State Univ. Press, 1996).

[7]   Peter Brown, *The Body and Society: Men, Women, and Sexual Renunciation in Early Christianity* (New York: Columbia Univ. Press, 1988) pp. 33ff.

[8]   Section 8 of the *Roman Catechism*, cited in Uta Ranke-Heinemann, *Eunuchs for the Kingdom of Heaven*, trans. Peter Heinegg (New York: Penguin Books, 1990) p.248.

[9]   W. Norman Pittenger, "Process Thought: A Contemporary Trend in Theology" and Shubert M. Ogden, "The Reality of God," *Process Theology*, ed. Ewert H. Cousins (New York: Paulist Press, 1971) pp. 3–35

[10] Michael Crosby has elaborated the idea of the Church as an addictive system and sexual abstinence as a form of institutional control in two books, *The Dysfunctional Church* (Notre Dame: Ave Maria Press, 1991) and *Celibacy: Means of Control or Mandate of the Heart?* (Notre Dame: Ave Maria Press, 1996).

[11] Augustine, *De fide et operibus* 6,8, cited by Uta Ranke-Heinemann, Op. cit., p. 98.

[12] Jerome, *Epistles* 48, 15, cited by Ute Ranke-Heinemann, Op. cit., p. 98.

[13] Origen, Select. in *Ezech.* chapter 7, cited by Ute Ranke-Heinemann, Op. cit., p. 98.

[14] Uta Ranke-Heinemann, Op. cit., p. 142.

[15] Ibid., p. 155.

[16] Ibid., p. 191, Thomas Aquinas, *Summa Theologica* II/II q.55 a.8 ad 1.

[17] Michael Crosby, Celibacy, Op. cit., p. 48 from Peter Damian, *De Celbatu Sacerdotum*, PL 145.410ff.

[18] Ibid., p. 56.

[19] Walter Davis, Op. cit., pp. 28ff.

[20] Matthew Fox, *Original Blessing: A Primer in Creation Spirituality* (Santa Fe: Bear and Co., 1983).

[21] Carter Heyward, Op. cit., p. 99.

[22] Christine Gudorf, *Body, Sex and Pleasure* (Cleveland: Pilgrim Press, 1994) pp. 82–83.

[23] Ibid., pp. 86–87.

[24] Ibid., pp. 87–88.

[25] Heyward, Op.cit., p. 99.

[26] Thomas Moore. *The Soul of Sex* (New York: Harper Collins, 1998).

[27] Ibid., p. 13.

[28] Andre Guindon, *The Sexual Language* (Ottawa: Univ. of Ottawa Press, 1977) pp. 53–59.

[29] Elizabeth R. McAnarney, "Adolescents and Touch," *Touch: The Foundation of Experience*, eds. K.E. Barnard and T. B. Brazelton (Madison: International Universities Press, 1990) 497–515.

[30] Michael Crosby, *Celibacy: Means of Control or Mandate of the Heart?* (Notre Dame: Ave Maria Press, 1996) p. 141.

[31] Mary Anne McPherson Oliver, *Conjugal Spirituality: The Primacy of Mutual Love in Christian Tradition* (Kansas City: Sheed and Ward, 1994) pp. 63–64.

❖ Chapter Three

Chastity Is Not Enough: The Poetics of Intimacy and Sexual Virtue

Act-Centered and Virtue-Centered Ethics

Frank and Mary, married for eight years, have two young children. Mary is a financial consultant and Frank is a high school science teacher. Both were raised in stable families and taught traditional Christian moral principles about marriage and sexuality. During the past year, their marriage has become difficult. Mary is often irritable, short with Frank, and rarely playful or in the mood to be intimate. Frank is baffled by Mary's recent mood swings but continues to hope things will work out. Mary is aware of the changes in her feelings toward Frank. She knows that much of her irritability and uptightness are symptomatic of stress at work. But she also feels that Frank is not as interesting as she once found him. She prefers spending time with some of the male partners at her firm and derives more personal satisfaction and intellectual stimulation from them. Robert, in particular, is quite attractive and responsive to her. He makes her laugh, relax, and can engage her in interesting conversation. Robert invited Mary to his vacation home for a weekend getaway. He suggested she use the pretext of a business trip to prevent Frank from being suspicious. Mary refused the offer, although she would have enjoyed the time with Robert and has desired having sex with him for quite some time. She doesn't believe it is right to have sex with someone other than her husband. When Robert pressed her further for reasons, she said, "I know it sounds old-fashioned, but I would feel like God was watching and would punish me. And besides, I am afraid of what would happen if Frank ever found out. I don't want our family to come apart."

The above scenario enables us to examine the relationship between two aspects of morality: morality as concerned with the rightness and wrongess of acts and morality as concerned with the character or virtue of those acting.[1] In many respects, Mary is acting morally upright because she has refused to compromise her marriage by having sex with another man. She knows that adultery is wrong, and she fears the consequences of violating a moral rule. But in other respects, Mary's internal dispositions are not ideally what they ought to be. While not physically having sex with Robert, Mary is not emotionally honoring her relationship with Frank either. She is so absorbed at work that she cannot be emotionally playful and lighthearted, necessary dispositions for sustaining intimacy. It appears that she is more emotionally involved with Robert, but it's equally possible that she's (perhaps unwittingly) using the mystique and intrigue of a new relationship to stimulate her out of her obsession with work. She seems more concerned about punishment for wrongdoing than about the substance of betraying Frank's trust.

Mary's concern not to compromise a moral rule by having sex with Robert and her fear of punishment or losing her family are what we would typically call act-centered morality. Such concerns are not without merit, and they function as a deterrent to doing things that will clearly be harmful to oneself and to others. Mary may feel morally upright about not having sex with Robert. She may feel relieved that she has not lost her family through sexual misconduct and that she is strong enough to resist the temptation of a weekend with Robert. But these confidences mask other serious problems. Mary's work habits undermine her ability to relax, play and be intimate. These habits weaken her relationship with Frank, are a violation of his trust, and make it difficult for Mary to sustain genuine intimacy with him or anyone else. These internal dispositions are what we call virtues or character goods (or in this case, vices). They are acquired habits of acting well (or failing to act well). They are character goods which need cultivation, and they dispose us or enable us to do the right thing for the right reasons.

Classical moral philosophy and traditional Christian morality placed much more emphasis on the cultivation of virtue than does contemporary morality. In our modern zeal to determine what are morally good and bad actions, we often fail to give adequate attention to virtue. Virtue concerns may have diminished under the influence of Roman Catholic penitential practices which involved the confession of sin and imposition of penances. For priests to impose the right penance it was important to know the specific type of sin and the circumstances which might further specify its gravity or type. This led to an emphasis on the specification of sinful acts.

The juridical manner of confessing and forgiving sins often eclipsed the developmental stages of the moral life. For example, it mattered little in the confessional whether, when a teenager confessed to having had sex with his girlfriend, it was the only time this had happened, it was part of a regular pattern, or it was a significant decrease in frequency. Roman Catholic moral theology taught that all sexual sins were serious or grave matter and, while some circumstances could make something more or less serious, in sexual matters all sins were theoretically "mortal," severing one from God. The contemporary Roman Catholic practice of a more conversational approach to confession diminishes the act-centered focus and permits priests who are attuned to developmental issues in morality to discuss them with penitents.

Since Martin Luther's criticism of the Roman Catholic practice of granting indulgences, Protestants have reviled the quantification and specification of sin. For Protestants, we are all sinners but are forgiven and redeemed by the grace of God. And while Protestants have avoided some of the pitfalls of a penitential approach to morality, their reliance on Scriptural texts to identify what constitutes a sin has also eclipsed a virtue approach to the moral life. The enthusiasm with which some contemporary Protestant groups cite the Bible in condemning particular acts gives the impression that the moral life is primarily a matter of conforming to a set of moral rules, not a matter of acquiring certain moral dispositions or attitudes (like compassion, concern for justice, forgiveness, or love).

Contemporary professional ethics has also contributed to an act-centered approach to morality. Professional codes of ethics and professional codes of conduct rightly focus on what kind of behavior is inappropriate given the principles and values associated with a profession. Professional conduct needs to be able to be measured, evaluated and censured when it violates ethical principles. Thus, there is a need to identify the kinds of acts which are right and wrong. But there has also been a renewed interest in professional virtue considerations, not because they can be measured, but precisely because professional life requires not just conformity to codes of conduct but the cultivation of dispositions which assure that the values and principles of professional life are internalized in the professional and are implemented even when there is little chance of being caught for wrongdoing and/or when the codes of conduct are not specific enough to dictate what the right course of action is. In situations which require judgment and application of values and principles, one hopes that the professional has dispositions (virtues) which will illumine his/her choices.

A virtue approach to morality is not uninterested in the rightness or wrongness of acts but is more concerned with focusing on what kind of person an individual is becoming in and through the choices and decisions he/she makes. Virtues are internal character goods, habits or dispositions that have been acquired or cultivated so that an individual finds it progressively easier to do the right thing. Virtues require right action—but right action done for the right reason.

For example, when an individual is punished for cheating on an exam and refrains from doing so in the future simply because she fears being caught and punished again, it is unlikely that she will forego the temptation to cheat in the future when she determines there is little risk of getting caught. In other words, when she decides not to cheat because she is afraid of getting caught, she has performed the right action for the wrong reason, and we should be concerned about the absence of the right internal disposition or vitue of honesty.

It is possible that this individual, in getting caught, will reassess her moral character and decide to work at being more honest. During the next exam, she may find it difficult to forego the temptation to cheat, and she might have to exert a good deal of internal discipline to not cheat. But gradually, as she practices honesty and overcomes inclinations to cheat, she will find it easier and easier to do the right thing for the right reasons. She will have cultivated the virtue of honesty.

Classical Emphasis on the Virtue of Chastity

Classical moral philosophers (Greek and Roman philosophers from the fifth century B.C.E. to about the third century C.E.) were less concerned about specific acts of sexual immorality and more concerned with sexual virtue. Most classical moral philosophers did not operate within a system of reward or punishment for sin (like Christian notions of heaven and hell). The reward for right conduct was the well-being it brought about, the personal excellence and happiness that accompanied doing good. Single acts of moral misbehavior might have social or legal consequences (corrupting someone else's property, goods or person), but they need not necessarily corrupt internal goods, personal dispositions or virtues.

The ancient Greeks and Romans looked at certain kinds of sexual behavior quite differently from the way Christian morality looks at them. Like Christians, the ancient Greeks would have discouraged sex between an adult married man and a prostitute. They would do so, however, not because it was adultery but because it demonstrated a lack of self-control on the part of the married man. Ancient Greeks thought that personal well-being was achieved when one had control over passions, particularly sexual ones. One could experience happiness and freedom only when the passions of the body were brought under control by reason.

Classical Greek and Roman moral philosophy did not usually express great moral concern about singular acts of self-indulgence, be they masturbation, sex with a prostitute, a slave, or a teenage boy. What mattered was a pattern of activity. If a man had a habit (a disposition) of engaging in acts of sexual self-indulgence, it was problematic because he suffered a "pathology," rule by the passions, *"pathe."* In other words, the immorality of these acts consisted primarily in their impact on the character or internal dispositions of the individual, not in that they compromised some external good or rule. Married women were an exception. Their sexual misbehavior was more seriously judged since it violated their husbands' reproductive proprietary rights. And married men were not to have sex with the wives or eligible daughters of other free men because these acts had serious social consequences.

Thus, the goal of sexual morality in classical Greek and Roman philosophical schools of thought was two fold. First, it was concerned with the cultivation of self-controlled and self-possessed rational individuals, free from the disruptive and unsettling influences of the passions. Second, it was concerned with preserving social order and resources through the institution of marriage where households were managed, women, children and slaves were governed, family patrimony preserved and passed on, and population sustained through reproduction. The first concern was a virtue concern; the second was concerned with specific sexual acts and external goods.

Moral education, then, consisted in cultivating the kinds of dispositions which would enable individuals to achieve these two goals. Chief among the virtues associated with sexuality was self-control. Sexual urges were considered irrational and antithetical to self-mastery. Sexual self-indulgence was not only inimical to personal excellence, it threatened goods associated with social order and household management. A good husband and father had to be sexually self-controlled, providing an important example to those who were thought to be innately less capable of moral virtue—women, children and slaves. He had to order and govern the household in accord with reason. Women, children and slaves had to possess the virtue of obedience and self-control, since they were not to indulge themselves but act in accord with the reason and authority of the head of the household.

As noted earlier, classical marriage was much less centered around love and interpersonal intimacy. It was chiefly an economic and reproductive institution concerned with household management and the reproduction and education of children. Spouses did not necessarily marry for love. Many marriages were arranged by parents seeking matches which preserved economic resources and social status. Men sought emotional companionship with other men and women with other women. Husband and wife were not necessarily friends. Rather, they were partners in the enterprise of household life.

Early Christian Models of Sexual Virtue

Early Christianity inherited classical Greek and Roman philosophical beliefs about the irrationality of sexual desire and sexual pleasure and the need to control this irrationality with reason through the virtue of chastity. Chastity was simply the term used to describe the moderation, curbing or "chastising" of sexual desire with reason. Since it was assumed with classical Greek and Roman philosophy that the only rational use of sexual desire and pleasure was in marriage for the sake of having children, the sexually chaste individual was the one who restricted his/her sexual pleasure to heterosexual-marital-and-repro-ductively-intentional acts. But at the same time, chastity was a lifelong process, and it was assumed that one could only gradually learn to moderate sexual desire and pleasure. Greeks did not harshly judge an individual who, otherwise striving to be chaste, occasionally indulged **him**self (women were not accorded this luxury!).

But, when Greek and Roman philosophical beliefs about the irrationality of sexual desire and sexual pleasure were incorporated into the Christian world view, they underwent significant changes. First of all, during the first century, many Christians believed in the imminent apocalyptic destruction of the world and the establishment of the Kingdom of God. Since marriage was viewed as a socially preserving institution, some Christians believed it was unimportant for an apocalyptic age and chose not to marry. Paul probably had this in mind in 1 Corinthians when he recommended celibacy.

Second, when the hoped for apocalypse did not occur, the Kingdom of God was increasingly spiritualized as a heavenly reality. It was assumed that in heaven sexuality was either unimportant or nonexistent. Human beings would live spiritually, as the angels. Some Christians believed that Jesus came from this spiritual realm to rescue human beings from entrapment in the material flesh-world. These so-called Gnostics believed that once one had been born again in Christian Baptism one was to live spiritually. Since marriage and reproduction further entrapped souls in the material flesh-world, Gnostics believed it was sinful to marry and have children. So they advocated complete sexual abstinence. They assumed that Jesus had been celibate and had provided an important moral example for his future disciples.

The world negating spirituality of Gnostic Christians was intoxicating. It provided a powerful coping mechanism during periodic persecutions, and it enabled unprecedented commitment and devotion to God and Christianity. Even after Gnostic beliefs were condemned as heretical, the practice of lifelong sexual abstinence continued in some circles, and those who achieved it were considered heroic in spiritual virtue.

The practice of lifelong sexual abstinence was rare among Greeks and Romans. The virtue of chastity, as lived among Greeks and Romans, consisted in a gradual process of moderating sexual desire so that one might eventually become "*apatheia*," without passion. It was assumed that during youth and early adulthood one's sexual passions were stronger and even suitable to one's duties in marriage. Even though sexual pleasure was supposed to be restricted to its rational purpose, heterosexual-marital-reproductively-intentional acts, it was assumed that many young adults would not be able to avoid instances of sexual self-indulgence. As long as these instances respected other men's wives and were not part of a pattern of dissolute living they were not considered very serious.

But within Christian groups that practiced lifelong sexual abstinence, the virtue of chastity, understood as a gradual moderating and curbing of sexual desire and pleasure, gave way to concern about individual instances of breaking one's vow of total abstinence! Chastity was viewed less as a disposition one had to cultivate and more as an obligation not to engage in sex at all, at least for anyone committed to sexual abstinence.

Christian morality was also influenced by apocalyptic descriptions of a final divine judgment. Several Christian writings, notably the Book of Revelation and several passages from the Gospels, speak of a final judgment. Most Greek and Roman religious and philosophical descriptions of death do not include such a notion. Thus, the motive for moral life within Greek and Roman society was honor before one's fellow human beings and the personal well-being or excellence one enjoyed in doing the good. Morality was a matter of cultivating personal excellence, not an accounting of sins. But for Christians, the notion of a final judgment meant that one's moral life would fall under the scrutiny of God. One would be called upon to account for one's actions. And while Jesus' descriptions of this judgment focused on the virtues of compassion, charity, and justice, popular moral sentiment shifted to the fear of having to account for individual moral acts. And as noted earlier, this was exacerbated when the practice of individual and frequent confession developed in the Roman Catholic Church after the sixth century.

One of the reasons that contemporary Christian sexual morality is in crisis is that it has failed to recover an appreciation for sexual virtue. Popular debate about sexual morality focuses on the identification of morally good and bad acts. For example, should the divorced be permitted to remarry, should young adults have sex before marriage, or should gay men and lesbians engage in sexual intimacy? And while some of this debate is important, it often misses the heart and soul of sexuality, the dispositions which enable people to initiate and sustain psychologically healthy relationships of intimacy. Too often debate about sexual morality is grossly act-centered. It focuses on rules without connecting them to the personal well-being and development of the people involved. A good illustration of this problem is debate about sexuality education.

Traditional Christian sexual morality teaches that sex before or outside of marriage is immoral. Thus, the focus of traditional sexuality education has been to teach self-control (chastity) and emphasize the wrongfulness of premarital sex. This approach typically does not include lessons on contraception, safe sex (to avoid sexually transmitted disease or HIV), how to make sense of one's sexual feelings, how to be in an intimate relationship with another person, or how to discern one's sexual orientation or sexual identity. Young people who strive to follow these teachings on chastity must make every effort to repress their awakening sexuality and, when they begin to develop affection for another person, must strive to disassociate their emotional feelings from their sexual ones.

If these teenagers and young adults lived in an age where marriages were arranged and consisted in household management and reproductive partnership, they would be fairly well-prepared for successful sexual life. But these young people will have to find suitable life partners on their own. The lifelong commitment they will be asked to make involves more than agreement to be a partner in household management and reproduction. They will agree to be companions in life, sharing emotional and sexual intimacy with one another, sharing power with each other, and supporting each other's personal and professional development. Unlike their early Christian and classical Greek/Roman counterparts, they will look forward to a life span of more than eighty years, requiring new skills for sustaining love and intimacy through many different seasons of life.

What kinds of internal dispositions or character goods will they need to find a suitable life companion, become vulnerable enough to share emotional intimacy, assure each other that that vulnerability will be honored and respected, share power with each other, and sustain their love over time and through many professional and personal changes? What kinds of internal dispositions or character goods will they need to balance the demands of economic and professional life with domestic concerns? Modern psychology has taught us that most adults have emotional issues which are buried in the unconscious and which surface in relationships which involve emotional intimacy. Classical Greco-Roman and early Christian models of marriage did not necessarily include the expectation that spouses would share that kind of emotional intimacy. Modern marriage includes emotional intimacy, and young people preparing for marriage need to develop the skills or dispositions that will enable them to navigate the conflicts and tensions that are invariably part of modern intimate relationships.

In the light of these concerns, it should be rather obvious that sexual self-control (chastity) is insufficient to prepare young people for successful sexual lives. Chastity is important in avoiding premature sexual involvement, in foregoing sexual involvement that would be hurtful to oneself or disrespectful of another's feelings or vulnerabilities, and in sustaining fidelity when one's feelings and desires tempt one away from one's commitments. But chastity alone does not enable personal or relational excellence. Christianity must develop a richer notion of sexual virtue, one that is more suited to enabling individuals to initiate, cultivate and sustain contemporary intimate relationships. Only when it does so will it move beyond its current crisis and again be a compelling voice for moral and spiritual development.

The Poetics of Intimacy: Initial Considerations

Today, people need a rich formation in the poetics of intimacy in order to sustain successful and graceful intimate relationships. As noted in the introductory chapter, I first encountered the concept of a poetics of intimacy in an article by James T. Sears.[2] Sears laments the inadequacy of both the morally nihilistic approach of hygienic sexuality education programs, with their focus on prevention of teenage pregnancy and sexually transmitted disease, and the moralistic ones, focusing on the wrongfulness of sexual intimacy before marriage. Neither of these approaches help young people develop the kinds of internal skills needed to understand their sexuality with all of its rich human interpersonal meaning. What is needed, he suggests, is a rich poetics of intimacy.

In the following pages, I will elaborate what I consider a poetics of intimacy to include. Then I will compare and contrast it with the best examples of contemporary chastity-based models of sexual virtue. I hope to be persuasive in showing that a chastity-based model of sexual virtue is inadequate, given contemporary religious and social scientific understandings of sexual relationships, and that Christian models of sexual virtue must be reformed and amplified.

First, and perhaps most obviously, a poetics of intimacy is grounded in the conviction that sexuality enables human beings to share deep emotional intimacy with one another. While classical philosophy and poetry occasionally praised the romantic and intimate graces of sexual love, this was overshadowed by social and philosophical models of sex which focused on the rational purposes of sex, namely reproduction in well-ordered households. As noted earlier, Christianity inherited this rational approach to sexuality and, under its influence, the role of sexuality as a rich exchange of interpersonal intimacy was eclipsed.

One way of coming to appreciate the poetics of intimacy is to notice the changes that come about when adolescents experience the awakening of sexual desire. This awakening includes a heretofore unnoticed capacity for deep interiority. Without sexual desire, human beings would probably have a more diminished sense of inwardness or soulfulness. A poetics of intimacy would include the celebration of sexual desire as, in the words of Carter Heyward, the embodied experience of our desire for mutuality,[3] for a sharing of the deepest parts of ourselves with one another. Sexual desire is one of the most intense ways that we experience our capacity for intimacy. Adolescents begin to notice each other in new ways. Relationships with peers become more complicated as sexual energy changes their perception of what interpersonal relationships might include.

Why is our civilization so fearful of this rich human experience? Why do we fear that which enables us to become aware of our deepest capacity for love and provides the impetus for much of our spirituality? Many of the mystics have described love for God in very sensual terms. Indeed, it is next to impossible to speak about love for God without reference to the human experience of longing for deep union with the beloved, a desire for an intimate sharing of oneself with the beloved. Why, then, do we fear and attempt to suppress eros?

There is, most assuredly, an apprehension that comes with the awakening of sexual desire during adolescence. One's sense of self is not yet well-defined. What one hopes for and desires begins to change and expand. Earlier certainties give way to new complexity and wonder. This wonder is both elating and burdensome. While life's possibilities deepen and expand, they become more challenging and complex. One becomes more aware of and concerned about acceptance, loveability, and interpersonal compatibility than before the awakening of one's sexuality. The sense of self not only changes with respect to one's peers, it changes with respect to the world. Adolescents gain a new awareness of the sensual qualities of the world around them. They begin to see new textures and notice the sensual dimensions of light, heat, cold, color, water, earth and sky. Their bodies begin to gain a heightened sensitivity and connectivity to their surroundings. Adolescents begin to have the capacity for genuine poetic feeling, expressing and imagining deeper personal moods, emotions, feelings, and tonalities of life.

The changes that take place during adolescence suggest that sexuality awakens within us a deep poetic sense of the self, the world, and of various relationships. A poetic sense of the self and of relationships is contrasted with an essentialistic view of human nature and human relationships. A poetic sense of the self celebrates the multidimensionality of personal life and the difficulty of defining, objectifying, possessing, or comprehending human subjectivity.

One comes to appreciate that persons are subjects, not objects or products. As a subject, a human person enjoys a unique, inexhaustible, and ultimately unpossessable interiority. A human person cannot be known the way objects are known. In many respects, a person is not a noun; he/she is a verb, a life, a narrative in progress. Even the ability to know oneself, to take hold of oneself, to engage oneself is elusive. At best, one knows oneself in the rich narrative breadth of one's life and, since that narrative is being revised in a living daily active manner, self-knowledge is always incomplete and developing. The human person is a mystery, a living reality that is always transcending itself and always more than any effort at description or objectification.[4]

Personal life is deeply relational. The human subject comes into existence in a rich constellation of relationships which, according to the insights of modern psychology, deeply shape the interiority of the individual. As an individual seeks to author his/her own life, he/she comes to realize that it is already deeply shaped and influenced by the conflicts and issues of one's family of origin. This is further complicated by other contextualizing factors of personal life, such as one's religious heritage, ethnic and cultural particularities, geography, historical epochs, politics, social institutions, and language. Thus, as Martin Heidegger stated, the human person is a situated subject.[5] As a subject, one is challenged to be authentic, that is to be the author of one's life. But as a situated subject, one must author life contextually, that is within a particular set of givens.

Like poets, human persons must employ rich imagination and creativity in authoring their personal narratives. One's life is not already set, predefined, predetermined. As subjects, human persons are invited to give personal shape and form to their lives. The invitation to be a person, to author one's life, is accompanied by anxiety. Anxiety arises, in part, because the horizon against which one authors one's life is infinite, and this means that self-authorship is never complete, never perfect, never secure.[6] One is constantly confronted with new insights about oneself and new depths that beckon engagement and expression. Since the experience of a deep and unperfectable interiority awakens simul-taneously with the awakening of sexual desire, and since this produces not just anxiety but a type of sadness and disappointment (at not being able to complete or satisfy the self), we can understand why some people have advocated the supression of eros as a means or strategy of self-possession and peace.

Anxiety also arises because personal life is inextricably intertwined with other persons and with events that are beyond one's control.[7] Both intimate relationships and social and professional ones require a sharing of power, a type of coauthorship. One's identity is always both self-constituted and socially-constituted. As Martin Buber noted, the term "I" is derivative of the primary words "I-thou" or "I-it."[8] I cannot know myself except as a being-in-relation. And because I cannot control these relationships without eclipsing the reality of the other (or myself), self-authorship is always coauthorship and thus filled with a good degree of anxiety. Since sexual desire is the most intense embodied experience of our longing for mutuality and relationship, it is again understandable why some have advocated the suppression of eros or sexual desire as a means of gaining peace, focus, direction, and a secure hold on one's individual identity.

But, the suppression of eros or sexual desire eclipses the rich poetic, multidimensional and inexhaustible depth of personal life. It must be seen for what it is, a futile attempt to gain self-control and self-possession, limiting the unsettling, disruptive and ever deepening dynamic of personal life. The irony of this is that the supression of eros within religious moral systems is purportedly motivated by a desire to cultivate spirituality and access to the divine. But the effect of the suppression of eros is quite the opposite. It stifles many of the resources that make spirituality possible.

As noted earlier, a poetic approach to personal life stands in contrast to essentialistic models. Essentialistic approaches to human life claim that one can define the essence or reality of human personal life. Essentialistic models minimize the historical, cultural, embodied, existential, and relational reality of personal life in favor of the rational and abstract. These are often regarded as extraneous to the core of who one is.

James Keenan highlights this in his revisionist work on the cardinal virtues.[9] Keenan argues that it is impossible to propose one model of moral excellence. Moral excellence is personally, culturally and historically plural. Keenan reminds us that the Church has canonized saints who embodied many different types of moral excellence. And, although many cultures confront similar moral issues and have common language to describe personal moral dispositions (virtues) like courage, patience, and justice, these are lived out differently in accord with culturally specific notions of excellence.[10] ". . . People can only become morally excellent persons by being themselves. The saint has always been an original, never an imitation."[11]

Most essentialistic philosophies have defined the human person as a rational animal. An assumption is made that what distinguishes human animals from nonhuman ones is reason. Thus, it is concluded that what is essentially human is reason. The bias toward the rational dimension of human existence favors the suppression of emotion and sensuality in favor of abstract reason and self-control, supposedly the perfection of the greatest human faculties, reason and free will. This, in turn has favored rationalistic models of morality or human excellence. The rational life is thought to consist of an undisturbed mind, one which clearly comprehends reality and orders one's life in accord with it.

It is not difficult to see how essentialistic models of human excellence would be projected onto models of God. Human beings have always described God in terms of what they considered their own greatest attributes and possibilities. If the highest form of personal life was an undisturbed, self-possessed, rational mind and, if God is greater than human life, God must at least be self-possessed, undisturbed, and rational.

When Christianity distanced itself from its original Jewish roots, it adopted Greek philosophical categories to describe God. Where the Jewish people described God in rich anthropomorphic and poetic language, Christians gradually employed essentialistic and rationalistic terms like truth, the one, unmoved mover, first cause, supreme good, or the infinite one.

Fortunately, the continued reading of Jewish and Christian Scriptures sustained a more poetic image of God.[12] God is the one who is always beyond comprehension and objectification. Thus, references to God are metaphorical. They suggest that God is **like** a father, a mother, a rock, flowing water, light, and shepherd. None of these metaphors is used as if God were literally father, mother, rock, water, light or shepherd. As Sallie McFague remarks, metaphorical language about God must remain necessarily plural. When any one metaphor is taken as if it alone expresses the reality of God, we begin to literalize it and objectify God in that literalization. Multiple metaphors complement each other and help prevent objectification and idolatry.[13]

According to Christianity, the mode of God's self-disclosure is also metaphorical and, very importantly, embodied and relational. God's word is communicated poetically in the life of Jesus. The Christian revelation was not primarily or exclusively a matter of dictating the words of God. Rather, the life of Jesus poetically expressed the way God loves and the way God calls us to love. The power of Jesus' witness to the love of God was not in his ability to theologically define and categorize doctrine but in his ability to tell stories that poetically illustrated God's way of being. They captured the imagination and heart of listeners in ways that conceptual language could never have accomplished. Poetic language engages the mind, spirit, soul and body. The power of Jesus' witness was also deeply rooted in his embodied gestures of love, solidarity, and vulnerability. More is communicated, for instance, in Jesus' actual instances of interaction with women (despite strict prohibitions in Judaism) than if Jesus were to have given a discourse on the inadequacy or inappropriateness of purity codes. If this were not so, God could have simply dictated the right teachings in some document that once and for all encapsulated the truth of God's being. But Christianity claims that God chose to be self-disclosive by establishing an ongoing relationship with human beings poetically modeled in the life of Jesus. And it is probably right to conclude that this mode of self-disclosure distances itself from rationalistic models of God.

The God modeled by Jesus is not unmoved, undisturbed, invulnerable, self-sufficient, in control, unchanging, or complete. God becomes vulnerable by sharing in our very existence. And if God indeed invites us into relationship, then God is not an unmoved, unchanged, or self-sufficient and self-controlled being. Relationships involve movement, change and a sharing of power. If Jesus is indeed fully human and fully divine and, if he is so not temporarily but forever (as suggested in descriptions of the Church as the body of Christ and as the dwelling place of God's Spirit), then the being and reality of God is intimately linked to our lives, to our choices and decisions, to our history, to our world.[14] And this means that descriptions of God are inadequate when they omit the relational and ever changing dimension of God's being, as rationalistic ones do.

Similarly, if human beings enjoy a spiritual transcendental subjectivity (in other words, an ever deepening and self-surpassing interiority), then our being and our relationships cannot be expressed any more categorically and objectively than God's. While some features of God and of human beings can be captured categorically and conceptually, we make them into idols, unduly objectifying them, if we think that these notions have indeed captured their being. We must turn to poetic and metaphorical language, to ritual and relationship, to engage deeper levels of the mystery of our being.

An illustration of this might be something like the manner in which family life is lived through rituals and celebrations. It is not enough for us to describe or define our family or what it means. We **live** our family relationships in the rich poetic and symbolic exchanges of gifts, gathering together for special meals, celebrating life transitions, exchanging gestures of affection, support and forgiveness. My family relationship is not accessed through definitions. Rather, I know and participate in that relationship through a rich multidimensional and plurally metaphorical shared life.

Inadequacy of Chastity-Based Models of Sexual Virtue

Chastity-based models of sexual virtue are grounded in essentialistic and rationalistic models of human nature, not poetic ones. Ironically, contemporary philosophical and religious attempts to sustain chastity-based models of sexual virtue appeal to personalistic rather than essentialistic models of human nature. This attempt to make chastity-based models of sexual virtue more appealing because they are couched in personalistic terms ultimately fails.

Pope John Paul II, first in his philosophical work, *The Acting Person*, and then in numerous addresses, encyclicals, and Vatican missives, calls attention to the manner in which the individual is self-determined in his/her acts. The human person is the object of his/her acts:

> Every actual act of self-determination makes real the subjectiveness of self-governance and self-possession; in each of these interpersonal structural relations there is given to the person as the subject—as he who governs and possesses—the person as the object—as he who is governed and possessed.[15]

In other words, no matter what the ends of our action are, one unavoidable end is ourselves. We are the goal or object of our action since we are shaped and constituted by our actions.

For John Paul II, this process of self-determination is good when it conforms to truth. He argues that the only way that human beings gain clearer perception of the truth and act in accord with it is through self-mastery, through control of the passions.[16] The passions are said to cloud reason and inhibit right choice, a legacy of Augustinian and Stoic thought. Self-control enables authentic freedom, not freedom from coercion but freedom to do the truth, to do the good. And indeed, according to John Paul II, the freedom to do the good is one that enobles and causes the human person to flourish and obtain his/her humanity in all its richness.

Sexual virtue, according to this model, is grounded in self-mastery and in respect for the "truth" of the person with whom one shares sexual intimacy. This requires self-discipline, temperance, continence, self-denial and purity.[17] It is important not just for abstaining from immoral sexual intercourse, but as an essential virtue for love. Janet Smith describes it thusly:

> . . . if one is driven by one's passions, one will treat one's spouse as an object designed to satisfy those passions, not as a person to be loved. Self-mastery does not free one from one's passions but enables one to put them into the service of one's loving response, of one's best judgment . . . . Self-mastery enables Man to gain some control over his sexual passions and thus some measure of freedom that allows him to respond to the objective realities of his passions and his love.[18]

On the surface, this line of thinking makes sense. It appeals to those experiences of ours which suggest that passion is sometimes confusing, conflicting, intense, and disorienting. We are aware that through sexual desire we are often drawn first to the physical attractiveness of another person, and so it is easy to understand how desire can eclipse other personal aspects. Developing the ability to suspend action in order to determine what is really good, and not just apparently so, is the mark of a wise and good human being. A certain degree of self-control and asceticism, promoting delay of gratification, is certainly in order. But chastity-based models of sexual virtue show little appreciation for the manner in which intimacy and love are served through the art of becoming emotionally and physically vulnerable to the other, requiring a letting go of control.

Sexual desire and sexual passion remain frightening to Western culture, addicted as it were to strategies of self-control, precisely because it is the ground for experiencing our vulnerability before the other. Sexual desire breaks down our illusions of self-sufficiency and beckons us to mutuality, love. Sexual desire rises up from the deepest regions of our soul and exposes us to the other. It is vital for our capacity to become intimate.

The limitations of the chastity-based model of sexual virtue become more obvious when it attempts to specify the "truth" of the other that frees sexual passion from being merely self-serving or self-indulgent. Drawing on the Augustinian tradition of identifying the sacredness of sexuality in its cooperation with God's creation of a new human being (a new spiritual soul), John Paul II concludes that this procreative good is the primary orientation of sexuality and remains central to understanding the personal value of the other. If the essence of one's sexuality is to serve life, to serve this cooperative venture with God, then one cannot give oneself totally, nor love the other truthfully, unless sexual intimacy is an expression of this fundamental essence. Accordingly, sexual intimacy outside heterosexual-marital-and-reproductively-intentional acts renders it dishonest and inauthentic. According to John Paul II, the only way that sexual desire can be kept from being self-serving or self-indulgent is if it serves the complete truth of the other, including the so-called "nuptial meaning of the body," its procreative orientation.

> The union of persons in love does not necessarily have to be realized by way of sexual relations. But when it does take this form the personalistic value of the sexual relationship cannot be assured without willingness for parenthood. Thanks to this, both persons in the union act in accordance with the inner logic of love, respect its inner dynamic and prepare themselves to accept a new good, an expression of the creative power of love. Willing acceptance of parenthood serves to break down the reciprocal egoism—(or the egoism of one party at which the other connives)—behind which lurks the will to exploit the person.[19]

This citation from John Paul II's work illustrates the conclusions that chastity-based models of sexual virtue make. Assuming that the essence of human nature and personal good can be identified, sexual moral rules are clear. One does not genuinely love another person when their truth and good is not respected or affirmed.

Human nature, according to this line of thinking, includes sexuality. But the bias of rationalistic philosophy prejudices the description of sexuality. Rationalistic philosophy asks what makes human sexuality human and not animal? What uses of sexuality are consistent with the specific excellences of human nature, that is, consistent with reason? The answer traditionally given has been reproduction. And, accordingly, one cannot genuinely love another person if the sexual exchange falls outside of heterosexual marriage and is intentionally contraceptive.

But reproduction is the purpose of animal sexuality as well. How does this use of sexuality really make human sexuality human? For rationalistically based theories, the answer is that free will and reason make human sexual reproduction human and not animal. The genuinely human use of sexuality is not instinct driven; it is freely chosen and chosen for the right purposes and in the right contexts. Thus, for humans to engage in sexuality humanly, they must have control over their animal instincts and urges, engaging in sex only for its reproductive purposes and only in those contexts in which the well-being of children can be assured, that is, in stable heterosexual marriages.

This, of course, was the moral doctrine of Greek and Roman Stoicism and the official Christian moral teaching about sexuality until the last couple of centuries. It was the official Roman Catholic approach to sexual morality until the 1960's when Vatican Council II finally admitted that love was a coequal end or purpose of human sexuality (with procreation). What makes human sexuality human is not just that it is engaged in with free will and reason but that it is loving. Human sexuality is human because it engages the soul, it involves a sharing of the deepest parts of ourselves in ways that only human beings seem capable of doing. Human sexuality is human because it is personally self-disclosive. It is not just a superficial rubbing of genitalia; it involves an affection for the other as a person, a desire to know the other as person, a desire to share oneself with this other person, a desire to be known and loved by this other person.

Contemporary chastity-based models of sexual virtue have attempted to update traditional moral teaching by affirming that one of the purposes of sexuality is love. But, as I hope to show, chastity-based models, particularly those which are grounded in rationalistic and essentialistic models of human nature, are incapable of being sufficiently upgraded to account for the rich meaning and significance of sexuality as an expression of human love.

An interesting illustration of this is in a statement in the 1995 Vatican instruction entitled: "The Truth and Meaning of Human Sexuality." The document states: "It must never be forgotten that the disordered use of sex tends progressively to destroy the person's capacity for love by making pleasure, instead of sincere self-giving, the end of sexuality and reducing other persons to objects of one's own gratification."[20] The term "disordered use" encompasses contraceptive sex between spouses, sex between unmarried adults, sex between gay men or lesbians, and sex between those who are divorced and remarried (not to mention any number of sexual acts that fall into various categories of paraphilia).

This document, like traditional Christian sexual morality, appeals to human nature as the ground for the truthfulness of its claims (not the authority of Scripture or church offices). In other words, this is a nonsectarian claim, one that assumes that reasonable people reasoning reasonably will find it reasonable. Thus it must submit its claims to the same scrutiny as any other nonsectarian claim. So is it the case that people who engage in the above mentioned categories of sexual intimacy progressively lose their capacity to love? There is little anecdotal evidence to support the claim. There are no studies that I am aware of that have measured the differences in the ability to love between heterosexual couples who practice birth control and those who don't or between people who have divorced and remarried and those who have remained married. So-called practicing homosexuals show no greater preponderance to being any less loving or less self-sacrificing than their heterosexual counterparts. Indeed, their statistical overrepresentation in helping professions is anecdotal evidence to the contrary. A recent study also showed that gay people were more generous in donating time and money to charitable organizations.

Although some disordered uses of sexuality might progressively undermine one's ability to love genuinely, I suspect that most reasonable people reasoning reasonably would not include in such a category of disordered uses contraceptive marital sex or sex between the divorced and remarried. Some might think that sex between gay men or lesbians is disordered, but more people are now aware of gay and lesbian couples whose relationships are indistinguishable from heterosexual couples in terms of commitment, longevity, and love. How is it possible for these couples to sustain a loving intimate relationship if their sexual intimacy is essentially disordered and progressively undermines their ability to love?

As intimated earlier, the weakness of chastity-based models of sexual morality lies in their essentialistic models of the truth of human personal life and in the belief that it is possible to be fully self-possessive and affirming of the complete truth of one's sexual companion. The Vatican instruction and John Paul II's sexual anthropology are both illustrative of this. "Love between a man and woman is achieved when they give themselves **totally**, each in turn according to their own masculinity and femininity."[21] (emphasis added) From the papal exhortation on family life, the Pope writes, ". . . sexuality, by means of which man and woman give themselves to one another through the acts which are proper and exclusive to spouses, is by no means something purely biological, but concerns the innermost being of the human person as such. It is realized in a truly human way only if it is an integral part of the love by which a man and a woman commit themselves **totally** to one another until death."[22] (emphasis added) The Pope goes on to say, "The only 'place' in which this self-giving in **its whole truth** is made possible is marriage, the covenant of conjugal love freely and consciously chosen, whereby man and woman accept the intimate community of life and love willed by God Himself . . ."[23] Richard Hogan and John LeVoir emphasize this point when they say that "there are two possible ways for people to relate to one another: love and use. Love is a complete and total self-gift."[24] It would appear that unless one gives oneself completely, according to this line of thinking, sexual intimacy would involve "use" and not "love."

There are two flaws in the foregoing comments. First, the nature of a spiritual transcendental subject does not permit a "total" self-gift, much less a "total" self-possession or self-mastery. The mystery of human subjectivity is such that it is always deeper and more profound than any attempt to possess or objectify it. Indeed, if the human person is "capax Dei," a patristic concept referring to the human capacity for union with God, then our own self-possession and self-mastery is impossible. As God-oriented (spiritual) beings, we cannot be possessed, mastered, or objectified without violating our human dignity. In fact, the "use" of another involves an unjustifiable "objectification." Loving another person, if it is something other than use, requires that we always respect the unfathomable and unpossessable character of their person. Sexual virtue based primarily on the concept of "self-mastery" for the sake of being able to give oneself "totally" does not correspond to either the best Christian or humanistic anthropology. If by "total" the Pope means "unreserved" or without qualifications, then his concept is closer to most people's experience of sexual intimacy. It is interesting to note that in "Gaudium et Spes" (from Vatican Council II), the language describing marital love never uses the term "total" but rather "mutual self-giving."[25] In the light of these concerns, the virtue of self-mastery or self-possession through control of the passions is at best an inadequate way of conceptualizing sexual virtue.

Second, the "nuptial meaning of the body" is a phenomenological claim that the body is essentially heterosexual and reproductively oriented. As a phenomenological claim, it suggests that reasonable people reasoning reasonably should find this a reasonable and fitting account of the truth of the human body! But striking (and converging) evidence is being produced in contemporary psychological and biological research which shows that the body is not universally heterosexual, that it is either biologically diverse or socially and personally malleable, such that an essential and universal heterosexual nature can no longer be affirmed with phenomenological or reasonable/scientific methods.[26] As noted earlier, there are many who are incapable of reproducing and others who choose to forego reproduction. They seem to flourish best when they find ways to be fecund, that is, creative and life nurturing. Thus, the language of the body is not exclusively nor essentially heterosexual or reproductive. It is, however, sexual and fecund. There are different ways that people are able to be fruitful and creative in the context of committed sexual relationships.

For the Christian tradition, indeed for Western culture in general, this is profound and, for many, uncomfortable information requiring nothing less than a Copernican-like shift in sexual anthropological paradigms. Recalling the words of John Paul II, we should not make the same errors that theologians did in condemning Galileo. When new information from clear and certain reason forces us to shift our ways of thinking, as uncomfortable and frightening as it may seem, we must do it or compromise the nonsectarian character of Christianity.

Covenantal Mutuality and an Amplified Model of Sexual Virtue

The language of heterosexual-marital-reproductively-centered morality is too impoverished to account for the richness of human sexual life. The vocabulary of sexual virtue needs amplification.[27] Any approach to sexual virtue that **reduces** moral sex or holy sex to heterosexuality and, moreover, to heterosexual-reproductively-intentional acts, is a reification and objectification of sexuality, compromising the truth and reality of other persons. This reduction is appropriately criticized as sexist, heterosexist,[28] and procreationist.[29]

But perhaps most importantly, the notion that sexual mutuality involves a "total" gift of the self is very problematic. The language of contemporary Christian sexual morality has shifted away from institutional-reproductive-household management models of marriage to a more personalistic notion of mutuality. Accordingly, marriage cannot be merely a matter of consent to sexual acts for reproductive purposes (as it was, for example, in the 1917 Code of Canon Law) but must be a consent of one's heart, a joining of two persons in a covenant of mutuality, of love. In order to form a communion of persons no less than an unreserved gift of oneself is required. Spouses make a commitment to share intimacy, to share their deepest selves.

But as well-intentioned as this reform is, it fails to appreciate an important feature of covenantal mutuality. The covenanted parties can neither express themselves nor appreciate each other totally. There is always more of oneself and more of the other to love, to discover, and to appreciate.[30] There are seasons in personal life and covenantal mutuality. An individual cannot be reified, encapsulated in a moment, or encompassed in his/her totality. Persons are dynamic spiritual entities, perhaps better described as processes or subjects rather than "truths" or "objective" things.[31]

Not only do the covenanted parties undergo change and elude possession, but relationships themselves include seasons such as illness, poverty, fortune, births, deaths, youth, old age, tragedies, triumphs, and celebrations. Margaret Farley expresses this as follows:

> Yet I do not have anything like total power in respect to my love. I experience myself as fragmented and conflicted, conditioned as well as self-determining, "swept away" as well as "self-possessed." No, there is no such thing as despotic control over any of my emotions by my freedom of choice. Belief in such a possibility probably rests on a faulty model of the human self, a popularized brand of Stoicism which would make reason the conqueror of emotion, rationality the mark of freedom—or the opposite, a runaway romanticism which would collapse freedom into my spontaneous emotions. It is surely blind to my complex experience—where I know that I can choose my love, but not always. I can shape my love, but oh, so slowly. I can cultivate my love, but only through long and patient attention. I can discipline my love and liberate it; but sometimes it still slips through my heart or disrupts my ordered life.[32]

Love then must take these various moments and shifts into account. What kind of virtue enables people to love this way, to love covenantally rather than instrumentally? How do we learn to love rather than use?

The Pope's answer is through a control of the passions and a restriction of sex to heterosexual-marital-reproductively-intentional acts. All other sexual intimacy constitutes "use." His answer, to some extent, parallels traditional Christian concepts of sexual virtue as well. But the control of erotic passion also severs the covenanted parties from the embodied resource that draws them lovingly toward each other. Eros, as Heyward notes, is our embodied yearning for mutuality.[33] It is the body's way of drawing us out of ourselves and toward delight in the other.[34] What keeps eros from degenerating into self-indulgence is not self-mastery or the "totalizing" of the self or the other. It is commitment which sustains eros in its regard for the reality and wonder of the other.

Commitment is a decision and a promise that we make, cognizant of the fluctuations or fickleness of our hearts.[35] It is the decision to attend to the other even when I am not always inclined to do so. It is only when I sustain my attention that I approximate a complete self-gift and a complete other-regard that characterizes genuine mutuality. Margaret Farley states: "Commitment is love's way of being whole while it still grows into wholeness."[36] But at any one moment of this mutual attending or love, total self-gift and total other-regard is impossible. At best, we practice a poetics of intimacy.

Good sexual companions, like good poets, have to have both imagination and a command of language.[37] Sexual companions must be able to perceive and to "image" the reality that is to be expressed. If one's sexual companion is grieving, it is inappropriate to express sexual intimacy as celebration, play, or fecundity. Rather, one is challenged to embody intimacy in gestures that communicate consolation and solidarity. This requires both sensitivity to the other's state and a good command of the rich possibility of embodied gestures of intimacy. One learns this through attentiveness to one's own emotions (one learns to be sensitive to another through personal awareness of what the other is probably experiencing) and practice in communicating such sensitivity in tender embodied fashion.

Popular culture mitigates against the poetics of intimacy when it banalizes intimacy in TV sitcoms, reducing sexual intimacy to a narrow range of emotions and expressions. Sexual expressions become pedant without poetic imagination and linguistic art. The poetics of intimacy is also undermined by the encouragement of detachment from emotions. This doesn't make one a more faithful lover; it severs one from the sensitivity that would enable compassion with and awareness of one's sexual companion.

Good sexual companions, like good poets, know how to arrange life, how to confer form and make visible the contours of a particular life moment and relationship.[38] Covenantal sexual relationships are not abstract conceptual essences but relationships that are being constituted and created in the intimate language and life of the partners. The covenanted parties arrange and shape their intimate sharing of life through poetic imagination and expression. There is not a single covenantal essence which is the proper form for all relationships. Each relationship must incorporate the unique life narrative of the parties involved.

For example, two invididuals who become covenanted at an older age need not attempt to give a traditional reproductive form to their love. They might, however, attempt to give creative shape to the life nurturing or outward turning orientation of love in other ways, including mentoring of younger families in the neighborhood, volunteering for after school programs, or supporting youth organizations. Or relationships which include a party who has been sexually abused in the past might have to find creative ways to give shape and form to their intimacy, forms which are more patient, healing and tender.

Judith Wallerstein and Sandra Blakeslee have identified different kinds of marriages or committed sexual relationships.[39] They describe four different types: companionate, romantic, rescue and traditional. We might think of these types as either different poetic forms or different poetic voices. A successful relationship might require a shared appreciation for the kind of relationship into which the parties have entered. If one individual is seeking a companionate relationship and the other a traditional one (with children and a household), the prospects of their successfully nurturing and sustaining intimacy are diminished, unless they become aware of the different poetic/relational forms that are in question. Few people are even aware of different forms of marriage, and this lack of awareness is a consequence of the lack of a poetic formation in intimacy.

A parallel comparison might be made to friendships. In his most recent book, Andrew Sullivan laments the lack of attention given to friendship in our culture and in philosophical and literary works.[40] He draws attention to Aristotle's treatment of friendship in the *Nichomachean Ethics* where three types of friendship are described: those based on what is pleasant, those based on what is useful, and those based on what is good.[41] Each of these types arises in different circumstances, enjoys a different narrative, and requires different kinds of attentiveness. How many of us were educated as to the different forms or poetic voices of friendship? How many of us would be able to make much better sense out of our friendships if we were more aware of these different forms and nuances? It is our lack of formation in the poetics of intimacy which leaves us ill equipped to make sense of the richness of our friendships.

Good sexual companions have to be sensitive to the sexual likes and dislikes of each other. A genuinely loving sexual relationship is not sustained by merely performing sexual acts. They must be performed in ways that respect and attend to the particular forms of sexual joy, delight, and pleasure of each other. This includes an appreciation and sensitivity to the seasons and cycles of each other's emotions. There are times, for example, when one's sexual partner needs more emotional and physical space, when physical affection needs to be less intense and unitive. There are other times when the same individual may delight in closeness and smothering affection. Some expressions of sexual intimacy are more deeply pleasurable and enjoyable to certain individuals but not so to others. Some individuals need and want more playful, sensual or rough exchanges. Others need and want more tender, cuddly and less genitally focused exchanges.

When a partner feels that his/her lover is not sensitive to these preferences nor seems interested in becoming more sensitive, it is often interpreted as more than just an annoyance or disappointment. It is often taken as an unwillingness or inability to respect the emotional and physical vulnerability that is part of a relationship where intimacy is shared. Sexual intimacy is one of the important ways that couples communicate emotional intimacy and, if it is insensitive or self-absorbed (focused merely on one's own sexual preferences), it undermines the sharing of emotional intimacy.

In former ages, when marriage was primarily a household-management-and-reproductively-centered institution, sharing of emotional intimacy was not as crucial. Thus, an appreciation and sensitivity for the varieties of ways that couples could share physical intimacy as a way of communicating emotional intimacy were predictably lacking. But since modern marriages have placed much more importance on the sharing of emotional intimacy, the accompanying ability to communicate that in sensitive, rich, and physically satisfying ways is much more important and needs to be included in the ways that we prepare people for marriage. Sexual intimacy is, dare one say, the sacrament of the love and intimacy of spouses. Just as the Church works at making sacraments rich, colorful, multidimensional, appropriate to the liturgical season, sensitive to the cultural particularities of the people involved, and celebrated by those who are trained at expressing what the sacrament communicates, we should not shy away from cultivating rich, colorful, multidimensional, seasonally appropriate, personally sensitive, and deeply communicative forms of physical sexual intimacy between couples.

The issue of seasons is an important consideration. John Bradshaw highlights the issue of relational seasons in his book, *Creating Love*.[42] Relationships follow similar patterns of development and include different seasons or stages. Bradshaw notes that most couples begin in what is described as a codependent stage, where the parties make every effort to accentuate and discover common perspectives and interests. The second stage involves a period of counterdependence, where couples discover and focus on differences, disagreements, and even conflicts. This is often followed by an independent stage, where the attempt to reconcile different perspectives is relinquished in favor of independence. If a couple make it through these various stages, they often discover and create a relationship of interdependence.[43] If one is not sensitive to these stages or the seasons of a relationship, one might not be able to move beyond the counter dependent or independent phases. Poetic sensitivity requires an awareness of these seasons and thus enables faithfulness, a faithfulness that might not be possible if the "truth" of a relationship is thought about in single categories.

Thomas Moore highlights another kind of poetic richness in *Soul Mates*. He distinguishes soul from spirit. Spirit refers to the part of ourself that seeks to rise above, to be rational, to be independent, to be spiritual. Soul refers to the part of ourself that enjoys rootedness, connectedness, union, relationality, and emotionality. Since we are both spiritual and soulful we must learn to cultivate and balance both. This has profound implications on the seasons and contours of relationships. They need room for union and independence, emotional connectedness and rational spirituality.[44] Without poetic appreciation for this, relationships suffer crises when either the soulful or spiritual dimension is unattended.

Helen Vendler states that "every artwork exists to evoke pleasures that are easier to feel than describe."[45] Sexual intimacy is a way of expressing aspects of love that are often easier to feel than describe or conceptualize. Sexual intimacy is a creative and artful joining of bodies to express more than can be expressed in words. It is a way of evoking pleasure or delight, not just as a response to physical stimulation but as an embodiment of a deeper emotional intimacy. The unveiling of the body through shedding clothes evokes pleasure and delight in the self-transparency it makes possible. The caressing of the body evokes pleasure and delight as a form of caressing and affirming the other. When the other kisses one's body in the most intimate of places, it is an expression of the pleasure and delight of sharing the most private and vulnerable parts of each other. In effect, the lovers are saying to each other in the language of this embodied intimacy that they will be tender and respectful of even the most fragile and vulnerable layers of each other's emotional lives.

The use of poetic language requires appropriate contextualization. As Vendler states, "the meaning of the word in a poem is determined less by its dictionary definition . . . than by the words around it."[46] In sexuality, this means that the context of sexual expression may constitute its meaning more than some abstract essential form or meaning. Suppose two individuals know each other casually and are very physically attracted to each other. Suppose they engage in genital sexual intimacy some evening after having gone to a show and dinner. For traditional sexual morality, such an act would constitute a violation of the covenantal or conjugal meaning of genital sex. But in such a context, the two do not necessarily intend for the act to express a covenantal commitment or relationship. It is an expression of their physical attraction. And we might suppose that they both have contextualized the act as such and not as an act of long-term commitment. If one of them took the expression to be more than that it would constitute a miscontextualization of the intent of his/her partner.

Traditional sexual morality argues that one cannot give some sexual acts a meaning they are incapable of embodying. Genital sexual intimacy cannot be merely an expression of physical attraction without compromising its inherent "essential" meaning (traditionally understood to be an expression of heterosexual marital procreative love). Consequently, the habitual misuse of sexual language risks jeopardizing its good use in the future. It is often hypothesized that casual or recreational sex leads necessarily to a superficial or impoverished (dishonest) understanding of sexual language.

But there are many people who have engaged in sexual intimacy in casual or recreational contexts who later form long lasting and faithful committed sexual relationships. Others, of course, remain stuck in superficial encounters. Wherein lies the difference? I believe there are two crucial issues.

First, sexual intimacy is capable of embodying a rich range of meanings. It does not have one essential meaning. As noted earlier, even marital sex represents different meanings as couples express play, passion, consolation, reconciliation, tenderness, and healing. What keeps sexual language from being corrupted is the ability of the individual to appropriately contextualize various sexual expressions. And this requires a rich poetic sensitivity.

Second, many so-called casual, anonymous or recreational sexual encounters are not as superficial as they might initially appear. In many instances, they are attempts to reach out and connect emotionally and soulfully with another human being. And while individuals do engage in sexual intimacy for recreational and/or casual intimate reasons, the openness to something more keeps the encounter from being grossly "utilitarian." While it might not be "love," it need not be mere "use."

I don't want to be misinterpreted as encouraging casual, anonymous and recreational sex. This kind of sexual intimacy is dangerous since one's physical and emotional vulnerability are more at risk of being taken advantage of and, to whatever extent an individual intentionally avoids real emotional intimacy, anonymous and recreational sex can become addictive and increase dissasociative tendencies in the individual. This usually undermines the process of personal and interpersonal maturation. Nevertheless, traditional Christianity's harsh condemnation of sex outside of marriage as necessarily corrupting of sexual virtue is based on the belief that sexual intimacy has only one reasonable purpose and that it can only embody that one meaning without being corrupting and vitiating. This is simply not the case.

Developmental Approach to the Poetics of Intimacy

How is sexual virtue cultivated? How do people become poets of intimacy? I would like to propose a general outline of such a development and then use subsequent chapters to elaborate specific considerations of how sexual virtue is cultivated in different seasons of one's life.

Grammar. Children must first learn the grammar of sexuality. They must learn the vocabulary, syntax, and grammatical rules of sexual intimacy. As in learning one's own language, learning the language of sexual intimacy occurs first in simply hearing (observing) others speak the language. The behavior and modeling of healthy adult sexuality is the most important form of sexuality education! It is how one gets a sense of appropriateness, timing, boundaries, and the various categories of life.

Children must gain a sense of the goodness of their bodies through the security they derive from adults. They should receive affection and be protected from physical or sexual abuse (healthy boundaries being respected). By learning that their own bodies are good and pleasurable it is hoped that they will learn to respect the boundaries of others. When they explore their bodies they should not be shamed into thinking that certain parts are dirty or bad. If they show evidence of self-stimulation (common in infants and children), they should not be made to feel shame about the pleasurableness of their bodies but grow to appreciate the appropriate context for such stimulation.

The process by which a child acquires a vocabulary and is able to name the world is politically charged. Language is filled with ideological and power perpetuating dynamics. Language is a way of naming and describing and shaping a world. It is impossible for language to be free from perspectival biases. But it would be wrong to deliberately instill biases that will be socially and personally disabling in the future. Exposing a child to a rich vocabulary of gender and sexual identity is empowering. Sexuality is a complex reality. It is frustrating to attempt to forge a sexual identity with a limited vocabulary. Boys and girls must be presented with a variety of examples of different ways to live out their gender so that, as they begin to develop their own identities, they are not constricted by artificial limits or constructions. They must learn to affirm varieties of sexual identities with respect to both gender and orientation. Their storybooks should include examples of women fully integrated into the workplace and into various positions of leadership. Men should be portrayed in nurturing roles as well as in stereotypical male roles. Depictions of romance and family life should include gay and lesbian relationships.

Critics of sexuality education programs that include affirmation of the diversity of sexual identity, gender roles, sexual orientation and diverse family configurations charge that such an approach confuses children and represents the breakdown of civilization as we know it. They often remind us that civilizations such as Greece and Rome failed **because** of their sexual immorality. These sorts of myths need to be countered with more accurate analysis and information about the collapse of former civilizations. It may very well have been the case that militarism, economic injustice, ethnic rivalry and social intolerance were more responsible for the collapse of imperial systems than affirmation of gay relationships. Ancient civilizations may have included a good deal of sexual immorality, but they never shed their fundamental heterosexist and sexist ideologies.

Affirmation of sexual and familial diversity in our current culture does represent a shift in cultural values, a fundamental change in our civilization. These changes involve a rejection of patriarchal beliefs about the inferiority of women. They involve a rejection of rigid gender roles that have impoverished societies by not allowing people's innate voices and gifts to ennoble their communities. These changes involve a rejection of heterosexism and its erroneous assumption that the only normal way for men to be men is through sexual intimacy with women and vice versa. These changes envision a society free from the psychological and physical abuse that has so deeply scarred our sexuality and has been legitimized by heterosexist, sexist, and sexual-phobic morality. Yes, civilization as we know it may change. Perhaps that would be a blessing.

The grammar of healthy sexuality is not the imposition of rigid gender roles or sexual identity but involves, rather, an appreciation for how to love covenantally. It involves learning what it means to be loved because one belongs, not because one conforms to others' expectations. It involves learning how to love others because they belong, not because they are advantageous to us. It involves learning how to love those who are different, particularly those who may suffer social prejudice. Families should model covenantal love. Imagine the rich poetic future of a child who sees his white father hug a black child at a birthday party. Imagine the appreciation for commitment and inclusive love that a child acquires when her parents invite her uncle and his male partner to dinner to celebrate the gay couple's anniversary. Imagine a household where the husband is just as likely to iron his wife's dress as she is his shirts. This kind of family and sexual morality is not confusing. Rather, it is centered firmly in gender equality and inclusive covenantal love.

If one of the central features of committed sexual relationships was the struggle to share power together, the grammar of sexuality would involve learning how to negotiate conflict with others. Children should be taught the grammar and vocabulary of peace and justice. Healthy adult sexuality is impossible if one's approach to conflict is aggression or passivity. Children must learn how to appreciate the perspective of others and gain a sense of how negotiation can lead to win win conclusions.

Children should witness a broad spectrum of affection associated with a variety of relationships. The vocabulary should be rich enough to accommodate a continuum of embodied expressions of mutuality. We tend to overly genitalize explicitly sexual relationships and undervalue the importance of so-called nonsexual relationships. We should prepare children for adolescence by equipping them with a richer vocabulary for affection than abstinence or genital intimacy. Children should witness adults expressing affection for each other in a variety of simple embodied ways.

Composition. With the onset of adolescence, sexuality education involves learning how to compose narratives of sexual intimacy. Composition involves bringing together various elements in a creative and balanced form. Andre Guindon wrote that sexual maturity involves the integration (or composition) of two basic dimensions of sexuality, the "sensual" and the "tender."[47] Sensuality involves all of the embodied features of sexuality, the urges and physical inclinations of our sexuality. Tenderness encompasses the capacity to establish interpersonal relationships. Sexual maturity involves relationships that are sensually tender and tenderly sensual. Sexual immaturity consists in relationships that are sensual but not tender or tender but not sensual. But these elements of sexuality are not innately integrated; they require a personal integration.

The exigency of integrating tenderness and sensuality occurs at adolescence. The awakening (or rather, reawakening) of one's sexuality during adolescence becomes a profound challenge. One's body begins to change dramatically, confounding all of the gracefulness and self-esteem one may have established as a child. Sexual desire begins to increase, manifesting itself at inopportune times (particularly with the spontaneity of male erection). One also begins to experience a depth of desire or interiority that longs for deep companionship and recognition. The syntax of adolescence is incoherent and confusing. One is left with a profound sense of the urgency to make something out of oneself, to give shape and form to this powerful emerging energy and inner self.

The goal of sexuality education for adolescents is ideally that of enabling the art of composition, putting together disjointed and competing urges into a coherent and graceful form. This is no easy task, and perfection is not expected. A young poet is prone to awkward composition; exaggerated use of some metaphors and neglect or ignorance of others; inappropriate timing, syntax and punctuation; and a still limited vocabulary.

The young poet must endure the humiliation of reading his/her work and realizing how far from excellence it is. How many adolescents look back at their failed attempts to love and realize the mistakes they made? These mistakes are usually little more than lack of experience. They involve situations where one equated sexual desire (sensuality) with genuine intimacy (tenderness) or where one's vulnerability was not honored or respected by the other. They are the hard lessons one must learn in order to become an accomplished poet of sexual intimacy. Some of the lessons are quite illuminating. One begins to learn how to embody mutuality in more and more graceful and effective ways.

Invariably, the question about sex and teenagers arises. In preparing this book, many parents of teenagers agreed with me in theory but felt apprehensive about actually encouraging adolescents to practice the composition of sexual language. The risks are very high for HIV transmission, pregnancy, and emotional trauma. Not suprisingly, parents of daughters are more concerned than those of sons. Risk for pregnancy, notwithstanding contraceptives, remains high and invariably leads to a constricting of life options for young women who become pregnant.

Isn't the idea of the immorality of sexual abstinence counter intuitive for our own day and age? I want to continue to reiterate a resounding no!

First, learning how to compose (integrate) the tender and the sensual dimensions of one's sexuality is indispensable for achieving a graceful adult sexual life. Adolescents who fail to learn how to do so are deficient in the kinds of skills needed to form good and sustainable adult sexual relationships. It is more difficult for them to distinguish sexual infatuation from emotional intimacy without having learned the compositional lessons of adolescent relationships. This may lead to tragically flawed choices about marriage during their late teens and early twenties. Or conversely, they may find it difficult as adults to express and embody warmth, affection and tenderness in ways that solidify and strengthen mutuality. This can lead to the breakdown of otherwise good marriages. While there are clear risks associated with sexual intimacy (pregnancy, AIDS, STDs, and emotional vulnerability), there are real dangers associated with the failure to practice and learn the language of sexual intimacy.

Second, the composition of sensuality and tenderness during adolescence invariably involves discovery of one's sexual orientation. We have come to appreciate in sociological studies of gay men and lesbians that the repression or suspension of sexual self-discovery during adolescence leads to a delayed adolescent period during adulthood. In the case of those who have married, this often involves the discovery that one is in an unsustainable committed sexual relationship. The ending of these marriages involves terrible consequences for all involved. Learning how to integrate sensuality and tenderness during adolescence enables adults to avoid making tragically flawed commitments and to mature in age appropriate phases.

Third, during adolescence sexuality (as the capacity and desire for physical and emotional intimacy) is intense. Young people feel a deep need to connect on emotional and physical levels. The belief that practicing the composition of sexual language is immoral leads many young people to anesthetize themselves with drugs and alcohol in order to mitigate their sense of responsibility. This actually leads to increased risks for AIDS, STDs, pregnancy, and physical and emotional trauma, not less.

Fourth, teens need to begin to address personality, character, and family of origin issues. Such issues inevitably surface in the conflicts associated with intimate relationships. These include learning how to be faithful, compassionate, sensitive, courageous, responsible, and a person of integrity. These are virtues which develop in a number of contexts, but are intensely tried in the chrysalis of intimate relationships. The tension between autonomy and mutuality is another issue teens must face as they become adults. They are at one and the same time becoming more independent vis-a-vis their parents but are forming relationships which include more mutuality and accountability. This forces the emergence of all sorts of lessons and insights into one's own personality.

If there are indeed serious risks associated with not learning how to integrate sensuality and tenderness during adolescence, these should be weighed in a calculus with other obvious dangers. While adolescent sexual abstinence may prevent AIDS, STDs, pregnancy and emotional and physical trauma, it may increase the likelihood of an impoverished and/or tragically flawed adult sexual life.

A poetic approach to adolescent sexual morality should involve a recognition of **all** the dangers associated with sexuality, both those occurring through sexual involvement and those associated with abstinence. Young people need to learn how to compose sexual lives that respect these dangers. A writer learns to work within certain grammatical and linguistic parameters but must also keep alive a creative and imaginative mind, trying new metaphors and revising awkward composition. The adolescent should be encouraged to set certain parameters within which she/he will attempt to compose a rich narrative of embodied relationships. This should include learning about risks of sexual intimacy and how to prevent untimely pregnancy and transmission of disease. It might also include setting certain benchmarks for different levels of sexual involvement. Since sexual language involves a composition of sensuality and tenderness, one should ideally attempt to match physical intimacy with the level of emotional intimacy and trust.[48] As Guindon noted in the 1970's, learning to speak the language of sexuality well requires that young people make every effort to integrate and balance sensuality and tenderness. A promiscuous and sensual sexual narrative, devoid of its relational ("tender") context, undermines the long-term project of fluent and graceful adult sexual life.[49]

The challenge of adolescent sexuality is manifold. First, the adolescent must come to terms with physical and sexual changes in his/her body. Some changes can be embarrassing and awkward, and adults can help teens by being frank (without being intrusive) and honest about these changes. Parents who are comfortable with their own bodies and who have modeled a rich poetic manner of expressing affection in embodied ways will make teens much more at ease about changes in their bodies and about continuing to be affectionate with their parents.

Young teens, particularly boys, will begin to discover the pleasurableness of their bodies during this age. For boys in particular, masturbation is part of the rite of self-discovery. Traditional sexual morality shamed adolescent masturbation. This has had the effect of alienating boys from their feelings, emotions, and bodies, and the resultant sexual violence of Western cultures may be directly associated with this anti-sexual and anti-pleasure bias. There are no documented psychological or physical health risks associated with masturbation. As an adolescent imagines him/herself with another and masturbates, this is part of the emergence of both a poetic and moral imagination. One begins to imagine oneself with another and begins to think about how to integrate the physical and emotional dimensions of sex.

The adolescent must come to terms with the deepening interiority and desire for intimacy. Young teens are not capable of the kind of interpersonal depth that normally accompanies sexual intimacy. Sexual intimacy at this age can be psychologically dangerous because there are risks for disassociative or addictive patterns steming from intense physical pleasure devoid of its concomitant interpersonal depth. Context is very important, and young teens who have a rich variety of relationships centered in a number of different kinds of social activities (sports, arts, social organizations, school, neighborhood, extended family, etc.) are less likely to be tempted to use sexually intimate relationships as a way to validate themselves or express their emerging need for significant relationships.

Sexuality education programs for young teens should in no way encourage sexual involvement. But neither should young adolescents be frightened about their emergent sexuality. Physical changes should be explained with tact and candor, questions answered confidentially and completely, and young adolescents should have opportunities to read about and discuss issues associated with friendship, loyalty, and intimacy.

Poetics. The final stage of development is adult poetic sexuality. Ideally, adult sexuality is a time for the flowering or flourishing of one's capacity for poetic intimacy. This stage will be elaborated more extensively in subsequent chapters.

Young adults, like adolescents, continue the process of learning how to be intimate, how to initiate and sustain relationships of sexual intimacy. Young adult relationships have the capacity to be profoundly pedagogical. Young adults come to know more clearly how they are in relationship with others. They come to know both their abilities and disabilities for healthy relationships.

In intimate relationships young adults gain a deeper sense of the poetic richness of their own personality and that of others. They learn about the various dynamics of intimacy, the seasons and stages of relationships, ways to communicate affection, support, love, fidelity, and tenderness. They learn how to accept love from others, how to become vulnerable in order to share personal intimacy.

Although adult poetic intimacy is the culmination of a developmental process, it involves its own development. Couples who are in long-term committed sexual relationships have the capacity to continue to discover new aspects of each other's lives and refine their abilities for graceful and poetic intimacy. Couples go through new seasons of love facing new challenges and unexpected successes. Indeed, the ever changing character of vital relationships challenges the notion that the moral excellence of adult committed sexual relationships can be expressed in the reductionistic categories of traditional sexual morality.

In the next several chapters we will examine the various challenges and achievements of adult poetic intimacy. But first, we should ask a methodological question: is a poetic approach to sexual morality, particularly as proposed in the subsequent chapters, Christian?

Notes

1   Although this categorization of ethics has become commonplace, I am indebted to Margaret Farley for its basic form.

2   James T. Sears, Op. cit. p. 14.

3   Carter Heyward, Op. cit., p. 99.

4   Thomas Moore, *Soul Mates: Honoring the Mysteries of Love and Relationship* (New York: Harper Collins, 1994) xiv-xv.

5   Martin Heidegger, cf. Walter Davis, Op. cit., pp. 114–119.

6   Walter Davis, Op. cit., p. 131.

7   Ibid., p. 115.

8   Martin Buber, Op. cit., pp. 53–54 and 74.

9   James F. Keenan, "Proposing Cardinal Virtues," in *Theological Studies* 56 (1995) 709–729.

10   Ibid., pp. 711–714.

11   Ibid., p. 713.

12   Sallie McFague, *Models of God* (Philadelphia: Fortress Press, 1987) 31–57.

13 Ibid. pp. 38–40.

14 Edward Collins Vacek, *Love, Human and Divine: The Heart of Christian Ethics* (Washington: Georgetown University Press, 1994) 87–106.

15 Karol Wojtyla, *The Acting Person*, trans. Andrzej Potocki, *Analecta Husserliana*, vol. 10 (Boston: D. Reidel Publishing Company, 1979) p. 108.

16 Karol Wojtyla, *Love and Responsibility*, trans H.T. Willets (New York: Farrar, Straus, Giroux, 1981) pp. 194–200.

17 Janet Smith, *Humanae Vitae: A Generation Later* (Washington: Catholic University Press, 1991) pp. 234–235.

18 Ibid., p. 235 and 237.

19 Karol Wojtyla, *Love and Responsibility,* Op. cit, p. 230.

20 "The Truth and Meaning of Human Sexuality," Dec. 8, 1995, Pontifical Council for the Family, English translation found in *Origins*, Feb. 1, 1996, paragraph 105.

21 Ibid., paragraph 14.

22 *Familiaris Consortio*, paragraph 11.

23 Ibid., paragraph 14.

24 Richard M. Hogan and John M. LeVoir, *Covenant of Love* (Garden City: Image Books, 1986) p. 160.

25 *Gaudium et Spes*, paragraphs 47–51.

26 Dean Hammer and Peter Copeland, *The Science of Desire: The Search for the Gay Gene and the Biology of Behavior* (New York: Simon and Schuster, 1994) and Simon LeVay, *The Sexual Brain* (Cambridge, MA: MIT Press, 1993).

27 Robert Solomon, "Sex and Perversion," in R. Baker and F. Elliston (Eds.), *Philosophy and Sex* (Buffalo: Prometheus, 1975).

28 Patricia Beattie Jung and Ralph F. Smith, *Heterosexism: An Ethical Challenge* (New York: SUNY Press, 1993).

29 Christine Gudorf, *Body, Sex, and Pleasure* (Cleveland: Pilgrim, 1994).

30 Vacek, Op. cit., pp. 44–49.

31 Again note the important essay of Thomas R. Kopfensteiner, "The Metaphoric Structure of Normativity," *Theological Studies*, 58 (1997) 331–346.

32 Margaret Farley, *Personal Commitments: Beginning, Keeping, Changing* (San Francisco: HarperCollins, 1986) p. 33.

33 Heyward, Op. cit. p. 99.

34 Margaret Farley, Op. cit., pp. 34ff.

35 Ibid., p. 34.

36 Ibid., p. 34.

37 Helen Vendler, *Poems, Poets, Poetry: An Introduction and Anthology* (Boston: Bedford Books, 1997) p. ix.

38 Ibid., pp. 25–29.

39 Judith Wallerstein and Sandra Blakeslee, *The Good Marriage: How and Why Love Lasts*, (Boston: Houghton Mifflin Co., 1995).

40 Andrew Sullivan, *Love Undetectable: Notes on Friendship, Sex and Survival* (New York: Knoff, 1998).

41 Ibid., pp. 188–189.

42 John Bradshaw, Op. cit., pp. 314–316.

43 Ibid., pp. 314–316.

44 Thomas Moore, *Soul Mates* (San Francisco: Harper Collins, 1994) pp. 3–21.

45 Vendler, Op. cit., p. 67.

46 Ibid. p. 147.

47 Andre Guindon, *The Sexual Language* (Ottawa: Univ. of Ottawa Press, 1977) pp. 53–59.

48 Guindon, Ibid., p 59.

49 Ibid., pp. 83ff.

❖ Chapter Four

Is This a "Christian" Sexual Morality?

Christianity and Philosophical Dualism

Questions about long-term and lifelong sexual abstinence and the proposal for a poetic approach to sexual virtue are directed, in part, to the Christian community. I believe traditional Christian sexual morality no longer functions as a compelling and graceful norm for living out one's sexuality in contemporary postindustrial societies. Many people have left organized Christian religion over sexual moral matters, particularly the divorced and remarried, married couples who use contraception, women alienated by sexism, gay men and lesbians alienated by heterosexism, and young adults who fail to find a discerning wisdom in the moral absolutism of traditional Christian moral teachings.

As an ethicist I am almost embarrassed to present a Christian sexual ethic because those terms are practically synonymous with anti-body and sexually phobic perspectives. New insights in neurobiology, biology, genetics, evolution, psychology, sociology, and other natural and human sciences have dramatically undermined the reasonableness of dualistic models of human nature. Dualism supported the belief that women were inferior to men, that women needed to be governed by men, that emotions and sensuality needed to be controlled by reason, that the body was dangerous and at odds with the soul and spirit, that sexual desire and sexual pleasure were dangerous for the development of spirituality and love of God, and that nonprocreative sex was inevitably self-indulgent and hence immoral.

The collapse of dualism has brought with it many changes in sexual practices and institutions. Women have gained greater equity with men, men and women increasingly share power in marriage, women and men share power in political and commercial institutions, we no longer disparage emotions or sensuality, stoic self-control and individualism are no longer moral ideals, we consider it important to be vulnerable in intimate relationships, we believe marriage should be more than a household management and reproductive partnership, we believe that sexual pleasure is good and contributes to physical and emotional well being, we believe that sexuality is not antithetical to spirituality, and we believe that nonprocreative sex (both in marriage and outside marriage) can be an important means of communicating love and intimacy or sharing physical pleasure.

The sexual ethic proposed in this book is reflective of this profound cultural shift in consciousness about human nature, about our bodies, about sexual desire, sexual pleasure and the nature of intimate relationships. Much of this change took place as a protest to traditional Christian sexual moral teachings. Thus, it is difficult to claim that the ethic proposed in this book is "Christian." Indeed, many of the positions proposed are in opposition to official Church teaching in both Roman Catholic and Protestant denominations.

One can, of course, distinguish between official institutional teaching and the belief of the membership of an institution. Is Christian morality what the institution proposes as normative or what Christian people believe and hold to be their faith? Without prejudice to such an issue, I would like to consider how some of the shifts in the sexual moral beliefs of ordinary practicing Christians is consistent with some of the central themes and patterns of belief of traditional institutional Christianity.

In brief and outline fashion, I want to show that Christianity and dualism are not necessarily or intrinsically linked and that Christianity is actually more compatible with a body affirming and eroto-poetic sense of interpersonal intimacy and love. Consequently, I hope to show that the ethic proposed in this book is reflective of some of the deepest insights of Christianity and has features which indeed make it distinctively Christian.

Christo- and Humanocentric

Jesus of Nazareth, the one we call "Christ," is the foundation of the Christian tradition and must be the point of convergence and link that connects various epochs of Church history. It is noteworthy that there is a resurgence of interest in "Christology" in contemporary Christian writings. Christology is the study of what the Church believes about Jesus. It includes both a study of the so-called historical Jesus and the Church's process of making sense of his life.

The recent explosion of studies and books on Jesus is in part a result of new archeological discoveries, particularly those at Qumran and Nag Hammadi, and decades of historical critical study of Biblical texts. New information has required us to rethink some of the assumptions about Jesus. But the explosion of books is also a response to the challenges raised by the modern and postmodern world views. New information about our world requires rethinking assumptions that support traditional beliefs. If our beliefs depend upon those assumptions, and they are no longer valid, what happens to our beliefs? Is Jesus still relevant? If so, how? What is it about Jesus' life that might illumine or bring coherence to contemporary existential problems?

One result of the recent interest in studying Jesus has been the discovery of the plurality of Christologies that were part of early Church life. A new book by Gregory Riley, *One Jesus, Many Christs: How Jesus Inspired Not One True Christianity But Many*, illustrates this point.[1] When the early Church decided which accounts of Jesus' life they would include in the canon of Scripture (the official list of sacred writings), they included four different accounts (The Gospels of Matthew, Mark, Luke and John)! It is amazing that even when the Church was attempting to consolidate and enforce orthodoxy through creeds and councils, it did not fear some degree of plurality. It authorized four different versions of Jesus' life, each with its own theological perspective. Some of these perspectives are more difficult to reconcile with each other than we might initially believe.

Plurality within religious traditions is important because experience of the divine is not something which can be easily conceptualized and described. We need a plurality of images and metaphors to account for the multilayered and multidimensional character of religious experience. Our lives, the reality of God, and our relationship with God all require metaphorical and/or poetic language because conceptual language never adequately expresses the richness of these realities.[2] It is only appropriate that when we begin to develop a sexual ethic that it, too, be poetic or metaphorical. In other words, if sexuality is our capacity for intimate relationship with one another, then it cannot be adequately described without reference to the poetic or metaphorical character of our lives and our relationships.

The Council of Chalcedon taught that Jesus is fully human and fully divine. This had profound implications for how the Church thought about human nature. First of all, it suggested that humanity and divinity were not incompatible. Humanity has the capacity to share fully in the divine, and God has chosen to be self-disclosive in our very being. As Karl Rahner taught, this means that our thought about God (theology) is always also thought about humanity (anthropology) and our thought about ourselves (anthropology) is always also thought about God (theology).[3] This vision is profoundly antidualistic. It suggests that human embodied life is not antithetical to spiritual divine life. One doesn't have to leave the body to be divine. One doesn't have to develop a detachment from bodily pleasures to be holy. One doesn't have to escape the messiness or complexity of human relations to encounter God. God is God among us, Emmanuel. God's life is fully accessible to us in our own being and in our ordinary existence.

This intuition about the union of the human and divine in Jesus influenced how Christianity would think about the relationship between faith and reason and between theology and science. If Jesus was (and remains) fully human, then human nature and human reason become indispensable criteria for authentic Christian belief. Nothing can be genuinely Christian if it contradicts the truth of human nature or contradicts clear and certain reason. Christianity's early appeal to reason (natural law) in the elaboration of its moral teachings is evidence of this fundamental affirmation of the sacredness and goodness of humanity. Christianity understood its message to be good news to human beings, a message whereby human beings could flourish and realize the full dignity of their humanity.

Thus, when we seek to develop an authentically Christian sexual ethic, it must be at one and the same time authentically human! In early Christianity, views about human nature were elaborated along Greek philosophical lines, particularly those of Stoicism and natural law. As noted earlier, Christian moral teachings were presented as if reasonable people reasoning reasonably would find them reasonable. But the assumptions which supported Stoic and natural law views of human nature have been questioned by contemporary findings in psychology, neurobiology, sociology, genetics, and other human scientific studies. We have a deeper appreciation for the evolutionary character of human nature, of its cultural and sociological particularity, and of the problems associated with dualistic anthropology. New discoveries in genetics and sociology are forcing us to revise assumptions held for thousands of years.

For example, traditional Christian sexual morality taught that same gender sexual desire was the consequence of sin and that sex between people of the same gender was essentially self-indulgent and under-mining of their vocation to love. Scientific studies about sexual orienta-tion show that sexual orientation is probably not a conscious choice, that it is a given and something over which very few individuals have much control. Thus, Christian sexual ethics cannot continue to teach that same gender sexual desire is a sin without contradicting its own basic assumptions about how we determine authentic Church teaching. Social scientific studies about gay people show that, when social prejudices and discrimination are removed, gay men and lesbians achieve the same level of well-being in their personal and relational lives as heterosexuals. There is no evidence to suggest that gay and lesbian couples are any less loving than heterosexual ones. Thus, Christian sexual ethics cannot continue to teach that same gender sex undermines gay men's and lesbians' capacity to love without, again, contradicting its own methodo-logical principles.

If Christian sexual ethics is going to be faithful to its Christological foundation, which requires an affirmation and incorporation of every-thing that is genuinely human, it cannot ground its moral teaching in an anthropological theory which is no longer reasonable or substantiated by the various disciplines through which we study human nature. During early Christianity, sexual morality was rooted in the best available anthropological theory and information, dualistic philosophy. But the relationship between Christianity and dualism was a contingent and historical one, not a necessary or essential one. The Church's imperative in elaborating anthropological foundations for its teachings is to utilize the best information at hand and seek to show how Jesus' life and teachings illumine human existence.

As is obvious, the earliest attempts at reconciling the ministry of Jesus with the human condition were made in the context of a culture imbued with dualistic philosophy and dualistic assumptions. Thus, most of the traditional texts (Biblical and non-Biblical) take this dualistic context for granted. And for those of us who live in an age with different assumptions and perspectives the challenge is how to be faithful to our heritage. This produces a dilemma: how does one elaborate an ethic which affirms the best information we have about the human condition (required by a Christology which is radically human and divine) and is consistent with earlier Christian ethical teachings which were influenced by information about the human condition which is no longer valid? Or, in other words, if the findings of science are taken seriously, which they must be, how do we reconcile them with other sources of Christian belief, like the Bible or traditional statements made by previous Church authorities? Can we propose as authentic Christian belief something that contradicts the Bible or Church tradition?

First, a little perspective. Earliest Christianity did not struggle with this problem in the same way we do. The Church of the first two centuries did not have a Bible! Earliest Christians, particularly those who were Jewish, relied on the Torah and the Prophets as sacred texts but had already begun to think critically about those texts in the light of Jesus' teachings about freedom from the law. The composition of what we call the "New Testament" took place over about thirty to fifty years. There were many Christians in the first couple of centuries who were not familiar with all of the writings you and I read on a regular basis in the Bible. Moreover, the process of deciding which books were part of the official list took several hundred years to complete. Early Christians relied on the authority of the community more so than on official Church writings (which would later become the Bible).

Of course, the Church-based notion of authority became problematic as power addicted leaders began to abuse authority. The Reformation was, in part, a reaction to the abuse of power in the Church. Consequently, Protestant churches relied more heavily upon the Bible as the criterion of authority. According to the Reformers, Church leaders were themselves accountable to God and to God's word. Their authority was not higher than God's. The Bible, according to Reformers, was the most concrete expression of God's word and thus binding on the Church.

But Catholic and Protestant appeal to Biblical authority has been paradoxically unpredictable. One notorious fiasco was Roman Catholic condemnation of Galileo over his belief that the world rotated on its own axis. This scientific belief was not consistent with a literal reading of descriptions of the earth in The Book of Genesis, a [flat] world planted firmly on its foundations. The Roman Catholic Church appealed to the divine authority of Scripture to condemn Galileo's findings. This, of course, has proven embarrassing. And Protestants acted similarly in response to scientific discoveries about evolution, condemning evolutionary science as invalid because it contradicts the Bible.

Both Catholics and Protestants have had to work through the issue of Biblical authority. The following is a gross oversimplification. Protestants began to handle contradictions by increasingly distinguishing between the world of faith and the world of secular politics and commerce. In other words, each of these spheres of activity have their own principles and points of reference. Ironically, this gave rise to an unprecedented freedom for Protestants to pursue academic and commercial interests free from restraining concerns of religion. The so-called Protestant work ethic is a result of this.

Catholics strove harder to retain an organic or integrated understanding of religion and political and commerical life; hence, the Catholic Church opposed the development of democracy and secular states. Catholic higher education retained a closer connection to the liberal arts and sought continued integration of philosophy, religion, psychology, and natural sciences.

In doctrinal matters, Catholics felt freer to elaborate beliefs without appealing to the Bible. Belief in the immaculate conception of Mary, in her perpetual virginity, in her assumption, in papal infallibility, and in the existence of some of the sacraments have been supported by extra-Biblical sources. Protestants have not felt so free and had been initially more creative in looking for ways to accommodate the Bible to contemporary problems. A good example is the increased openness in Protestant churches to permit divorce and remarriage, notwithstanding Jesus' prohibition. They appealed to other texts in the Bible that could be construed as moderating Jesus' strict position on this matter. Catholics, ironically, have been more "Biblically literal" in their interpretation of divorce, but less Biblically grounded in the issue of artificial contra-ception and reproductive technologies.

A more extended consideration of this problem is found in the chapter dealing with sexual orientation. Both Protestants and Catholics have used the Bible to resist changing teachings on homosexuality, and both have used the Bible in ways that are not customary for their traditions. For example, while Protestants will permit remarriage after divorce because it is better to do so than burn with desire and potentially fall into more serious sin (appealing to Paul's statements), they do not seem to think this applies to gay men and lesbians. And the Catholic Church, which has traditionally appealed to reason in grounding its sexual ethic, clings tenaciously to dubious Biblical texts about homosexuality in sustaining its condemnation.

The convenient use and misuse of the Bible to suit one's vested interests betray other agendas at work in the sustaining of traditional Christian sexual morality. Pope John Paul II, in his apology for how the Church treated Galileo, stated that, when there is a contradiction between clear and certain reason and the teaching of Scripture, the interpreters of Scripture must find a new way of interpreting the texts. He concludes that what drove the leaders of the Church in their condemnation of Galileo was their unwillingness to rethink prevailing assumptions about the world that had been ingrained in their thinking for centuries.[4]

Contemporary Protestants and Roman Catholics face the same dilemma the Church did in the seventeenth century. Can we let go of ways of thinking that are supported by assumptions no longer valid, or will we permit our vested interests to cloud our commitment to truth and justice? A Christian sexual ethic must be, first and foremost, the fruit of a genuine and honest search for truth, a truth that frees and enables people to achieve the well-being and flourishing God intends for them to enjoy! If we perpetuate a sexual ethic that cripples and enchains people under rules which are arbitrary and not life enabling, we are no better than the legalistic perpetrators of Jewish moral law of which Jesus seemed so critical! When there is a contradiction between contemporary information about human nature and the teachings of past Church authorities or Biblical texts, we must find ways to interpret these past texts which enable us to affirm the important information we have today. The best way of doing that is to contextualize traditional documents and teachings. What they teach is often connected with anthropological assumptions. Take those assumptions away and one would be constrained to come up with a different teaching. We must be able to ground our ethic in fundamental methodological principles, not in particular historical and cultural conclusions which eventually become outdated.

This also means that we cannot claim for our contemporary ethic any more universality than is warranted by our anthropological assumptions. Human beings are deeply social, cultural and historical creatures. This means that while there are some features of human existence which are rather universally manifest, most human beings have to make sense of and author their lives in particular cultural and historical contexts. Thus, this poetic approach to sexual morality is reflective of postindustrialized Western societies and probably not relevant in other societies. I don't believe that weakens the claims. It simply suggests that human excellence is achieved in these particular societies through certain patterns of thought and action, but that human excellence could be achieved in other ways in other cultures and contexts.

Body-Affirming (Incarnational)

It is very strange that Christianity became a body-phobic and sexual-phobic religion, given the centrality of the doctrine of the incarnation, God become flesh![5] From the beginning of the Church's attempt to make sense of Jesus, it moved toward an incarnational Christology. Jesus is the Word of God who became flesh, who is God among us (Emmanuel), who shared fully in our human condition, who died, who now enjoys a resurrected "body," and who assembles the people of God into his body (the body of Christ)!

Jesus is, according to the Church, God's self-disclosure, God's way of expressing God's love, God's way of joining us to God's very inner life. One implication of this is that the human body is capable of being the medium by which connection between persons and connection between God and human beings is communicated. Jesus is described throughout the Biblical texts as one who ate and drank with people, who embraced and was embraced by people, who reclined at table with friends, and who displayed emotion.

Some contemporary scholars even suggest that it is quite probable that Jesus was married.[6] Jewish moral law expects Jewish men to marry and have children. This is one of the divine commandments. When a man does not marry, particularly one who is a public figure (a rabbi, for instance), elaborate explanations are given for why he is exempt from the commandment to have children. Since there is no elaborate defense of Jesus' celibacy in Biblical texts, in fact there is no mention of his celibacy at all, the presumption should be in favor of the fact that he was married. All of his "twelve" companions were presumed married, although little is mentioned of their wives.

While this issue might never be resolved, it is clear when one reads the Biblical texts that Jesus did not practice a dualistic form of spirituality or asceticism. Apart from his reported forty days in the desert, he was not noted for abstaining from food and drink, nor did he appear to shun opportunities to celebrate at banquets or feasts. Every indication was that Jesus was "at home" in his body, that he did not consider life a process of detaching himself from his body. Rather, his embodied life was an opportunity to establish intimate connection with those around him, to establish the kinds of bonds which were self-disclosive, one to another, and to tenderly touch those around him so that they might be made whole, that they might be affirmed, that they might know that they were loved. This pattern of embodied intimate self-disclosure is consonant with Carter Heyward's description of eros as our embodied yearning for mutuality.[7] Eros is the embodied experience of the longing to make connection with one another. It is one of the most intense ways we experience our vocation to love, and Jesus displays a comfort and at-homeness with that embodied movement toward others. Indeed, if Jesus is the incarnation of God, then one could easily conclude that God's way of becoming intimate with human beings is in and through embodiment.

The body-affirming implications of the incarnation were eclipsed by the body negating perspectives of Gnostic, Neo-Platonic, and Stoic philosophies so prominent in classical civilizations during the first several centuries of Christian history. We must reclaim the centrality of the body- affirming novelty of Jesus' life! It is antithetical to the original experience of Christianity to perpetuate a disdain and distrust of the body.

Justice-Oriented

There is increasing concern in contemporary sexual ethics to affirm the importance and centrality of justice.[8] Justice concerns first arose in the light of women's reflections on their experience of alienation and disempowerment. It is amazing to think that even in the twentieth century women did not have the right to vote, they were excluded from many professions, they could not enter certain types of graduate programs, in some jurisdictions they did not have the right to initiate divorce, they were expected to submit to the authority of their husbands, and they were paid less money for the same jobs that men performed. In almost every religion and denomination women were systematically excluded from leadership positions.

Dualism supports discrimination against women inasmuch as it portrays women as inferior to men. Dualistic descriptions of human nature include prejudice against emotions and organic bodily processes. Since women were believed to be more intimately associated with organic processes like menstruation, gestation, and lactation, and, since women's way of thinking was considered to be more holistic than abstract, women were considered innately inferior to men and in need of their governance and protection. This, in turn, left women economically and socially dependent on men.

A poetic approach to sexual virtue avoids rigid gender role descriptions. Although we have come to appreciate that sexual identity is greatly influenced by social patterns of meaning, we have also come to appreciate how varied the experience of gender is from person to person. One's own sexual identity is a rich process that is constituted both socially and personally, and we have come to recognize that rigid gender expectations are often alienating and destructive of personal well-being.

A poetic approach to gender identity has emerged in part because as women gained more social and economic freedom they were able to author different personal narratives which included roles traditionally assigned to men. Social equity also favored more gender equity in committed relationships, particularly in marriage. It is rare, today, to find a young couple describe their marriage in terms of patriarchal power. Husbands and wives think of themselves as equal partners, sharing power in relationship. Men are more willing to take on responsibilities traditionally assigned to women without feeling inferior or unmanly. Consequently, their children are less likely to subscribe to rigid traditional gender roles.

The Southern Baptist Convention recently encouraged a return to traditional gender roles in marriage during their 1998 summer convention declaring that women should submit to the authority of their husbands. They and other fundamentalist Christians believe this is a more authentically "Christian" approach to marriage. But justice in sexuality was a hallmark of the Biblical description of Jesus' life.

Two features of Jewish moral law were particularly alienating and disempowering for women: the ritual impurity associated with female organic processes and women's vulnerability to being divorced by their husbands. Jesus' ministry directly confronted these alienating tendencies.

Much of Jewish moral law centered around maintaining ritual purity. This is a complicated concept, and it is far beyond the scope of this chapter to make sense of it. Nevertheless, the fundamental sense of ritual purity was that of identifying states of transition or personal unsettledness which rendered one less suitable for presenting oneself to others and to God. Ritual impurity rendered one unsuitable for worship in the temple and it was often thought of as a state of un-wholeness or unholiness. Being holy meant being whole, being in a state of composure, able to direct oneself wholly to God.

Coming into contact with someone ritually impure rendered one also ritually impure. Since women were more vulnerable to ritual impurity through menstruation and birth, men were encouraged to avoid social interaction with women, particularly women in public about whom they did not necessarily know their state. It was as if they were to assume all women were ritually impure. Gender segregation left women more socially and economically marginalized, reinforcing their inferiority and dependence on men for social, economic and religious power.

In the Gospels, Jesus is reported to have interacted with women in disregard for the concerns of ritual purity. His approaching the woman at the well and his permitting of a prostitute to anoint his feet with her hair and oil are just two examples of how Jesus seemed to be critical of how these laws alienated women. Holiness, for Jesus, was not a matter of maintaining external purity (by conforming to purity codes) but a matter of maintaining right relationship with his fellow human beings, males and females. Right relationship involved affirming the intrinsic dignity and goodness of people regardless of how society had labeled them.

Jesus is also reported to have prohibited divorce and remarriage. Indeed, his statement reported in the synoptic Gospels (Matthew, Mark and Luke) distinguished Christian sexual morality from Jewish and Greco-Roman. Christians, unlike the Jews, Greeks and Romans, did not permit divorce and remarriage. The exceptions to this rule are reported in the chapter on poetics of intimacy and married adults.

What is notable about Jesus' position is its implicit concern about the injustice women suffered under Jewish divorce law. Under Jewish law, men could initiate divorce for any reason.Since women had no economic or social independence, divorced women suffered greatly. Divorce was often initiated when children had not been born in a marriage. Two statements Jesus makes in reference to his teaching imply that he is concerned about how divorce impacts women. First, he emphasizes the unity of husband and wife, presumably in contrast to the commandment to be fruitful and multiply. Second, he mentions that some men become eunuchs for the sake of the kingdom. Eunuch could mean, literally, one who had been castrated. But in Jewish culture, it also meant one who had no children. Jesus seems to be inferring that the center of marriage ought to be the love between husband and wife. This contrasts with the prevalent cultural belief that women where reproductive property of men.

Thus, a genuinely distinctive Christian sexual ethic, one based on the unique vision and ministry of Jesus, ought to strive to eliminate the way purity codes ostracize people and ought to strive to foster a society where women are not treated as reproductive property. Women and men should be encouraged to form loving partnerships, ones where they share power equally.

As will be noted later, if Jesus' primary reason for discouraging divorce was its unjust impact on women, then attempts to permit remarriage in our own day, out of concern for the well-being of both men and women, would not be a violation of Jesus' original intent.

In addition to concerns about sexism, a Christian ethic which is justice centered would also seek to dismantle heterosexism, bias against gay men and lesbians. Again, within Jewish law, gay men were considered ritually impure. And certainly within traditional Christian sexual ethics, gay men and lesbians have been socially and ecclesially vilified and alienated. Western society permits people to discriminate against gay men and lesbians in housing, employment, social services, and church membership. Dualism supports heterosexism both in its insistence that only heterosexual-marital-and-reproductively-intentional sex is virtuous and in its insistence that men realize their masculinity only in sexually loving women and women realize their femininity only in being loved sexually by men. Inasmuch as it associates abstract rational self-control with human excellence and argues that men are more innately suitable for achieving such excellence, dualism supports the notion that men realize their masculinity by exercising authority over women. Gay men and lesbians do not fit these rigidly described gender roles and are, consequently, discriminated against by those who seek to perpetuate dualistically grounded models of sexual morality.

So even though gay men and lesbians were traditionally condemned in Christian literature, the information upon which such a condemnation was made has now been superseded by new information, and our Christian commitment to sexual justice would demand it.

Love-Centered

A poetic approach to sexual morality is love-centered. The human vocation is to love. A poetics of intimacy is concerned with enabling people to engage the deep interiority of their lives with one another, indeed, to bring about an ever deeper soulfulness through the intimate relationships they establish. One of the ways we enable people to love deeply and authentically is to help them sort out the many lessons learned in intimate relationships, help them develop a richer vocabulary of intimacy and deeper appreciation for the mystery of intimate relationships.

Rodney Stark notes that what distinguished Christians from their Greco-Roman contemporaries was the importance they gave to love as the central Christian virtue.[9] The centrality of love was so important that it probably gave Christians an actual and perceived edge in facing two severe outbreaks of the plague during the first several centuries of Christian history. Their Greco-Roman neighbors saw how Christians took care of one another and how they flourished accordingly. One might argue that love is the distinguishing mark of Christianity.

A Christian sexual ethic should be love-centered. But it is curious that throughout the history of Christian sexual morality, influenced as it was by Greco-Roman dualistic philosophy, love played such a secondary role in thinking about sexuality. Christians followed shared Greco-Roman cultural values about marriage as a household management and reproductive institution rather than as a covenant of intimacy and love. Our contemporary shift to a love-centered approach to sexual life is not antithetical to Christianity; indeed, it may be more distinctively Christian.[10]

Christian life has always been portrayed as a movement toward union with God. Jesus summarized the moral law as one of loving God with one's whole heart, soul and mind and loving one's neighbor as one loves oneself. Traditionally, under the influence of dualistic philosophy, loving God meant detaching oneself from earthly loves and from the embodiment and sensuality that typically characterize sexual love. To love God was equated with becoming rational and spiritual, loving supreme truth and supreme good. The spiritualization and rationalization of the love of God was the fruit of dualistic influences on Christianity.

Jesus' life should remind us that God's love for us and our love for God are fully implicated in the fundamental goodness and sacredness of embodied human life. God chose to become intimate with us by sharing our very flesh, sharing our very being, joining God's being with ours. Jesus reminded his followers that one cannot love God without loving one's fellow human being. I don't believe Jesus meant this in the way we often think of it, that our neighbor is a means to God. If I love my neighbor, God will be happy with me and invite me into heaven. Rather, I believe Jesus was teaching us that God has joined God's being with ours and that God isn't an abstract, separate, distant being. Rather, God is fully present, Emmanuel! And when we are alienated from one another we are alienated from God. Loving one's neighbor is not a means to loving God, it is a direct participation in the very being and reality of God.[11]

Moreover, if learning to love with greater integrity and depth means having to pass through the chrysalis of difficult and intimate relationships, then one cannot love God with integrity unless one has learned to love other human beings with integrity. This is where Thomas Aquinas was wrong about the question of the immorality of sexual abstinence. Giving up sexual intimacy is not primarily a matter of giving up the opportunity to have children. Sexual intimacy is one of the richest contexts for learning to love more deeply and more authentically. Thus, long-term or lifelong sexual abstinence jeopardizes the vocation to love, central to the Christian model of moral excellence.

The Christian community needs to ask what impact long-term or lifelong sexual abstinence has on one's journey to God, cognizant of new understandings about the lessons and transformations that are enabled in committed sexual relationships. Given new insights, we should be more concerned about the risks or dangers associated with long-term and life-long sexual abstinence. That is not to say that some individuals might not be able to access the same resources in other contexts. But we must assume that alternative routes to learning to love are extraordinary and require extraordinary circumstances and resources. We cannot assume that these are universally or even ordinarily accessible.

A love-centered ethic must be respectful and attentive to the good and well-being of others. But as should be obvious by now, the reality of our humanity is poetic and metaphoric, not essentialistic and determinate. Learning to love one another requires learning to be sensitive to the poetic and metaphoric dimensions of each other's lives. Although traditional sexual morality sought to guard against the "use" of each other by stipulating certain truths about each other which must be respected lest they be eclipsed by the passion of sexual desire, a poetic approach to sexual morality claims that reductionistic identification of the "truth" of each other is equally eclipsing of personal truth. A poetic approach to sexual morality is not an encouragement to utilitarian love; rather, it is an attempt to amplify and deepen our appreciation for what constitutes the reality of each other.

Fecund (Fruitful)

Traditional morality considered procreation to be the primary moral purpose of sexuality. Any nonheterosexual, nonmarital, and non-reproductively intentional sexual pleasure was an affront to the moral purposefulness of sexuality. It has been argued that love cannot be sustained if it does not extend beyond itself, if it does not reach beyond self-gratification and become self-gift and creative.

When the Roman Catholic Church officially prohibited artificial contraception in marriage during the 1950's and 1960's, many Catholic scholars and laypeople argued that procreation is but one form of a more inclusive or general notion of fecundity. They agreed that love must be fecund, but they disagreed with the notion that fecundity is exclusively realized in procreation. Married couples' love is fecund not only in having children but in raising them, nurturing them, and confirming them in life. Consequently, couples who are infertile are able to realize the fecundity of their love in many different ways such as through voluntarism, working with children, improving the quality of life in their communities, and through confirming life in those around them.

Andre Guindon was one of the first to think about fecundity in different contexts, i.e., marital fecundity, celibate fecundity, and gay and lesbian fecundity.[12] His argument is both a priori and a posteriori. In other words, by definition (a priori), fecundity would appear to be a more inclusive term than procreation. By experience (a posteriori), we know that people live out the fruitfulness of their love in many different ways. We know, for example, that gay couples and lesbian couples flourish and that they flourish, in part, because their love is not solipsistic (turned solely inward). Gay men and lesbians find many different ways to turn their love outward, beyond themselves, in service to life and to justice.

If it is appropriate to think about sexual intimacy poetically because human beings and human relationships are not ultimately comprehended by essentialistic categories but rather are lived and experienced through a rich multiplicity of metaphors, dimensions, seasons, voices, and goods, then fecundity and/or sexual reproduction are best regarded as one of many poetic dimensions of sexual intimacy. As already noted in chapter three on sexual virtue, it is impossible to have total possession of oneself or total knowledge of another. No single act can express all of the poetic dimensions of oneself or one's relationships. Thus, while fecundity and sexual reproduction are genuine aspects of sexual intimacy, they need not be intentionally present in each and every sexual act any more than any other poetic dimension must be present in each and every sexual act.

In Summary

A Christian sexual ethic will not be Christian merely by reiterating past ethical codes or past models of sexual virtue. Both Christian Scripture and tradition are culturally and historically particular. We must distinguish between the "good news" and the medium in which it was expressesd. A Christian sexual ethic is first and foremost one which enables human beings to flourish and achieve excellence with respect to one dimension of their lives, sexuality. A Christian ethic cannot be genuinely Christian if it proposes norms which undermine the well-being and flourishing God intends for us to enjoy.

There are certain marks which are characteristic of "Christian" moral thoughtfulness. Christian morality is human affirming, consistent with the best information we have about human nature and human life, it is rooted in the witness Jesus gave to God's enduring love, it is body affirming or incarnational (inasmuch as God chose to become united to human history in Jesus), it is justice-oriented, love-centered, fruitful and ultimately enabling of human well-being. When a particular set of moral teachings is inconsistent with the best information we have about human nature, when it is anti-body or anti-sexual, when it marginalizes particular groups of people, when it does not bear fruit or enable personal and social well-being it cannot be celebrated as an authentic expression of the Good News!

Traditional Christian sexual morality was an expression of a synthesis with the best information that earlier Christian generations had about human nature, the best information they had about their tradition, and a response to the socio-cultural exigencies of their respective ages. We have an obligation to forge a similar synthesis, one which integrates new information we have about human nature, one which incorporates new information we have about the historical Jesus and the socio-historical context of early Christianity, and one which responds to the socio-cultural exigencies of our day. Faithfulness to a previous Christian form should not be equated with faithfulness to a tradition which includes these constitutive methodological values.

The following chapters present some considerations toward reforming traditional Christian sexual morality so it can be more consistent with these distinctive marks. Specifically, the following chapters outline what a poetic approach to sexual virtue might look like with respect to different groups of people within the Church.

Notes

[1] Gregory J. Riley, *One Jesus, Many Christs: How Jesus Inspired Not One True Christianity But Many* (San Francisco: Harper Collins, 1998).

[2] Sallie McFague. *Metaphorical Theology*, Op. cit.

[3] Karl Rahner, Op. cit. pp. 24–25.

[4] John Paul II, *The Galileo Affair*. Op. cit.

[5] James Nelson, *Embodiment* (Minneapolis: Augsburg, 1978).

[6] William E. Phipps, *The Sexuality of Jesus* (Cleveland: Pilgrim Press, 1996).

[7] Carter Heyward, Op. cit., p.99.

[8] Marvin M. Ellison, *Erotic Justice: A Liberating Ethic of Sexuality* (Louisville, KY: Westminster John Knox Press, 1996) and Carter Heyward, Op. cit., pp. 22–23 and Martha C. Nussbaum, *Sex and Social Justice* (New York: Oxford Univ. Press, 1999).

[9] Rodney Stark. *The Rise of Christianity* (San Francisco: Harper Collins, 1997).

[10] Edward Collins Vacek, Op. cit.

[11] Carter Heyward, Op. cit., pp. 22–23.

[12] Andre Guindon, *The Sexual Creators* (New York: University Press of America, 1986) pp. 163 ff.

❖ Chapter Five

Poetic Morality of Single Adult Sexuality

Traditional Moral Approaches to Single Adult Sexuality

The sexual universe of traditional Christian morality was heterosexual and martially-centered, although the ultimate goal of sexual morality was often described as a movement toward a nonsexual way of loving. Single adults had two morally sanctioned options: marriage or religious celibacy, and both of these ideally ought to lead to the elimination of the disruptive and unsettling power of sexual desire and sexual pleasure! With the exception of Gnostic Christians in the early Church and Quakers in the later, most Christian denominations discouraged a protracted single life. It was generally assumed that sexual desire needed a remedy, a moderating and legitimizing institution, and it was believed that marriage or religious life provided this *remedium*. Single adults were either feared (for their unchanneled sexuality) or pitied (for not having found a suitable spouse).

Divorce was rarer than it is today, so large numbers of divorced and unremarried adults did not exist. However, divorce and/or spousal abandonment was common enough to warrant remarks from Luther and other reformers. They recommended remarriage as a way of avoiding more serious problems like promiscuous nonmarital sex or the personal dissolution that can accompany postmarital life.

Single adult sexual morality was described in relationship to marriage. When unmarried adults engaged in sexually intimate behavior it was described and condemned as "premarital" or "extramarital."If Christian sexual morality is shifting toward a new moral paradigm, and if that new paradigm is no longer heterosexual and martially-centered, what kind of implications might this have for how we think about single adult sexuality? Before we proceed, we need a bit of terminological clarification.

Adulthood

When does an individual become an adult? The answer to this question varies from society to society and is relative to the kinds of activities, responsibilities or opportunities one considers. Historically, women were of legal age to marry in their early teens, but few societies would have considered them adults. Indeed, women were often regarded as perpetual children, always in need of the protection and guidance of males, be they fathers or husbands.

Adulthood might be defined as the age when a society accords adult responsibilities to individuals, responsibilities like voting, military service, or the right to dispose of property or manage commercial affairs without a guardian. For some earlier societies, this coincided with physical marks of maturation such as menstruation for women and a beard for men. But this is certainly not the case in contemporary Western societies.

Postindustrial societies display a good deal of ambivalence about when individuals become adults. Contemporary teenagers are more physically mature at earlier ages than their predecessors. Physiological markings of adulthood, then, occur at younger ages. But contemporary societies discourage young marriage with the average age at which men and women marry projected well into the later twenties.

Jewish and Christian rights of passage, such as Bar/Bat Mitzvahs and Confirmation, occur when young people are from fourteen to sixteen. But few parents are really willing to accord them adult status at this point. Individuals are not permitted to vote until they are eighteen. In the United States, one cannot legally drink alcohol before twenty-one, although prior to this one could die in war, marry, raise children, own companies, and pay taxes.

Personal maturation obviously varies from individual to individual. Some older teenagers are very mature and responsible, sometimes as a result of having to face formidable personal challenges and crises. Some so-called adults, well into their twenties or thirties, display very little personal maturity or responsibility.

From the perspective of a poetics of intimacy, adulthood coincides with the capacity for deep interpersonal intimacy. There is no magical date or moment at which one achieves adulthood. Personal maturation occurs along a continuum. However, generally speaking, individuals begin to achieve this capacity for deep interpersonal intimacy in their late teens, usually from seventeen onward.

Singlehood

The term "single adult," in the past, would have referred to the unmarried, excluding ordained clerics and religious brothers and sisters. The practice of concubinage during the classical era raised interesting questions about the term "single." Men and women who cohabited without intention of marrying were not, strictly speaking, single. But they wouldn't have been accorded the status of "married" either. Children born in concubinate relationships did not have rights to inheritance or the surname of their fathers. The practice of cohabitation in classical times raises interesting questions about cohabitation in our own.

For example, contemporary couples who live together without formal marriage often do so without intention to refrain from marriage in the future, something uncharacteristic of historical concubinage. But like concubinage, contemporary cohabitation usually includes sexual exclusivity and emotional intimacy.

Another category of sexual relationship in classical culture was betrothal or engagement. Prior to marriage, individuals promised to marry one another and/or their parents or guardians arranged for a future marriage through betrothal agreements. Technically, these individuals were not "single" even though no marriage ceremony had taken place. In some societies, couples who were betrothed could engage in sexual intimacy without moral or legal recrimination. Contemporary society includes the practice of engagement, but traditional Christian sexual morality does not accord these couples the moral right to sexual intimacy.

Contemporary societies also include coupled gay men and lesbians. In most instances, these couples are not accorded legal marital status, but they function as couples, not singles.

Single Adulthood—A Definition

In this chapter, a single adult will be defined as an individual who is seventeen years of age or older and who is not in a long-term committed sexual relationship. Couples who have an ongoing romantic relationship but who do not live together nor have made a formal commitment to one another will still be considered "single."

How to Think About the Morality of Single Adult Sexuality

The question before us is that of thinking about the morality of single adult sexuality. Traditional Christian (particularly Roman Catholic) morality would have focused on specific kinds of acts or on the development of sexual virtue, chastity. Act-centered questions considered what kinds of physical acts of sexual intimacy were morally permissible or not outside of marriage. Virtue questions considered what kind of behavior fostered the cultivation of chastity.

As already noted earlier, both act-centered and chastity-centered morality are inadequate given both the poetic/metaphorical nature of human personhood and relationships and given the kinds of long-term committed sexual relationships contemporary society encourages adults to form. Act-centered concerns are usually reductionistic, failing to appreciate the poetic richness of relationships. Chastity-centered concerns do not adequately address the kinds of dispositions needed to sustain satisfying and graceful adult relationships of intimacy and mutuality.

Traditional Christian sexual morality sought to specify which acts violated fundamental sexual moral norms. It was assumed that sexual intercourse certainly violated the no-sex-outside-of-marriage norm. But what about kissing? What kinds of kisses were acceptable or not? What about touching or nudity? Each of these questions was answered with respect to the fundamental moral norm of no-sex-outside-of-marriage or, in more technical discourse, no sexual pleasure outside of marriage.

Absent from traditional sexual moral discourse was any understanding of or concern about the poetics of intimacy. If, for instance, a certain kind of touching was morally acceptable with respect to the no-sex-outside-of-marriage norm, was it always acceptable, or did it still need to be thought about with respect to the poetics of intimacy, to the developing relationship of a couple?

Let me propose an example. Ken and Janet have been going out for six months. They are both twenty-three. They have grown emotionally close to one another. Ken derives a good deal of emotional and physical satisfaction from having Janet sit close to him. He likes to put his arm around her, hold her hand, and even lay his hand on her thigh. Janet usually likes the affection and closeness, but occasionally feels irritable and wants some space. Ken doesn't seem to appreciate this and, when Janet pulls back, he either forces her back close to him or punishes Janet with passive aggressive anger.

Traditional act-centered sexual morality would be hard pressed to come up with the categories or conceptual language adequate to evaluate or assess the moral appropriateness of Ken's and Janet's physical intimacy. The moral acceptability/nonacceptability of these acts doesn't address the more serious issue here, Ken's insensitivity to the poetics of intimacy. He appears very immature in terms of recognizing when his affection needs to be less intense and when it is okay to be intense. While he might have developed a good deal of self-control with respect to more sexually intimate expressions of love, he hasn't developed a poetic sense of appropriateness with respect to so-called morally acceptable expressions of love.

Janet's friends might counsel her to overlook Ken's insensitivities. He's obviously a self-controlled person. He hasn't pressed her to go further. He seems to respect her and, while somewhat insensitive on one level, is well-behaved and considerate on another. In other words, their relief that Ken is within bounds in terms of traditional sexual moral norms blinds them to the potential problems Ken is likely to demonstrate once he and Janet are married. Ken's lack of poetic sensitivity will be amplified once he and Janet are married. He is not developing the kinds of dispositions which will enable him to sustain a long-term intimate relationship.

The above example illustrates that traditional moral categories about single adult sexuality are insufficient for illuminating and giving shape to the rich potential of interpersonal intimacy. However, it doesn't demonstrate that traditional moral categories are irrelevant with respect to single adult sexuality or even to the poetics of intimacy.

We must ask a second type of question. Is there an inner logos, an inherent orientation or character of adult intimacy which serves as a criterion for what is appropriate/not appropriate in single adult sexuality? Or perhaps more specifically, is there any truth to traditional Christian sexual morality's claim that single adult sexuality is oriented toward heterosexual marriage and must be evaluated with respect to it? Should moral questions about single adult sexuality be thought about in terms of how they impinge upon the movement of those individuals toward marriage?

Let's consider Ken and Janet again. As before, Ken and Janet are twenty-three. They have been going out for six months. They have become emotionally very close. They have a lot of common interests. They are both law students. They have similar political leanings. They both enjoy the arts, and they have very compatible personalities, notwithstanding Ken's insensitivity to Janet's need for space from time to time.

Neither is currently interested in marriage. Both have several more years of law school and internship before they realize any substantial financial security or stability. Both enjoy their law work and want to devote a lot of time to it. Both doubt whether they are willing to give the time it takes to begin a family and have children.

Traditional sexual morality would have thought about their relationship as a premarital one, one that was at least open to further commitment. Some contemporary Christian ethicists would even argue that sexual intercourse would be acceptable between Ken and Janet if and when they came to the conclusion that they want to marry. In other words, sexual intimacy would be acceptable during engagement or what might be described as "preceremonial" marital intimacy.

But what if Ken and Janet do not think in these terms? What if Ken and Janet simply enjoy an intimate friendship, one which doesn't necessarily include an implicit or explicit direction toward marriage? How might we think about the morality of their interpersonal and sexual exchange? Must single adult sexuality always be assessed with reference to marriage?

For example, is there a relationship between single adult sexual patterns of behavior and the stability of marriage? Some traditionalists argue that sex before marriage, cohabitation before marriage, and contraceptive sex among single adults undermines the desirability of marriage and its eventual stability. In a heterosexual marital-centered moral paradigm, actions are judged good or bad with respect to whether they support and enhance the institution of heterosexual marriage.

But even granting the legitimacy of these concerns, statistical studies are ambivalent about the relationship between unmarried adult sexual practices and the institution of marriage. In the NHSLS survey of sexual practices in the United States, "virgins have dramatically more stable first marriages."[1] Although only 16.3 percent of men and 20.1 percent of women are virgins at marriage, apparently those who are are much less likely to divorce. Researchers are hard pressed to understand why this is the case. They assumed that those who have sex in order to select a compatible partner for marriage would have had greater success in marriage. But apparently this is not the case. If sexual intimacy among single adults jeopardized successful committed sexual relationships (including marriage), would this be sufficiently serious to warrant long-term sexual abstinence until marriage?

If successful marriage is one of the marks of genuine Christian love, and if sexual abstinence prior to marriage makes it more stable, the expectation that single adults practice sexual abstinence might not be as unjust as initially thought. However, several aspects of these statistics need closer examination. First, longevity is not synonymous with good covenantal mutuality or love. Many long-term married couples are embittered, hostile, cold, unaffectionate, and do not share power or intimacy with each other. They have perhaps completed successful reproductive-household-management-style relationships, but they have not necessarily achieved the richness of covenantal and poetic mutuality. The above cited statistics do not measure the correlation between happiness and having been a virgin at the time of one's first marriage. They do confirm, however, that those in long-term committed relationships (either marriage or cohabitational) are generally happier than those who are not or those who are engaging in sex with multiple partners.[2]

But we are not able to tell whether those who were virgins at marriage are happier in marriage than those who were not.

Second, the statistics do not control for the age of first marriage coupled with virginity. Are these virgins marrying young or old? On the surface, it would seem that sexual abstinence prior to a young marriage would be easier to sustain than prior to a later marriage.

Third, is it even reasonable to make a lifelong commitment to marriage without first having established a successful narrative of embodied mutuality and intimacy with one's future partner? If marriage is expected to be lifelong, and if it is centered in love and not merely in institutional and reproductive goods, one ought to know whether his/her partner will be able to become appropriately vulnerable, expressing vulnerability and intimacy in tender embodied sexual union. Expecting single adults to practice sexual abstinence deprives them of the context within which to make informed decisions and commitments. While some uninformed commitments might be successful, the odds are against it, and luck does not mitigate against the irresponsibility of being uninformed.

Sexual intimacy among single adults is the context within which the poetics of intimacy is learned and rehearsed. This is not a crude form of learning how to perform good sex, although that certainly must be learned. It is more importantly the context within which young adults discover their capacity for interpersonal intimacy, learn how to embody that appropriately and richly, and develop their own poetic intimate "voice." Rich poetry is the fruit of an artist understanding his/her voice. This refers to the particular style, composition, syntax, vocabulary, and metaphors that express and embody poetic imagination. This is critical for sustaining rich adult committed sexual relationships, and this voice is learned and constituted not as an individual but in relationship. It is established and matures through mutuality.

If the model of successful sexuality is covenantal mutuality, and if this is grounded in a rich poetics of intimacy, it is difficult to imagine how adults could make successful and informed commitments to marriage or other covenantal sexual relationships without prior experience with sexual intimacy. Or put differently, while many covenantal sexual relationships may be successful, their **excellence** is grounded in a rich poetics of intimacy. Sexual intimacy among single adults does not guarantee the formation of a rich poetics of intimacy, but its absence most assuredly jeopardizes its acquisition. In at least this sense, mandated sexual abstinence for single adults risks severing them from the resource and context by which they acquire the dispositions that will enable a richer, more excellent, and more sustainable living out of covenantal mutuality.

Here, the reader may notice an important, albeit subtle, distinction. Sex between unmarried adults does not guarantee the acquisition of those dispositions that enable rich covenantal mutuality and a rich poetics of intimacy. The question might be asked, what kind of sex between unmarried adults does and what kind does not? But this question cannot be asked by Christian leaders as long as the Church is committed to the principle that the only morally acceptable option for unmarried adults is sexual abstinence. The problem that the contemporary Christian faces is that its commitment to the principle of sexual abstinence for unmarried adults does not permit it to develop a pastoral strategy that would cultivate the acquisition of good sexual dispositions among those adults who are sexually active.

In this sense, the traditional norm requiring long-term sexual abstinence for unmarried adults is harmful. It provides a false illusion that the Church is fulfilling its duty to young adults by preaching an abstinence only message. Consequently, when sexually active adults feel shamed by the Church for attempting to establish successful narratives of sexual intimacy with potential lifelong sexual partners, they are compelled to make choices between practicing their faith and doing the hard work of learning how to love and searching for suitable life partners. Since sexual intimacy is so vital to the overall well-being of people, most will go about the process of learning how to love and try to deal with their faith later. Traditional Christian sexual moral norms, then, are a source of unnecessary ecclesial alienation. They undermine the life of young adults who feel alienated from their faith tradition, and they undermine the life of the Church which suffers the loss of their presence and contribution.

Christianity needs to develop a compelling sexual ethic that gives young adults the confidence that the Church is a community committed to their growth, maturation, and well-being. This should include the celebration that sexual intimacy is one of the primary blessings of God. This should also include the affirmation that successful covenantal sexual relationships require the acquisition of certain dispositions which are probably not learned apart from the difficult lessons of trying to establish successful narratives of sexual intimacy. And if that is the case, the Church must begin to think about how adults can engage in sexual intimacy in ways that will assure the acquisition of those dispositions rather than their loss. It can only begin to do this when it acknowledges that its expectation that all unmarried adults practice sexual abstinence is at least unreasonable, if not harmful and, hence, immoral.

Toward a Christian Moral Approach to Single Adult Sexuality

The Church must begin with a fundamental assertion: **sexuality is a gift that enables us to form satisfying and transforming relationships of mutuality. Sexuality includes a spiritual or mystagogical dimension** in that it awakens in us an awareness of our deepest capacity to love and be loved, and that inevitably points to the presence and reality of God. **Sexuality is educational** since, in our various attempts to form relationships of deep mutual intimacy, we inevitably discover both our strengths and our weaknesses and are challenged to love with greater integrity, authenticity, fidelity, and compassion.

Sexual desire is not an irresistible or an aberrant irrational urge. It is a grace and blessing that we must learn to listen to, learn from, and use wisely and lovingly. Sexual desire appears irresistible and irrational when we distrust it, fear it, and try to repress or control it. The operative sexual virtue is not control but integration and contextualization. And the process of integrating and contextualizing sexuality is a poetic one that is deeply imbedded in each person's life narrative.

Yes, self-control and self-discipline are part of the process of integrating and contextualizing sexuality, but they are not the primary ways that people become sexually virtuous. One cannot love deeply, intimately or warmly unless he/she has learned how to become vulnerable to another, and this is impossible if sexual self-control is the primary approach to sexual virtue.

An effective pastoral approach to sexuality might include providing spiritual directors or pastoral counselors who would be available to help young adults sort out the lessons learned in the course of attempting to establish successful narratives of sexual intimacy. Rather than preaching condemnation, guilt and shame, the Church ought to admit that there are many rich spiritual, personal, and relational lessons embedded in sexual relationships needing identification and confirmation. Obviously, mistakes will be made. Individuals will discover that they are not as loving, faithful or tender as they had hoped. But this is why sexual intimacy is so important. It is an intense mirror into the soul and forces one to look at oneself in ways that might be avoided in other types of relationships.

The Church should position itself as an ally in the spiritual journey associated with sexual intimacy. All too often the Church appears to be an enemy, a shaming institution, and a judging parent. If it succeeds in shaming and frightening young adults into sexual abstinence, it risks severing them from the resources by which they can become virtuous covenantal lovers. If it does not shame them but offends and alienates them, then these young adults lose the potential spiritual discernment the Church could offer, and the Church loses the rich contribution that young adults bring to the community.

Moral Wisdom and Adult Single Sexuality

What insights do Christian single adults bring to the issue of adult single sexuality? How might these insights inform moral guidelines for single adults?

The goal of Christian moral life is to love with ever greater integrity and depth. Sexuality should be affirmed as one of the gifts which enable people to grow in this capacity and to enjoy the richness of interpersonal mutuality.

Intentionally utilitarian, superficial and promiscuous genital sexual activity is not usually conducive to acquiring dispositions of, or abilities for, integrity and interpersonal intimacy. Compulsive promiscuous sexual intimacy is most likely a symptom of sexual addiction and/or disassociative psychological states which require counseling and therapy. Normally, promiscuity is a symptom of deeper intimacy problems; it is itself not the problem.

Single adult romantic relationships develop along two broad tracks. One group develops out of social and professional relationships. Friends, students, coworkers and associates may first develop relationships that later become romantic. Physical and emotional vulnerability is less risky in these kinds of relationships. Presumably, the parties involved know each other and already have a good sense of whether or not their vulnerability will be respected and safeguarded. In these kinds of relationships, genital sexual intimacy is secondary to an already established friendship or association. There is less danger that the pleasure of genital sexual intimacy will eclipse the growth or development of emotional intimacy and mutuality.

The second group involves relationships which are first sparked by physical attraction. Two individuals often notice each other and feel a spontaneous delight associated with the physical appearance of the other. If the response is reciprocal it may lead to conversation and/or a plan to get together. These kinds of relationships begin with little or no knowledge of each other. Hence, they involve an increased risk of physical vulnerability. Since sexual desire is the primary impetus of such relationships, there is often a greater sense of urgency to satisfy that inclination.

Although casual genital sexual intimacy is common among single adults, some individuals have begun to deliberately postpone genital sexual involvement in these kinds of relationships in order to get to know the other better, to reduce the risk of physical assault, and to encourage the development of emotional grounds for satisfying sexual intimacy.

The increased risk of HIV transmission and other sexually transmitted disease makes genital sexual involvement between single adults more dangerous. Many heterosexuals do not believe they are at great risk and do not practice safe sex. Recent statistical reports of increased incidence of genital herpes suggest that many single adults are not practicing safe sex.

One step in assuming more responsibility for practicing safe/safer sex is to anticipate situations where one might engage in genital sexual intimacy. The reluctance of some "good Christians" to plan for such eventualities because "they would not do something like that" leaves them ill prepared for situations which do develop. Several good rules for the road are in order. One, be prepared to refuse to participate in sex with someone who is not willing to practice safe/safer sex. Two, come prepared with condoms. Bringing condoms on a date does not commit one to having sex, but it certainly equips one with an important barrier to disease transmission should sex occur! Three, learn how to exchange physically enjoyable intimacy in ways that are safe. This requires being confident enough to talk with one's potential sexual partner about this. If one doesn't feel confident doing so, it might signal a lack of trust that should be there.

Protecting oneself against sexually transmitted disease, untimely pregnancy or physical assault is not the extent of moral consideration in single adult sexual relationships. It is not enough for relationships to be safe and consensual. There are other important moral/poetic questions that need to be asked. Some of these are:

- Why am I attracted to this person?
- How does this relationship fit into my own life journey and personal goals?
- How honest can I be with this person?
- Does this relationship compromise commitments I have to other persons?
- Is this relationship just? Are there gross inequalities of power, conflicts of interest, or potential for exploitation?
- What am I learning in this relationship?
- Is the other person able to be honest with me?
- Does the other person respect my emotional or physical vulnerability?
- Is the relationship excessively exclusive or does it naturally open outward to other friends, family and associates?
- Does this relationship invite each of us to excellence and growth or does it stifle us and/or lead us to indulge our worst tendencies?
- Are we able to integrate emotional and physical intimacy in a graceful and poetically rich balance or do we avoid physical intimacy and/or emotional intimacy?
- Are we able to be tender with each other?
- Are we able to express disappointment and disagreement in safe and constructive ways?

These are the kinds of questions that are really the heart and soul of emerging romantic relationships between single adults. Having or not having sex is really a very minor indicator of the morality of our relationships. Attempting to determine the morality of single adult relationships against this criterion alone distracts attention from more serious issues. Genital sexual intimacy does, however, strip bare some of the facades behind which we hide and forces couples to confront issues that might otherwise go unnoticed. This is one of the reasons why long-term sexual abstinence for single adults may be impoverishing.

The above set of questions is essentially a manner of asking about the soulfulness of an emerging relationship. We can well imagine that in the heat of sexual desire and passion these not the first questions that come to the minds of young adults. But why shouldn't they be? Why couldn't we encourage young adults to ask these kinds of questions rather than shaming them about nonmarital sex? And if our concern is to reduce promiscuity, we might well find that encouraging young adults to ask these kinds of questions would reduce the amount of casual and anonymous sex between them.

An Objection

A hesitation is sure to be voiced! "This all sounds good and pastoral; but, if the Church gives the impression that it is condoning sexual promiscuity or fornication, it is encouraging people to engage in sex that is destructive of their personal well-being." One is reminded of the distinction St. Paul made between not being bound by the Law but nevertheless recognizing that not all things are good for Christians. Servais Pinckaers distinguishes between "freedom of indifference" and "freedom for excellence."[3] Freedom can be considered in terms of the freedom to choose among a number of different options or the interior freedom that enables one to excel and flourish. While the Church might permit freedom to choose, it would be remiss in its pastoral responsibility if it encouraged behavior that ultimately enslaved people to passions that prevented their excelling and flourishing.

Does sexual intimacy among single adults enslave them in such a way that it undermines their achieving human excellence? It was assumed by St. Paul, Augustine, Luther and many others in the Christian tradition that sexual passion, divorced from its moral context, was enslaving. It constituted a form of self-indulgence which jeopardized the flourishing of love. It was a form of moral confusion which disoriented the soul from the source of genuine moral discernment and, hence, endangered freedom for excellence.

It was also assumed by St. Paul, Augustine and Luther that sexual intimacy's moral purposefulness was marriage and reproduction. Any sexual intimacy outside that context lacked moral purposefulness and, hence, could be nothing other than self-indulgence. This is why the

Roman Catholic Church has reiterated in numerous documents that contraception between unmarried adults encourages a selfish living out of sexuality that is ultimately enslaving and destructive of those individuals' moral well-being. The Roman Catholic Church has assumed that widespread practice of contraception among single adults would lead to a gradual diminishment of interest in and respect for marriage. The reasoning runs something like this: why would someone want to marry if they could enjoy sexual gratification without the responsibilities of commitment?

But is this the experience of sexually active single adults? Do they demonstrate diminished respect for and interest in making lifelong commitments? According to the NHSLS survey (confirmed in other parallel studies), "adults overwhelmingly continue to form long-term social and sexual cohabitational partnerships, as they have for decades."[4] The NHSLS survey admits that the "rate of formal marriage has fallen dramatically" and that the "proportion of first unions that are informal cohabitations has risen steadily from one cohort to the next."[5] But interestingly, having one or more sexual partners before the age of eighteen increased the statistical likelihood of forming a union in the 18-30-year-old age group.[6]

The surveyors note that many of the informal cohabitations convert to formal marriage. This would seem to confirm the hypothesis that sexual activity among single adults involves the attempt to establish successful narratives of sexual covenantal mutuality in order to make informed commitments. The statistical data would also seem to confirm that sexual activity among single adults does not diminish interest in making long-term commitments. There may be less interest in forming formal marriages but not in avoiding monogamous sexual committed relationships.

Why is there increased preference for making commitments to cohabitational unions and not to formal marriages? Let me make a couple of suggestions. First, since many cohabitational unions convert to marriage, there is not an overall preference for them but for the use of them as a way of establishing a successful narrative of sexual covenantal mutuality before a formal marriage commitment or union is celebrated. A cohabitational union is usually monogamous and is usually open to its development into something more formal. This could be interpreted as a greater respect for the seriousness of marriage even in the face of rising statistics of divorce.

Second, there may be a general disenchantment with traditional institutional models of marriage. If, in the minds of some single adults marriage is associated with reproductive household management concerns, unequal distribution of power (patriarchy), proprietary interests (she is "my" wife; he is "my" husband), and institutional obligations which eclipse other goods (like having to stay together even when there is abuse or gross loss of affection and mutuality), then cohabitational unions appear more genuine, equitable, and loving. Moreover, if among Roman Catholics there is no way to remarry after the end of a tragically flawed marriage, many young adults may be hesitant to formalize their relationships until they are proven to be sustainable.

The reputation and vitality of marriage may depend less on the sexual activity of single adults and more on the ability of the Church to cultivate and celebrate models of marriage that are more reflective of the belief of Christians about what constitutes a good marriage. This must include affirming the importance of mutuality, sharing of power, minimizing proprietary attitudes about one's spouse, and cultivating the internal dynamics that can sustain commitment and fidelity while recognizing that, if one cannot, one will not be forced into lifelong abstinence as a result.

Does the practice of "safe sex" affect the development of a poetics of intimacy? Or put differently, how do the strategies of hygienic sex impact single adult sexual intimacy? I have tried to argue that long-term or lifelong sexual abstinence among single adults does not serve the acquisition of the virtues or dispositions which enable a rich and graceful poetics of intimacy. But given the present risks associated with sex, single adults either need to be abstinent or practice "safe sex." I understand the term "safe sex" to refer to sexual exchanges which are virtually free of the risks of contracting a sexually transmitted disease, of the risks of untimely pregnancy, and of the risks of physical or emotional trauma.

Risks of physical and emotional trauma are reduced by avoiding anonymous sexual encounters, sex with strangers or with individuals about whom one has little knowledge. Physical and emotional trauma occur in both long-term relationships and in casual short-term ones, but the risk increases in short-term ones. Since a poetics of intimacy is not normally served in anonymous or promiscuous patterns of sexual intimacy, avoiding situations that are risky is not problematic and, hence, recommendable.

Risks of untimely pregnancy can be reduced by using contraceptives. Chemical contraceptives ("the pill") do not protect for sexually transmitted disease but are attractive to some because they do not interfere with spontaneity nor do they require any alteration of sexual practice. Given contemporary risks of serious disease transmitted through sexual contact, "the pill" is not an adequate measure to assure "safe sex."

This leaves us to consider the practice of "safe sex" through the use of condoms or through engaging in intimacy which does not involve the exchange of bodily fluids. These strategies involve a greater likelihood of impacting spontaneity and, thus, of impacting the poetics of intimacy. Let me propose an example.

Margarita is a college student. She has become conscious of the risks of HIV transmission and contracting other sexually transmitted diseases such as chlamydia, hepatitis, and herpes. She finds herself more reserved at campus parties, aware that too much alcohol can numb her decision-making faculties. She is more reserved about the signals she gives to men to whom she is attracted. Previously, if a guy came on too strong and she had sex with him, not to worry. But today, she wants to make sure that her sexual partners are going to practice safe sex, that they are going to take her well-being into consideration.

This makes conversations with prospective sexual partners more delicate. Margarita says, "If you really like a guy and are interested in being intimate with him, you have to first bring up the issue of safe sexual parameters. You might decide you don't want to have sex with him, but even bringing up the subject puts you in an awkward situation."

Traditional sexual ethicists would argue that two people who don't know each other very well shouldn't be having sex anyway. And their point might be well taken, even in terms of a poetics of intimacy. The current situation certainly forces people like Margarita to take her time and be more reserved about anonymous sex. This might actually be good for someone like Margarita. Perhaps the reservation she feels will force her to establish a greater knowledge of her sexual partners and serve the poetics of intimacy.

But let's consider another example. John is also a college student. John was raised in a very traditional family where he learned strict moral rules about sex. John was taught that sex before marriage was wrong.

He feels very guilty about sexual fantasies and occasional episodes of masturbation.

John finds himself sexually attracted to both men and women. This is very disturbing, and he has struggled to make sense of his feelings. He is not sure if he is gay or bisexual. Although he believes unmarried sex is immoral, he thinks the only way he will know if he is gay or not is to experience sexual intimacy with both men and women. But he is mortified about the dangers of catching a disease or contracting HIV. Periodically, John becomes attracted to someone and he/she to him. But when they become affectionate, John becomes very nervous and reticent. He can't relax and be vulnerable with his partner. He is worried about keeping the sex "safe," and he is worried about performing correctly, depending on the gender of his partner.

John is, of course, struggling with at least two issues: sexual orientation and how to share tender and satisfying sexual intimacy. Concerns about the mechanics of safe sex (making sure the condom is on correctly, making sure one's partner is committed to a safe sexual encounter, and exploring forms of affection which are sensual without sharing bodily fluids) make it difficult to relax, to be vulnerable, to be playful, and to communicate affection. These difficulties, in turn, make it more difficult for John to listen to his body and its signals about sexual orientation.

John needs some good advice. This might include a suggestion to worry less about identifying his sexual orientation. Our society overvalues the categorization and classification of life. This is a product of our addiction to control! Many researchers believe sexual orientation falls along a continuum.[7] Most people, while predominantly heterosexual or homosexual, periodically experience sexual attraction or have sexual experiences which are discordant with their primary orientation. John may be someone whose orientation is more ambivalent. His need to identify a fixed orientation may be more a product of social pressure to fit into a sexual group with well established sexual objects than a genuine need for establishing satisfying intimate relationships.

John also needs encouragement in establishing trust and verbal communication as the foundations for good sexual communication. Although some couples move from good sex to good verbal communication, most successful intimate relationships begin with verbal communication. Trust enables partners to relax and become vulnerable in sex.

This still leaves our first question unanswered. Do concerns about safe sex impact the poetics of intimacy? It is certainly the case that spontaneity and vulnerability in sex are more risky due to the epidemic of HIV and of sexually transmitted diseases. But spontaneity and vulnerability in casual and anonymous sexual encounters has always been more risky, both physically and emotionally. Thus, if concern about safe sex encourages people to spend more time establishing trust and communication before sex, this is a good thing.

But in relationships where trust and communication have been established, concern about safe sex can still inhibit the kind of relaxation, spontaneity, and vulnerability that make sex a powerful communicator of love and mutuality. On one level, this may be an ongoing limiting condition of sexual intimacy in the twenty-first century. It is not ideal, but it is real and must be taken into consideration so that sex is responsible/safe.

There are some ways to mitigate this limiting impact of HIV on the poetics of intimacy. One, correct information is critical. Information about which forms of sexual exchange are risky and which are not can enable people to make informed decisions and feel confident during a "safe" exchange. Learning how to use condoms appropriately or how to share sexual pleasure in safe ways frees one to relax during these encounters.

Two, young adults need to set boundaries for themselves. One needs to have decided, when approaching a potentially sexual situation, what one will or will not do. One has to have enough self-love to avoid serious risks. Making firm commitments to oneself about boundaries frees one to communicate more confidently with potential sexual partners. These personal self-commitments enable one to be more vulnerable or intimate, knowing what one will do if one's partner is not willing to practice safe sex.

Three, these boundaries need to include decisions about alcohol and drug abuse. Some substances help us relax, let go of our inhibitions, and meet new people. But over consumption renders one unable to make good decisions, and this leads to serious risks in sex.

Four, a poetics of sex is important. We need to develop a broader repertoire of ways to express sexual affection, ways that are less risky for HIV transmission but no less sensual, erotic, and pleasurable. Since the Christian tradition has cultivated a strong anti-pleasure bias, imagining new ways to enjoy sexual pleasure will seem impious to many. Only with time will we grow more comfortable with the idea that sexual pleasure is a grace, a gift, and one that we can seek to enhance without fear or shame.

Deliberately Chosen Singleness

I have stated that the primary concern of my thesis is that **mandated long-term and lifelong sexual abstinence is harmful and, hence, unjust.** But is there harm when someone voluntarily chooses to remain single and/or sexually abstinent? How does the notion that long-term or lifelong sexual abstinence is harmful apply to those who have freely chosen to remain single? Are they incomplete, immoral or vicious? Are their lives impoverished? Ought we mandate sexuality in reaction to the harms of mandated sexual abstinence?

There are several motivations for remaining single. When an individual chooses to remain single out of fear of the challenges and unsettledness of relational life, he/she has failed to embrace the path of intimacy and likely will be impoverished because of it.

Some may choose to remain single out of a recognition that they are not suitable candidates for long-term intimate relationships. This might involve some impoverishment, but it might create less harm than that caused by unhealthy or harmful relationships.

Others may choose to remain single as a response to serious physical and/or sexual abuse as children or adults. Many of these individuals lament the loss of intimate companionship but are too traumatized to become emotionally and physically vulnerable in a relationship. Certainly it is inappropriate to suggest that these individuals are immoral or vicious. They are victims who have suffered violence to the most intimate and interior parts of themselves. Unfortunately, in a world that centers around sexual coupling, these individuals often feel additional shame and inadequacy for not being coupled. Every effort should be made to avoid applying the thesis of this book in such a way that it further victimizes them.

Those who have suffered physical and/or sexual abuse are often already aware that sexual intimacy would enrich their lives, but the process of recovering from the deep scars of abuse takes a long time. Long-term sexual abstinence for such individuals is already part of the poetics of intimacy. It is a season of recovery, a season for constituting safe physical boundaries. Intimacy for these individuals is often sought in relationships which are not likely to become physically intimate or, if they do, probably not genitally. Many of these individuals are not committed to lifelong abstinence, but they certainly need the space and time to work through the deep wounds of abuse. This is often a grace-filled process!

Some of the most serious challenges to the thesis of this book rest with those who have deliberately chosen to remain single and/or sexually abstinent and who insist that their singleness, celibacy and/or abstinence is not impoverishing in the least! I want to consider three types of choices here: one, the choice to remain single and sexually abstinent after having been in one or more sexually intimate relationships; two, the choice to remain single but to engage in sexual intimacy from time to time; three, the choice to remain single or celibate for religious reasons.

Singleness after sexually intimate relationships. It has already been noted that some individuals choose to remain single after the death of a spouse or after the end of a long-term sexually intimate relationship. Sometimes such a choice is motivated by the need to process the lessons and challenges of earlier relationships. Many couples, particularly those married with children, remark that life seems to move so fast that it is often difficult to take time to be reflective and process insights and lessons. Singleness after such a relationship might involve a long period for reflecting on the graces and challenges of the relationship.

Others may have been in relationships where their own individuality and autonomy were not honored. They, too, might very well need a long period of time to recover a sense of themselves. Singleness might very well be a poetic season in their pilgrimage of intimacy. It is a time for deeper intimacy with the self. Others may have been in abusive relationships where the prospect of embarking upon another is unimaginable. This, too, is a season for recovering a poetic sense of one's own interiority and intimacy. One can well imagine someone whose life has been defined primarily in relationship to others (e.g., a spouse or children or parents). Deliberately chosen singleness might very well be an enriching discovery of one's own intrinsic self-worth and identity. This is an important step in becoming a poet of intimacy and should not be looked upon as immoral or impoverishing.

Deliberately chosen singleness which includes sexual intimacy. Some may choose to remain single for a number of reasons but may also choose to engage in physically or sexually intimate relationships from time to time. It has already been noted that the reasons for restricting sexual intimacy to marriage in traditional Christian morality was motivated largely out of proprietary concerns and/or reflective of dualistic theories about human excellence. It has also already been noted that there is no reason to condemn singles who engage in sexual intimacy in the process of attempting to establish a successful narrative of mutuality upon which to base a life commitment. But what about singles who do not intend to make a life commitment? Are moments of sexual intimacy for them predominantly a form of "use" rather than love?

If such individuals engage in a pattern of deliberately superficial and anonymous sex, it is difficult to understand how this serves the poetics of intimacy. Such a pattern is usually psychologically harmful and physically risky.

But some individuals may cultivate friendships that are enduring, mutual and intimate. There may be situations where physical touch and/or sexual intimacy is an appropriate expression of the emotional vulnerability and intimacy these friends share. The endurance and depth of the relationship provide opportunities for continued personal integration and physiological pleasure and well-being associated with intimate touch. Therefore, those who are deliberately single and choose to remain so need not suffer the impoverishment of long-term or lifelong abstinence, provided they have access to and cultivate these kinds of relationships.

This situation might occur more often in those who are older, who have been in one or more exclusive relationships, and who now recognize that the prospects of forming future cohabitational mono-gamous relationships are not likely or even desirable. As the population in Western industrial societies ages, this may become more prevalent. Cathleen A. Fanslow's research in touch and the elderly underscores the importance of physical and emotional touch for older people.[8] Those who through death of a life companion/spouse or the end of a relationship find themselves single may choose to remain single but recognize that sexual intimacy is still physically, psychologically and spiritually enriching and seek opportunities for sexually intimate mutuality.

Religiously motivated celibacy and sexual abstinence. As already noted in several parts of this work, the choice to remain sexually abstinent or celibate for the sake of spiritual perfection is theologically and psychologically problematic. It assumes that God is a separate objective entity with whom one can more perfectly unite when free from the unsettledness and challenges of sexual relational life with other persons. Such a motivation also tends to assume that sexual desire is a primary hindrance to self-possession. This rests on dualistic anthropological models that are less and less supported by contemporary psychological and neurobiological studies.

The motivation to give up sexual intimacy for the sake of spiritual perfection also risks either the cultivation of delusional images of oneself, free from the critical feedback one gets from intimate relationships, or disassociate patterns of relating to others where one's emotional life is repressed and cut off from interaction with others. This, in turn, risks developing characteristics of bitterness, coldness, lack of com-passion and unattentiveness to the emotional needs of others.

It should be noted that religiously motivated celibacy developed historically in the Church under the influence of dualistic models of human well-being and as a means of enforcing more control over clergy and the Church. Today, those who defend the continuance of the institutional mandate of celibacy for the clergy speak of celibacy as a counter sign to the cultural obsession with sexuality in Western culture. It is supposedly an eschatological sign of the nonsexual spiritual existence we are to live in the age to come. It is supposedly a sign of a less exclusive form of love, placing oneself at the service of the wider community.

But since religiously motivated celibacy has been institutionally linked with the clerical state in Roman Catholicism, and since the organizational structure of Roman Catholicism involves little systematic accountability of the clergy to laypeople, celibacy is seen less and less as a sign of love and more and more as a sign of privilege and unaccountability. Many laypeople recognize the profound challenges and lessons that are part of committed mutual sexual relationships, and they do not see that kind of accountability or growth evidenced in their celibate priests. Moreover, many of them notice that priests become more embittered, cold, self-absorbed, and uncompassionate as they grow older. If celibacy is a sign of eschatological joy and flourishing, it is less evident in the general profile of the average parish priest.

Nevertheless, there are religiously celibate men and women who demonstrate a profound sense of joy, well-being, compassion, warmth, and the capacity to be genuinely intimate with others, sharing power and being accountable to them. More studies need to be done to identify the resources these individuals have drawn upon to make this happen. One suspects that either these individuals have experienced a significant enduring sexual relationship of some sort in their lives or they have learned how to make themselves emotionally vulnerable to others in tender and embodied ways. As several priest psychologists have noted, these kinds of celibates are genuinely rare.[9]

The institutionalization of lifelong sexual abstinence in the Roman Catholic priesthood implicitly lends a degree of legitimacy to traditional moral norms requiring the divorced, gay men and lesbians and single adults to practice long-term or lifelong sexual abstinence. Increasingly, the credibility of institutional celibacy is being questioned by overt symptoms of immaturity, self-absorption, sexual misconduct, and compromising sexual behavior among the clergy. Protestant denominations are more prone to recognize the problems of long-term and lifelong sexual abstinence and will likely reform their official sexual moral norms accordingly. Most notably, they will continue to affirm the importance of blessing remarriage after divorce, will move toward recognizing the moral and spiritual quality of gay and lesbian relationships, and will tacitly accept patterns of adult singlehood which include serious relationships of sexual intimacy. The Roman Catholic Church will have a more difficult time moving toward these affirmations precisely because of the institutionalization of celibacy and the identification of ecclesial power with celibates. It will continue to be important to identify in what sense long-term and lifelong sexual abstinence is problematic and usually harmful.

The Poetics of Intimacy in Nonsexual Adult Relationships

Most adult relationships do not involve genital sexual intimacy, but they include rich possibilities for intimacy. Christianity and Western post-industrial societies have not given much attention to the dynamics of friendship or other kinds of social relationships and their role in enabling one to love with greater depth and integrity. I want to explore some of the potential for a poetics of intimacy in nonsexual adult relationships.

Friendships.   Andrew Sullivan notes the absence of much writing about friendship in contemporary philosophical or moral discourse. This stands in stark contrast to classical appreciation for the importance of friendship in overall human well-being:

> Friendship, for Aristotle, seems to be the cornerstone of human society and flourishing, an integral part of happiness, and bound up inextricably with the notion of virtue. It is almost, it seems, prior to the notion of the individual himself.   Just as, for Aristotle, human beings are somehow not human beings unless they are part of a social network, so human beings cannot be fully themselves without the opportunity to befriend and to enjoy the activity of being with friends.[10]

Aristotle divides friendship into three categories: "friendship based on what is pleasant, friendship based on what is useful, and friendship based on what is good."[11] It would be friendship based on what is good that offers the richest possibility for the poetics of intimacy.

Sullivan speaks very highly of this kind of friendship. He contrasts it with sexually intimate relationships where a "sublime ... almost inhuman ... bliss of primal unfreedom" comes about through the loss of self-control. He describes friendship as "the complicated enjoyment of human autonomy."[12] Sullivan takes up the classical bewilderment about friendship. How can it be so important yet satisfy no vital human need? With the ancients, he describes the love between sexually intimate lovers as a relationship driven by need, passion, and longing. Friendship, on the other hand, is a choice; "it is a symbol of man's ultimate freedom from his emotional needs; love is a symbol of his slavery to them."[13]

Friendship, that is the good kind, is chosen not out of some need or purpose. It is chosen simply because it is good. The friend becomes a friend simply because of the goodness that he/she embodies. Sullivan notes that when we impose needs and purposes on friendship it often suffers. Precisely because friendship is free from needs and purposes "a friend can be far more honest than a lover."[14]

It would seem that this honesty is an important foundation for a poetics of intimacy. For if intimacy with oneself and with others requires an ever greater degree of self-honesty and integrity, then friendship provides an important window into the soul. But how is the honesty of friendship related to the radical honesty and self-transparency of a sexually intimate relationship?

There are many things friends can tell each other precisely because there is less fear of rejection, hurt, or betrayal. Many will recount how sex between friends ruined the kind of openness and exchange that was previously possible. For this reason, friends often cultivate a poetics of intimacy which is deliberately free from sexually intimate involvement. Preservation of certain boundaries provides the kind of space for honest exchange. This preserved space frees friends to be themselves without fear of the other requiring change. Friends who share living space and/or who travel together often find that the space which made honesty and friendship possible crumbles. Good friends can become irritable and disillusioned when previous boundaries are withdrawn. The irritability stems, in part, from a dissonance between friendship which accepts the other as he/she is and the intimate proximity that cohabitation creates, increasing pressure for interpersonal adjustment.

It is precisely the contrast between friendship and sexually intimate relationships which highlights the value of sexual intimacy. It is the context where self-transparency is most possible, not because one feels free to be self-disclosive (although that is often the case), but because in sexual intimacy one becomes self-transparent despite efforts of self-concealment.

But friendships are obviously a rich context for the growth and flourishing of a poetics of intimacy. They provide a complementary form of intimacy to that of sexually intimate relationships. In traditional and classical society, friendship was more important since marriage did not include the expectation that spouses be best of friends. But in contemporary culture, marriage has taken on many of the functions of friendship. And when friendships outside of marriage are not cultivated or sustained, marriages and other committed sexual relationships bear unreasonable pressure to provide both sexually intimate and friendly nonsexually intimate forms of intimacy.

Business Associates.   In postindustrial capitalist societies, many adults spend almost as much time with work associates as with anyone else. As economies shift from manufacturing to information and service industries the workplace becomes an intense place of interpersonal interaction. Team management models increase pressure for workers to form good working relationships with their peers. Companies provide workshops and retreats for employees to understand personality styles and manage conflict in positive and creative ways.

Consequently, workplace relationships are increasingly regarded as embodying many of the attributes of friendship. Admittedly, these friendships are more utilitarian than the "friendships of the good" in Aristotle. But their function requires self-disclosure and sharing which inevitably include levels of interpersonal intimacy. This may be accentuated in companies which emphasize extracurricular activities like sports, community involvement, company socials, and group business travel.

Work relationships do not normally include the kind of honesty and self-disclosure that is typical of good friends, but not a small number involve close sharing. How many of us have gone to lunch with an associate or had coffee over a conversation about difficulties at home or with our lover? Work relationships sometimes become places where we share confidences and seek advice. And to the extent that we get honest feedback, these relationships can be, like friendships, windows into the soul.

Moreover, through peer review and supervision, work relationships can become instrumental in confronting personality issues and patterns which impact, positively or negatively, our capacity for intimacy. Negatively, one might recall individuals who have little or no boundaries and expect coworkers to be their primary network of emotional support and/or who seek to establish levels of intimacy which are simply inappropriate in the workplace. Positively, one might consider individuals who have self-esteem issues and who discover attributes and qualities in the workplace which had not been affirmed in other kinds of relationships.

Many large American companies have initiated diversity management programs. These now go beyond the inclusion of different ethnic, racial and gendered workers. Diversity management programs now include affirmation of diverse personality work styles. It is not uncommon for teams to take the Myers-Briggs personality profile or to participate in Enneagram workshops.[15] These tests/models identify prevalent ways that individuals relate to others. As interpersonal profiles, they invariably address some issues of intimacy. Some insights gained in the workplace can illumine domestic relationships. There is always the risk that these profiles become another form of control, reification or categorization. But if approached soulfully, they can be a source of deepening integrity and poetic gracefulness in relationships.

Workplace relationships are important opportunities for addressing issues of power. Is one able to practice integrity in the face of unethical pressure from management? Is one able to share and delegate authority and power appropriately? Does one repeat a pattern of paranoia or defensiveness in workplace relationships?

The workplace can be an important place to deal with one's vocation, one's sense of what one can contribute to the world. What does one feel passionate about? What talents surface in workplace relationships and roles? How do some opportunities provide new options?

The workplace also becomes an important place where we meet different kinds of people. This challenges us to think about diversity and how comfortable we are with it. Working with people of different religious and/or moral persuasions forces one to assess one's own beliefs. This can be personally transformative whether one makes changes or not. One often learns how to work with people of different gender, different sexual orientation, and different ethnic or racial background.

All of these experiences form the context and grammar of a rich personal poetics. Both business and church have mutually alienated themselves from each other, buying into the so-called Protestant work ethic which separates the sacred and profane spheres of human endeavor. Many postindustrial corporations have further eradicated from the workplace any hint of soulfulness or spirit. In the name of efficiency, productivity, and organizational control, more and more of the worker's life is circumscribed by rules and regulations which suppress emotion, feeling, embodiment, sensuality, or imagination. What happens to an individual who spends eight to ten hours a day before a computer monitor interacting with digital information and/or entities in cyber-space? What happens to the poetics of intimacy when workers must, for legitimate reasons, suppress sexual feelings and thoughts in the workplace (out of concern for sexual harassment regulations)? When workers must turn off their emotional and sexual feelings for the better part of a day and then turn them back on when they return home, why are we amazed that so many couples feel detached and unaffectionate with each other? Why are we surprised that there are so many symptoms of superficial sexuality in our culture when the workplace demands detachment from the body and sensually rich stimuli? Much work needs to be done to address the complex question of how to sustain soulfulness in the modern workplace without giving up legitimate concerns for efficiency, productivity, and appropriate business boundaries.

In Summary

Single adults, particularly those in their late teens, twenties and thirties, have the opportunity to form many types of relationships (friend, business and romantic) that are deeply self-revelatory, self-transformative, and occasions for rich interpersonal flourishing. These various kinds of relationships have the capacity to deepen spirituality, sharpen one's poetic sensitivities for love, and refine one's capacity to confirm others' well-being through responsible and graceful relationships of mutuality. A Christian ethic, committed as it were to personal and social flourishing, should amplify appreciation for the poetic contours of single adult relationships, relinquishing essentialistic and reductionistic paradigms.

Notes

[1]   Laumann et al, Op. cit., pp. 502–508.

[2]   Laumann et al, Op. cit., pp. 351–367.

[3]   Pinckaers, Op. cit., chapters 14 and 15.

[4]   Laumann, Gagnon, et. al., Op. cit., p. 476.

[5]   Ibid., p. 476.

[6]   Ibid., p. 484.

[7]   Alfred Kinsey's 1950's study of sexual orientation produced a seven-point scale of sexual orientation, strongly suggesting that few people fall in the absolute heterosexual or absolute homosexual range (i.e. having only fantasies, erotic feelings, and sexual experiences with people of either the opposite or same gender).

[8]   Cathleen A. Fanslow, "Touch and the Elderly," in *Touch: The Foundation of Experience*, eds. K.E. Barnard and T.B. Brazelton (Cincinnati: International Universities Press, 1990) 541–557.

[9]   A. W. Richard Sipe, *Sex, Priests, and Power: Anatomy of a Crisis* (New York: Brunner/Mazel, 1994) and by the same author, *A Secret World: Sexuality and the Search for Celibacy* (New York: Brunner/Mazel, 1990).

[10]   Andrew Sullivan, *Love Undetectable* (New York: A. A. Knopf, 1998) p. 188.

[11]   Ibid., p. 189.

[12]   Ibid., pp. 209–210.

[13]   Ibid., p. 211.

[14]   Ibid., p. 214.

[15]   Helen Palmer, *The Enneagram in Love and Work: Understanding Your Intimate & Business Relationships* (New York: HarperCollins, 1995).

❖ Chapter Six

The Poetics of Intimacy in Committed Sexual Relationships

Changing Forms of Committed Sexual Relationships

As already noted, traditional sexual morality assumed that committed sexual relationships were heterosexual-monogamous-lifelong-patriarchal-household-management-and-reproductively-centered institutions. Love, affection, mutuality and emotional intimacy might be hoped for in marriage, but their absence did not undermine the essential purpose and function of marriage. These relationships were often initiated with an engagement or promise to marry followed by a formal religious or civil ceremony.

The profile of contemporary committed sexual relationships is more varied. While some individuals in Western postindustrial societies still enter into traditional marriages as described above, they are a distinct minority. Contemporary committed sexual relationships are heterosexual, bisexual and homosexual, patriarchal, matriarchal and nonarchal, formal and nonformal (no ceremonial beginning), reproductive and nonreproductive, lifelong and nonlifelong, cohabitational and non-cohabitational, monogamous and nonexclusive. The social context of committed sexual relationships is also varied. People now enter into committed relationships on the average at a later age and at different points throughout the lifespan. Many relationships today include individuals who are both working outside the household, often in professional careers which make sustaining relationships more difficult. Families vary in size, with smaller being more statistically normative. Most couples live together in nuclear households, but others live apart and/or travel extensively. Few couples live in multigenerational households. Many couples are made up of individuals who were in prior committed relationships, and many of these share custody of children from these earlier relationships. Most couples strive to practice monogamy, but, with a more sexually integrated workforce and society, there are more occasions for individuals to form significant relationships with others. Some couples are open to permitting outside significant relationships, but usually these are not physically intimate.

Some people regard the current state of affairs as catastrophic. They lament the loss of traditional marital forms and consider current practices to be symptomatic of moral decay. The mantra of "family values" has been a code word for the attempt to recover the lost innocence of family life in its so-called traditional heterosexual-lifelong-monogamous-patriarchal-household-management-and-reproductively-centered form. But when pressed to identify what is it about traditional family life they wish to recover, few traditionalists are really willing to recover the traditional form in its full integrity or relinquish the idea of romance-based relationships.

People expect their relationships to be centered in love, to include sharing of emotional and physical intimacy, to involve a sharing of power, and to enable each other to flourish both in relationship and as individuals with particular interests, friendships, and professions. Relationships of this type are much more fragile than those centered around household management and reproductive interests. The traditional form is more institutional, the contemporary one more interpersonal. Building committed relationships on mutuality, intimacy, sharing of power, and a commitment to enable the flourishing of each partner requires a more rarefied set of dispositions or abilities, chief among them being a rich poetic sensitivity, enabling one to appreciate the various seasons, levels, dynamics, and voices that are inevitably part of contemporary relationships.

Traditional sexual morality, grounded as it was in essentialistic and dualistic models of human nature and sexuality, is simply inadequate for enabling contemporary individuals to make sense of their sexuality and their committed sexual relationships. We need to amplify the vocabulary and metaphors of sexual morality so that it is more inclusive of the types of relationships people form, providing them with resources for sustaining those relationships gracefully.

Exclusivity and Commitment

Contemporary Christian descriptions of marriage employ the language of covenantal love. Covenants are agreements or contractual exchanges. But they differ from utilitarian contractual relationships in that what is exchanged is so central to the well-being of the parties involved that the relationship is ideally ongoing and includes serious obligations. There are many types of covenantal relationships, but this chapter is devoted to exploring the poetics of romantic or sexual ones.

Romantic love, unlike friendship, moves toward exclusivity and, hence, toward practices which are intended to confirm and assure exclusivity and fidelity. Born in an embodied longing for union, romantic/sexual relationships usually involve a deep soulful movement of the self toward the beloved. Western dualistic morality has taught us to distrust sexual desire as superficial and animalistic. As we have noted earlier in the text, sexual desire confounds our desire for self-possession and control because it draws us out of ourselves into complex and beguiling relationships with real persons. Under the influence of Western moral and religious bias toward self-control and abstract rationality, we are not encouraged to trust sexual desire as a grace. But far from being superficial, the movement toward soulful union with other persons is one of the most sublime possibilities and graces of human life. Again, this is why Carter Heyward argues that eros is one of our most profound experiences of the love of God.[1] Sexual desire becomes vilified and banalized when we decide to disassociate it from its soulfulness.

But not all sexual desire nor do all romantic relationships lead to committed ones. How do lovers discern that their attraction and affection for one another merit commitment? Is there a difference between soulful sexual desire and lust and how might we distinguish them?

There is some reason to argue that all sexual desire is soulful. If we think of sexual desire as our embodied yearning for mutuality, as Carter

Heyward remarks, then whatever its context, form, or season it is a window into the soul's yearning for relationship. When we find ourselves captivated by the striking features, the gait, the style of dress or undress, certain physical endowments, or the alluring eyes or mouth of someone passing on the street, we have been taught to think of that as "mere" sexual desire or lust. Our Christian moral tradition has taught us to suppress such attraction, lest we delight in it immorally. If we are already in a committed relationship with another, or seriously considering one, we have been encouraged to be even more suspicious and distrustful of it.

Alternatively, Thomas Moore describes the soulfulness of sexual desire masterfully in his book, *The Soul of Sex.*

> The body is a mythology, entire and complete in itself. Just as we can turn to any culture's traditional stories and rituals and find gods of war, nymphs of groves and streams, and spirits of place, so we can look at the body and find nurturing breasts, protective muscles, luxuriant hair, adventurous feet, and boyish buttocks. Each part of the body, differing slightly from person to person, is a window onto a world of meaning and allure. This stirring of fantasy and desire shows that the body expresses the soul, or even, in Blake's language, is the soul.[2]

Although cultures develop mythologies about the value or importance of certain features, sexual desire is experienced in very personal ways. One individual is attracted to strong muscular bodies, another to soft and pudgy ones. Some are moved by deep dark eyes, dark skin and hair, others by blonde hair, blue eyes, and fair skin. These differences are metaphors for some of the things we personally long for in relationships, such as strength, tenderness, depth, vitality, passion, security, or adventure.

Obviously, an obsession with and exaggerated objectification of some physical feature become problematic in terms of a poetics of intimacy. Fetishes may indicate deep-seated neuroses which need therapy. But sexual preferences are not the same as a fetish, and it could be argued that the inability to accept sexual desire as a movement of the soul toward mutuality fosters the development of obsessive sexual desire. An example or two might be helpful.

Alfred is a middle-aged fifty-five-year-old American male. He has been married twenty-five years. He and his wife, Jen, have three children. The children are all in college. Although happily married, Alfred has found himself unexpectedly attracted to young thirty-year-old women. He is particularly fascinated by those who are thin, have rich luxurious hair (light or dark), and who have firm thighs and large but taught breasts. At first he was disconcerted about his roving eye. He had not been this way before. But he began to analyze it and realized that he was middle-aged, his wife was beginning to gray and sag, and that this was his body's way of saying that he still longed for youthfulness and physical vitality. Fortunately, Alfred was able to contextualize his feelings, laugh at them, share them with his understanding wife, and find new ways with her to be creative, playful, and engaged in life. Had he sought to suppress and distance himself from those feelings they would have undoubtedly become more obsessive and troublesome. Listening to the soulfulness of his sexual desires, contextualizing them, and responding appropriately enabled Alfred to live out his sexuality in a soulful and poetically rich manner.

Another example involves Jane, a thirty-five-year-old woman married to David, an elusive, enigmatic, and introverted man. Jane and David have been married five years. They had been good friends in graduate school and eventually decided to marry. Both were professionals, extensively involved in pharmaceutical research. Jane has found herself increasingly attracted to female research interns. Initially, she was disturbed by her feelings. Why did she find one young woman's breasts so sexy or another's neck and short cropped hair so tantalizing? Why did she find herself fantasizing about sleeping next to them, exploring their bodies, kissing them passionately?

Jane had been seeing a therapist about depression. She decided to talk to the therapist about her feelings. The therapist asked Jane if she had been sexually attracted to women during adolescence or young adulthood. She thought she recalled some fantasies in high school, but in college she was too busy with her studies. She didn't even date seriously.

The therapist helped Jane recognize that she was probably, for the first time, getting in touch with her real sexual desires. Jane asked the therapist how this related to her marriage with David? They worked on this area and agreed that Jane had probably found David attractive because he was not sexually threatening or agressive, being a graduate colleague and friend. Jane admitted that their relationship involved little sexual intimacy. While Jane's sexual desires initially seemed lustful and in conflict with her marriage, they were soulful messages about how she could establish graceful and flourishing intimacy in her life.

These two examples only scratch the surface of how sexual desire is a deep window into the soul. Let me propose another example which moves us to consider another side of sexual desire.

Ken is in a committed sexual relationship with George. They are both in their late thirties and have been together for eight years. After some difficult struggles during the first four years of their relationship, Ken and George love each other very deeply and are sexually faithful to each other. Ken has more of a roving eye than George, but he is firmly committed to sustaining their relationship.

One New Year's Eve Ken and George are at a party. Ken is immediately taken aback by a tall dark Mediterranean man who caught his eye from across the room. Ken is disturbed by how spontaneously his feelings arose. What does this mean? What kind of person am I to lust after someone who is not my partner?

The young man, Robert, comes over to speak with Ken. Ken is gracious, even a bit flirtatious. He enjoys the attention, but soon realizes that Robert is very narcissistic and turns every topic of conversation around to himself. Ken excuses himself and goes to get a drink.

Afterwards, he thought about his response. He felt bad about seeking out the attention of Robert. He didn't think it was consistent with his commitment to George, and he needed to be more attentive to that relationship. But he also realized that Robert possessed some of the features he always found attractive. He liked men who had very distinctive dark features. They seemed to possess a kind of passion or vitality which Ken found attractive. George didn't have that passion, nor did he embody those physical characteristics. Ken realized that there was a part of himself that still longed for those in a lover.

One of the lessons we invariably learn in our sexual lives is that few individuals will satisfy all of the longings of our soul. There will be conflicting desires over the course of our lives. Some of these desires, like Ken's for Robert, pull us away from primary commitments. If Ken were to pursue a sexual relationship with Robert it's possible that it might not have any real impact on his and George's relationship. Robert is a jerk, and Ken would soon find that out. But if Robert had not been so narcissistic, a simple sexual liaison could become something much more and represent a compromise of Ken's long relationship with George.

Sexual desire is expressive of soulful longings for mutuality, even conflicting ones. But if covenantal mutuality is what we desire, that is, if we desire to share intimacy and life with another, we cannot pursue all of our sexual desires. We must ask what soulful movements our conflicting sexual desires are expressing. How important are these longings? How can we contextualize or appropriate them in such a way that they serve the intimacy or mutuality we desire? In some instances, like Alfred's, they are insights into a new season of life and encourage us to make adjustments in order to sustain graceful and flourishing intimacy. In others, like Jane's, they are indicative of important needs which are not being met and which touch upon the very foundation of one's capacity for intimacy and love. In Ken's, they are simply conflicting desires which need to be acknowledged but which cannot be acted on if Ken is to honor and nurture the rich relationship he has with George.

In relationships where sexual intimacy is accompanied by emotional intimacy, it is common for the partners to desire and expect sexual exclusivity. During the so-called sexual revolution of the 1960's and 1970's, it was more common to meet young adults who intended to sustain multiple sexual relationships at the same time. Today, young adults are more "traditional," and show more evidence of the desire for monogamous relationships. But it is also more common for young people today to have had a series of significant sexual relationships before they finally make a formal commitment to marriage or some other covenantal sexual relationship.

What distinguishes relationships which are passing and those destined to become committed? I would like to propose two ways of thinking about this question.

The first consists in a hypothesis that, when two people are attracted to each other and engage in sexual intimacy, many are theoretically open to the possibility that the exchange might develop into something enduring. An intentional rejection of such a possibility makes the exchange clearly more utilitarian or self-indulgent and probably does not serve the development of a poetics of intimacy, notwithstanding the fact that some deliberately superficial sexual exchanges do engage something soulful and become enduring.

Assuming that many sexual exchanges between single adults include openness to an enduring relationship, those that do not move toward a commitment most likely lack sustainable mutuality. One or both of the partners identify something which makes an enduring relationship improbable. This may include a lack of tenderness, respect, passion, sympathetic views, or common aspirations. It might also include a lack of "spark" or "chemistry." The soulfulness or depth of the exchange is simply missing.

A second way of distinguishing passing and enduring relationships focuses on the kinds of positive conditions which are prerequisite for committed sexual relationships. Such conditions are likely to vary among different cultures, ethnic groups, and individuals. As Judith Wallerstein and Sandra Blakeslee argue in *The Good Marriage*,[3] people marry (and enter into committed sexual relationships) for different reasons. If someone wants a committed sexual relationship that includes traditional household management and parenting opportunities, then he/she is likely to move to a committed relationship with a partner who values the same and is able to provide the kinds of material and personal goods that will make it possible. Some want a relationship which is more companionate; thus, they are likely to move toward commitment with someone who has become a good companion, who shares common values and interests, and who is interested in forming the same kind of relationship.

A poetic approach to intimacy and to committed sexual relationships must avoid reducing the conditions or grounds for marriage or commitment to a select list of items. The search for enduring love is too varied and poetically rich to be described categorically. However, some conditions or grounds are more common. These might include the following.

The desire to enter into a committed sexual relationship with another person is often born out of a realization that loving and being loved by this person is constitutive of one's well-being. There is both an expansiveness of oneself in the relationship and an ability to bestow and recognize increasing value on/in the other. In other words, enduring love is grounded in mutual transcendence. One's horizons are more clearly open and expansive in committing oneself to this person. Love draws us beyond ourselves into the rich mystery and depth of another. And this being so, one wants that self-transcendence to continue by making a commitment to nurture the mutuality within which one's heart and soul find growth.

Likewise, the other is beloved both for the values/qualities which are already apparent and for the value which love bestows on the beloved.

"The lover senses a horizon of value—we might call it an aura of mystery—lying in and behind every value that he or she already knows. This horizon of higher value may include new values or it may be a new depth in the values already felt. Thus, love always includes a sense of expectation and hope, and love grounds a trust that exceeds legitimate inferences from past experience."[4] Lovers are caught up in the beauty and goodness of each other. But their love is unlikely to move to a committed form unless they sense that each embodies goods yet to be discovered. In mutuality, lovers seek ongoing transcendence.

Although the term is overused, lovers also hope for a kind of unconditional acceptance. They hope that they will be loved for the people they really are. They hope that this person with whom they have become intimate and self-transparent still loves them despite the frailties and shortcomings they have discovered. The movement toward commitment arises, in part, out of confidence that having been self-disclosive one's lover has honored that vulnerability and will continue to honor it when new levels of self-disclosure evolve over the course of one's life. Thus, the movement toward commitment is grounded in a level of comfort, trust, and security that accompanies being with the other. And this trust is felt on both an emotional and physical level.

In summary, relationships which include an engagement of the two parties at deep interior levels are more likely to move toward commitment than those which do not. This deep engagement includes a type of "ec-stasis," a movement out from oneself, literally, a standing outside oneself in the other. Profound joy and delight in the presence of the other are manifestations of this experience. This most often includes a sense of being loved or touched deeply. When I become self-disclosive to the beloved, he/she accepts and affirms me for who I am. Lovers often express being able to "be themselves" more completely or deeply with each other. Signs of the contrary might include a sense that certain topics are not open for conversation or that one finds it difficult to share certain feelings or concerns. The way one's partner treats others is also indicative of future mutuality. If one's partner has few friends or treats them condescendingly, rudely or even violently, it is likely that the same pattern will emerge in an intimate relationship.

A poetics of commitment must take into consideration conventional wisdom about the length of time which normally ought to precede commitment. There is often initial shock, even horror, when couples declare their love for each other and announce intentions to marry or move in together after knowing each other for only weeks or a few months. Couples will often say, "We know it's short, but we have never felt this way about anyone before," or "I've been looking a long time, and I know what I want, and he/she's it!"

Personal maturity is an important foundation for rich mutuality in committed relationships. Age is not necessarily a predictor of maturity. Lamanna and Riedmann speak about four types of maturity: emotional, economic, relational and value.[5] Emotional maturity refers to the degree of self-esteem an individual has achieved and his/her ability to resolve emotional conflict rather than becoming defensive or threatening. Economic maturity obviously refers to the ability to support oneself financially. Many relationships are doomed to failure under the stress and strain of financial hardships. Relational maturity refers to communication skills which include the ability to recognize other views, to explain one's own view, to make decisions about changing one's behavior or asking for one's partner to change behavior when appropriate. Value maturity refers to an individual's recognition and confidence about personal values. A relationship which begins when two individuals are still working through their value systems may include conflicts which are simply too overwhelming to integrate into a shared life.[6] The rich poetics of intimacy builds upon personal maturity. Thus, these types of maturity need to be faced and constituted before intimacy can usually flourish.

In earlier forms of arranged marriage couples often had little or any prior knowledge of each other, and those relationships endured. But those relationships, as we have noted, were not necessarily built around a sharing of emotional intimacy. Rather, they were relationships centered around dynastic, economic, household, and reproductive interests. Why do we think it is normally wise for contemporary couples to spend substantial time dating before making commitments?

At least two considerations are valid. One, while contemporary relationships are love-centered, they also usually involve cohabitation and parenting. Cohabitation and parenting involve considerable material resources and practical logistical arrangements. Sometimes, young couples are caught up in the poetics of intimacy and have not adequately considered the practicalities of household management and parenting responsibilities. In postindustrial societies, these issues are more complicated requiring significant education, coordination of career steps, geographical transfer for job opportunities, financial resources for times of job transition, and other material matters.

A second issue revolves around the way in which the promises and challenges of intimacy become more transparent with time. Physical attraction, as soulful as it might be, is more intense and delightful at the beginning of many relationships. The natural tendency to celebrate commonality and shared perspectives in early stages of romantic relationships often masks underlying conflicts and dissonance. As will be noted later, conflict is an essential part of graceful committed sexual relationships, but too much conflict or dissonance makes sustaining intimacy difficult if not impossible. Couples who have been able to identify the types of conflict and differences which will accompany their relationship and have learned how to process them in love-sustaining ways will be more successful at making their commitment work.

Those who have not had the time to identify conflicts may find that they are insurmountable once they are already into a committed relationship. While this can ultimately serve the poetics of intimacy by revealing to the parties more about themselves, if they have already "moved in together" or formalized their relationship in a commitment ceremony it can add unnecessary suffering and grief to their lives.

Thus, conventional wisdom would seem to support the idea that couples establish a successful narrative of intimacy and mutuality prior to making a commitment. Such a successful narrative would include the delight and joy that accompanies intimacy and mutual transcendence as well as the inevitable conflicts, friction, different perspectives, and disagreements that also characterize such love. Couples should ask themselves whether they are able to love each other even recognizing the differences and unpleasantries of each other. Can I, for example, still accept that I am loveable when my lover discovers that I am not always as thoughtful, tender, smart, resourceful, or sensitive as I might have initially appeared. Do we harbor resentment? If so, mutuality will not be sustainable. Can we forgive and enable each other to grow? When my lover or I become vulnerable, is that vulnerability respected and supported or is it taken advantage of?

Couples ideally ought to have experienced seasons in their affection prior to making a commitment. Affection intensifies and wanes for a variety of reasons. Although young lovers cannot imagine such a change, it invariably happens. And whereas it is not always explicit, commitment includes the affirmation of the reality of the fickleness of our feelings.

A number of authors identify love as an emotion.[7] They distinguish feelings from emotions. According to Margaret Farley, for example, feelings adorn love. And while the emotion of love might perdure, feelings do not always remain the same. Commitment is a way of sustaining the emotion of love even when the adorning feelings are absent. Love can be sustained even when the feelings that often accompany it are absent. Commitment would be unnecessary if we were not susceptible to changing feelings. Thus, an informed commitment includes the anticipation that one's feelings may, and probably will, change. It is helpful for couples to have experienced shifts in their feelings prior to making such a commitment.

In other places in this book I have suggested that sexual intimacy is an important part of establishing a successful narrative of love and mutuality prior to making a commitment. I have stated that this is more than determining whether two individuals are sexually compatible. It is first and foremost the determination of whether one's potential future life partner is able to integrate and embody physical and emotional intimacy and vulnerability as well as respect and honor one's own efforts to do so.

In love and intimacy-based marriages, the expression of physical and emotional vulnerability in tender and affectionate sexual intimacy is integral to their sustenance and flourishing. In former household–management-and-reproductively-centered marriages, sexual intercourse was required (as evidenced by the declaration of nullity in cases of impotence), but sexual intimacy as a way of embodying and communicating love and affection was not required, even if hoped for. Thus, the mere ability to perform sexual intercourse is not sufficient for the constitution of contemporary committed covenantal sexual relationships. Couples must be able to communicate through sexual intimacy, and this requires some degree of sexual compatibility. And, if this is so, commitments made without such knowledge are uninformed and, hence, ill-founded.

What constitutes sexual compatibility and sufficient knowledge for well-founded and well-informed commitments? Essentialistic and dualistic approaches to sexual morality required only gender complementarity and physical sexual function. Sexual compatibility was constituted by a male's penis penetrating the female's vagina and the male achieving orgasm. The so-called consummation of a marriage, as stipulated in canon law and in many secular jurisdictions, only required male orgasm. If a marriage was consummated, it was valid, it existed, it had achieved its moral purpose and finality. Thus, couples only had to know that their future partner was of the opposite sex and capable of sexual intercourse for marriage to be valid. If sex was not particularly pleasurable or tender, this mattered little with respect to the morality and permanence of marriage.

Today, even the most traditional moralists are likely to find such an approach to marriage anachronistic. We hope couples will be able to communicate their love in pleasurable and tender ways. We understand that mere gender difference does not count for sexual attraction or good sexual experience. Men and women derive sexual pleasure in a variety of ways. We are more aware of the variety of sexual likes and dislikes that constitute peoples' sexuality and how these can either enhance or significantly undermine the communication of love and affection between two people. We encourage men to pace themselves so that their female sexual partners will achieve orgasm. We encourage couples to talk about what they like and dislike sexually so that sexual intimacy is more satisfying. We believe that good sexual intimacy between individuals helps sustain and nurture relationships.

If this is so important in contemporary relationships, absence of sexual experience before making a commitment exposes couples to the risk of substantial and insuperable sexual incompatibility. While it is true that couples continue to learn more about each other's sexual preferences, and sexual preferences even change with time, couples who have not begun to establish a successful exchange of sexual intimacy before making a formal commitment to each other risk making commitments which are not sexually sustainable. Let me give an example.

Maria and Alfredo grew up in traditional homes where sex before marriage was highly discouraged. Maria's father was very protective of his daughter, and he did everything possible to limit opportunities for Maria to have sex with her boyfriends. Maria internalized her father's moral position and resisted sexual involvement with the various men who pursued her.

Alfredo, being raised in a traditional home, also believed that sex before marriage was wrong. He began going out with Maria. They quickly fell in love. They share common interests, seemed emotionally compatible, and they enjoyed being with each other.

After six months of going with each other, Alfredo proposed to Maria. He had just obtained a good job with a local computer software firm. She was completing a degree in allied health. At twenty-two years of age, they both married in a traditional religious ceremony.

Both were sexually inexperienced and, when they began to share physical intimacy, this proved problematic. Alfredo was overly excited during their love-making and reached orgasm very quickly, leaving Maria frustrated. Alfredo could not look beyond his own self-gratification. Maria learned that she needed to avoid exciting Alfredo with foreplay; this only exacerbated the problem. Consequently, rather than their sexual intimacy being a rich exchange, it was very isolating. It was physically satisfying for Alfredo, but not for Maria. And although Alfredo could intellectually acknowledge this as a problem, he had no resources with which to address it.

Eventually, Maria and Alfredo went to a marriage counselor who recommended sexual counseling. It took many months for them to get over their initial resentment and disillusionment. Even after learning to communicate better about sex, Alfredo never managed to understand Maria's sexual needs nor how to pace his own sexual arousal. Maria became pregnant, and they had a boy. Maria threw her energies into parenting. She tolerated Alfredo's need for sexual gratification, increasingly resentful that he could not reciprocate.

Maria and Alfredo's story would not be terribly tragic in a house-hold-management-and-reproductively-centered approach to marriage. And, while Maria is sublimating much of her sexual energy into parenting, what happens when their boy grows up and leaves home? How will Maria and Alfredo sustain intimacy through the seasons of their lives, which will be quite a bit longer than couples in former ages? How did their premarital sexual morality serve the poetics of intimacy?

Had Maria and Alfredo shared sexual intimacy before making a commitment, their sexual problems would have invariably been part of the equation of their decision-making process. Maria might possibly have decided that she wanted much more in a life companion than that which Alfredo could offer. Alfredo, too, might have learned more about what kind of sensitivities and abilities he would have to cultivate before he could enter a covenantal sexual relationship.

Since we no longer regard women as reproductive property, physical virginity as a prerequisite for marriage is no longer a common concern. But uncommitted adult couples who are attempting to establish a successful narrative of intimacy do need to be concerned about untimely pregnancy, sexually transmitted disease, and physical or emotional trauma that might accompany premature sexual involvement. How are these issues related to a poetics of intimacy?

The term "safe sex" has arisen in the past twenty years to refer to sexual intimacy that is free from or relatively free from the risks of pregnancy, disease, and trauma. Precautions are taken to avoid these risks. First of all, it is important to limit one's number of sexual partners. The more sexually active an individual is the greater the risk of disease, trauma or other complications. From the perspective of a poetics of intimacy, promiscuous sexuality does not normally serve intimacy. But promiscuity is frequently a symptom of a fear of intimacy or a disassociative traumatic sexual experience in childhood which makes genuine intimacy fearful. Young people should be encouraged to limit the number of sexual partners both for hygienic and intimacy reasons.

Second of all, because sexual intimacy is an important part of establishing successful intimate relationships, young adults should learn how to be sexually intimate in ways that significantly reduce or even eliminate the risk of sexually transmitted disease, untimely pregnancy, or emotional and physical trauma. Discussion of the challenges of sustaining a poetics of intimacy in the light of the dangers of HIV transmission was elaborated in the chapter on single adult sexuality.

Additional considerations of a poetics of commitment include a regard for honoring vulnerability in each other. The deepest sinews of one's flesh intuit that intimacy will require change, will require self-disclosure and self-gift, and will require a whole new way of being in the world. Becoming naked with another is more than a superficial uniting of flesh. It is our embodied way of being self-disclosive. Sharing each other's breath in kissing, caressing, and stimulating parts of the body prone to intense pleasure are concrete ways that human beings embody self-disclosure and intimacy. We have to work hard at making sexual intimacy superficial and merely recreational. It runs counter to the language of embodied intimacy.

The self-transparency that accompanies sexual intimacy moves toward exclusivity and commitment for a number of reasons. One, with self-transparency there is personal vulnerability. Sexual partners know each other more deeply than most. One of the ways we express or embody respect for that vulnerability is to refuse to share that level of intimacy with another. One feels that one's vulnerability is honored when one's partner refuses to share profound intimacy with another.

Sexual self-transparency is at one and the same time self-gift. It is not a gift of some part of the self as we might do in business or friendship. It is a gift of the deepest soulful part of the self. And even though we are never in full possession of ourselves, self-gift in sexual intimacy is ideally without conditions or limits. An unconditional self-gift is difficult to express in merely recreational, anonymous, temporal or promiscuous forms of sexual relationship. Sexual partners intuitively know when the other is holding back emotionally. Genuine sexual companionship is difficult to sustain when there is emotional reticence. Sexual companions look toward exclusivity and commitment as a way of sustaining the context for ongoing self-gift.

Expansion of oneself in the other and enrichment of one's life by the other bring profound joy and delight. As with all profound goods, we long for these to be sustained. Soulful love naturally longs for permanency. We want this sharing of life and well-being to continue. We want this soulful flourishing to increase and deepen. In a world of many transitory goods, we seek to affirm and confirm sexual intimacy with a commitment.

As Margaret Farley notes, a commitment to love seeks to safeguard us against our own inconsistencies, what we perceive to be our possibilities of failure. If we are not naively confident that our love can never die, we sense the dangers of our forgetfulness, the contradictions of intervening desires, the brokenness and fragmentation in even our greatest loves. We sense, too, the powerful forces in our milieu—the social and economic pressures that militate against as well as support our love.[8]

Union and Autonomy

The inclination of lovers to declare their love, to make promises of exclusivity and commitment, is itself an acknowledgment of competing sexual desire. A poetics of intimacy must take seriously the dynamics of conflicting or competing desire. The desire for union is but one movement of the soul. There is also a desire for independence and autonomy.

As Edward Vacek notes so appropriately, it is tempting to think of profound love as moving toward an identity or union of lovers.[9] The desire for union is strong; but, without personal distinction, there is no participation. As an active participation in one another, love ceases to exist when the personal distinctiveness of the lovers is dissolved into union. As noted earlier, Vacek describes authentic love as unity-in-difference.[10]

Romantic or sexual love will certainly include the desire for union and identity, but it must also include the recognition as well as cultivation of difference and autonomy. How is this experienced and lived out?

In early stages of romantic love, lovers often experience an eclipse of other loves. The value or good of the beloved is so overwhelming that all other goods pale in comparison. Even love of oneself can be eclipsed by love of the other; but, with time, other values and goods become important again. Lovers must learn to reassure each other that they will balance these other goods and values with their love for each other. This is where poetic sensitivity is very important.

It might be helpful to consider different types of values and goods. We might think of these goods in terms such as sexual, friendly, familial, vocational, civic, and personal. In essence, these are further elaborations on the typology James Keenan introduced in his revision of the cardinal virtues to include justice, fidelity, and self-care.[11]

On the surface, other sexual values and goods would seem inimical to sustaining committed sexual relationships. How can one give oneself without reserve to another and/or feel confident that his/her vulnerability is being honored and respected without sexual fidelity? As long as our current social model of committed sexual relationships is romantic-based, sexual intimacy with others is likely to undermine the development and sustenance of one's primary sexual relationship. With the development of effective birth control in the 1950's, some heterosexual couples experimented with opening their relationships to outside sexual liaisons. Critics of artificial contraception predicted that birth control would drive a wedge into heterosexual marriage rendering it socially weaker.

Contemporary statistics, however, do not bear this out. Heterosexual couples remain, perhaps stronger than before, committed to sexual fidelity. One explanation might be that marriage has become decidedly less institutional and more love-based. Couples who are united out of love have less incentive to seek sexual satisfaction outside of the relationship than those who were united for institutional (household management and reproductive) interests.

Second, we often think we can have sexual intimacy with someone other than our primary partner without it affecting our commitment. Sexual desire for someone other than our primary partner can be motivated by powerful sexual attraction. We might think we can have sex with an attractive person without it compromising our fundamental commitment, but sexual intimacy is powerful and it invariably opens the heart. If the new sexual partner offers more than just a pretty body, the heart is turned. Couples intuit this and know they must hold themselves to their promise of fidelity in order to sustain their love.

Sexual desire may be motivated by a lack of personal satisfaction in one's primary partner. Here, sexual desire is an important window into the soul, and one must address why the primary relationship is not what one would have hoped it to be.

But there is another dynamic at work here that should be part of a poetic/moral approach to committed sexual relationships. As profound and satisfying as intimacy between two individuals may be, the poetic character of our personality guarantees that some facets of our emotional lives remain unintegrated or unincorporated into our primary relationships. Sexual desire for other persons is an embodied way of feeling longing for mutuality with persons who appear to be able to respond to other parts of ourselves.

We can listen to these longings for clues to enriching and deepening the mutuality with our primary partner. But we must also learn to recognize that no relationship is capable of engaging every aspect of our lives. Many descriptions of romantic-based relationships include the idea that one will eventually find one's soulmate, someone who fulfills and engages all of the longings and desires of the heart. Many young lovers experience an intensity of desire for each other and a deep satisfaction being with one another. This often leads to an eclipse of other significant relationships. Emphasis on the nuclear family and nuclear household accentuates the isolation many couples feel from other relationships. Great importance is placed on marriage and family fulfilling all of the emotional needs of its members. Under such weight, many marriages fail. They fail not so much because the conditions for a flourishing mutuality don't exist or that the individuals have not tried to make it work. They fail because emotional needs not able to be met in the relationship are left unattended. Couples can often strengthen their own relationship by forming friendships together and individually. A rich constellation of relationships feeds the many emotional needs of couples and discourages the formation of resentment when certain needs are not being met by one another.

Different Types of Covenantal Love

Committed sexual relationships can arise in a number of different circumstances, and these alter the poetics of intimacy. The above description is largely romantic or passionate. But couples can grow to love each other out of a prior friendship which, while intimate, did not include the level of intimacy normally associated with sexually intimate relationships. Couples may form what Wallerstein and Blakeslee call companionate marriages where there is less emphasis on the sharing of emotional intimacy (a face to face romance) and more of a desire to be companions (side by side) in life.[12] Romance and companionship are not mutually exclusive. Some romantic relationships include a deep sense of companionship, and some companionate relationships may experience moments of deep romantic intimacy. What is important is that couples have the poetic sensitivity to understand the differences of these types of love and recognize when they are at work during various times and seasons of their relationships. Many companionate relationships become progressively romantic.Many romantic relationships become progressively companionate. Being aware of these transitions enables couples to sustain faithfulness and joy in their relationships.

Some couples come together after experiences of great trauma, hurt, or loss. So-called "rescue" relationships may be more common in an age where divorce rates are high.[13] Human beings are able to provide enormous support, healing and comfort to one another and, in so doing, respond to deep soulful pain. The sharing and reponse to deep personal pain provide the opportunity for intimacy to flourish. Many relationships emerge out of these moments. They provide opportunities for each party to care for another very deeply and tenderly. And this exchange can become the foundation for an ongoing covenantal love relationship.

Wallerstein and Blakeslee also speak about traditional marriages, those formed around the desire to establish a traditional family and to raise children.[14] Many romantic, companionate and rescue relationships take on the form of traditional family life and may eventually include children, but so-called traditional marriages begin with these purposes. In these relationships, the covenanted parties may regard their relationship more in terms of partnership than romantic or companionate. And, as before, these terms are not mutually exclusive. Traditional mar-ried partners can experience times of deep romantic, companionate or even therapeutic love. And, conversely, romantic, companionate and therapeutic relationships can desire traditional forms of family life.

Conflict in Covenantal Intimate Relationships

Scott Peck and numerous psychoanalytic writers have highlighted the "frictional" character of intimate love.[15] It is impossible to speak about the poetics of intimacy in contemporary postindustrial Western societies without being attentive to the dynamics which psychoanalytic psychology identified. At least two trajectories can be followed in thinking about a poetics of intimacy from a psychoanalytic perspective.

First, since each of us begins our life in a matrix of relationships, our family of origin, our individual identity develops out of that primordial being-in-relationship. We are not first individuals who then seek out significant relationships. We are first relational beings who become gradually aware of ourselves as individuals. But our individual identity is secondary to our relational identity. The emphasis on the priority of relational being was highlighted by many of the existentialists including Heidegger and most notably Martin Buber in *I and Thou*.[16]

Second, the psychoanalytic school gave particular attention to the formation of the unconscious in the context of this primordial set of relationships. Infants and children need love, warmth, security, and gratification. In ways that are not entirely known, they perceive subtle and not-so-subtle conflicts and issues which members of their family of origin display in their interaction with one another and with the infant/child. The infant/child begins to internalize these various family issues and conflicts in order to "fit into" the family and secure the love and goods it needs.

According to the psychoanalytic perspective, erotic love stems, in part, from the deep relational needs we carry with us from our first sense of self-in-relationship. Again, we are not first individuals who form significant relationships. We are first relational beings. So the adult, who has become increasingly individualized, continues to long for the relational love and security out of which he/she became increasingly conscious of an individual identity. The adult typically replicates the kinds of relationships with which he/she was most familiar, those of his/her family of origin. And this is where "friction" or conflict emerge in romantic or intimate relationships. When two individuals share deep emotional intimacy, they expose deep family "baggage" repressed in the unconscious. Since this is full of conflict, it is often experienced in the conflict and vulnerability of adult relationships.

The psychoanalytic model of intimacy and its concomitant friction has been illuminating for making sense of romantic relationships. It illustrates some of the poetic tensions that exist in relationships, namely the tension between autonomy (independence) and union, between love of self and love of the other, the problem of narcissism, self-loathing and resentment, and the various issues associated with learning how to be vulnerable to another and sharing power in relationship. A balanced poetics of intimacy must acknowledge and celebrate this anticipated conflict as one of the blessings of love. Society has all too often romanticized marriage as a place of union, bliss, and self-fulfillment. While it may produce those feelings, it is also highly conflictual, and the conflict is a grace, challenging each other to love with greater integrity and constancy.

Social Dimensions of Committed Sexual Relationships

An exclusively romantic-based model of committed sexual relationships and their associated conflict may eclipse important social dimensions of committed sexual relationships. In other words, some of the poetic possibility and tension in adult committed sexual relationships stem from the social context of those relationships, not necessarily from family of origin issues. Let us consider a couple of examples.

Frank and Joan have been married for fifteen years. During the first ten years of marriage they worked through many issues which included Joan's experiences of sexual abuse as a child and Frank's family pressure to be successful. Frank has learned how to make Joan feel safe.

Joan has learned how to be vulnerable again. And Joan has been able to help Frank feel less pressure about measuring his success as his parents would have measured it. He has learned to accept his loveableness just as he is.

Frank took a job with a high profile law firm. He has done quite well, and both he and Joan enjoyed the social opportunities the job afforded them. But they have become increasingly concerned about the classist mentality that they and their children are being pressured to adopt in the affluent suburb where they live. When they were younger and less affluent they had a broader mix of friends, including some who were poor, some of different racial and ethnic background, and a few gay and lesbian couples. Now most of their social acquaintances are rich, heterosexual and white. This new context causes new levels of tension and conflict in their relationship.

John and Jack are a gay couple. They have been together for eight years. The last couple of years have been rough. They fight a lot and, after getting some counseling, they realize that many of the issues stem from childhood issues of abandonment and neglect. They are successfully addressing these issues.

But they are aware of other issues which have surfaced since they moved from a large city on the East Coast to a small town in the South for Jack's work. They are finding that they have to be much more careful about being "out." Jack's company is relatively progressive about gay issues in the workplace, but John's is not, and the town where they live has few openly gay people around.

The hostile environment makes them feel more entrenched. And while this has some positive benefits on their relationship in that they turn to each other for support and security, they have noticed, in counseling, that it has taken its toll on their self-esteem and sense of well-being.

What is at work in both these cases is more than psychoanalytic issues of the unconscious. The social context of these relationships creates stressors and affects the poetics of intimacy. As noted earlier, James Keenan has been developing models of virtue which take these intersecting levels of love and community into account. Keenan has identified what he considers to be cardinal virtues for the contemporary world in which we live: justice, fidelity and self-care.[17]

Justice involves our obligation to love or care for all human beings. It is a type of universal regard for others as human beings. In some cases this only requires basic respect of others' rights and well-being. But, in some instances, it may require active commitment on our part to work for the well-being of others, to work for the promotion of a more just society.

Fidelity involves our obligations to particular or special relationships. We have many types of special or particular relationships including friends, business associates, colleagues, members of special communities and, most importantly, in the context of a poetics of intimacy, those relationships where we make a commitment to share physical and emotional intimacy with another.

Care of the self is the obligation we have to love ourselves and to care for our own well-being. It has become increasingly obvious in contemporary psychological and moral discourse that love of others is impossible if we do not love ourselves. Love of self involves a sense of one's own dignity and goodness, the sense that one is loveable. Those who do not believe they are loveable either live out their lives in great self-loathing, in excessive attention getting (narcissism), or in angry and mean-spirited resentment. Without love of self, love of others is not genuine and not sustainable.

Ironically, love of self is a gift. It is made possible by the love that we have been shown by others. Children who are neglected, traumatized, or psychologically abused have a difficult time ever believing they are loveable.

According to Keenan, we all need a special virtue, prudence, which is the ability or the excellence of balancing justice, fidelity and self-care.[18] I believe this is similar to what is meant by a poetics of intimacy. It involves an artful living out of the values and tensions between justice, fidelity and care of self not according to some prescribed formula, concept or moral algorithm. Rather, the balancing of these three types of love requires attentiveness to the special circumstances, seasons, occasions, and people involved. Virtues are resistant to conceptual description. Rather, they are best presented in their personal manifestations or instances. Virtues are embedded in the real life relationships of others. A poetics of intimacy requires attentiveness to the manner in which the social context of relationships impacts their flourishing.

Balancing Goods Poetically

Naturally, the poetics of intimacy centers around the tension between fidelity and love of self without excluding regard for justice. As noted before, the poetic balancing of fidelity and love of self involves the issues of independence and union, of spirit (seeking rational and autonomous life) and soul (which roots itself in relationships, commitments, and places), and of the importance of sharing power in relationship. But this more fundamental challenge of intimacy is itself contextualized by other issues which make the poetics of intimacy more intricate. As noted by Wallerstein and Blakeslee, there are different kinds of relationships within which autonomy and union are lived out: companionate, romantic, rescue and partnership. Each of these has its own poetic voice and form.

Likewise, there are stages of intimate relationships. John Bradshaw speaks of the codependent, counterdependent, independent and interdependent stages. Couples who are attentive to the poetics of intimacy should anticipate these typical stages. The codependent stage involves the accentuation of sameness and commonality typical of new couples. There is a natural effort to celebrate shared perspectives, likes and dislikes, and hopes and dreams.

But eventually couples begin to discover their differences, and these become more apparent as time passes. Often couples enter a counter-dependent stage, one characterized by greater sensitivity to disagreements and dissonance. This can be very painful and disturbing. Many couples are not able to sustain their love through this stage. But if they are able to recognize this as a natural stage in the process of deepening intimacy, they will have a greater chance of navigating the rough waters.

Some couples get through the counterdependent stage by simply giving each other more permission for independence. Independence eases the tension and pressure associated with differences. For those who idealized a close relationship, independence can be frightening. But it, too, can be recognized as a stage in the movement toward deeper love, the so-called interdependent stage.

The import of Bradshaw's analysis is the identification that intimate relationships go through stages. A rich poetic sensitivity takes these into account and sees them in their larger dynamic and developmental context. Without the contextualization of these stages, couples can become disillusioned by the counterdependent and independent stages.

These stages are further complicated by the modern problem of reconciling careers in families where both individuals work professionally. Many contemporary couples go through various cycles of changing employment and professional training. Since it is difficult to synchronize these changes, often precipitated by layoffs, changing technology, or other factors, couples undergo stress as they seek to sustain their relationship amidst changes they didn't anticipate. It is difficult to balance love, relationship, intimacy and professional changes. Professional issues cannot be easily written off as superficial or of secondary importance. One's self-esteem and identity are often deeply connected to professional pursuits. So, the poetics of intimacy must take these identity issues of professional life into account.

Relationships also include seasons. These are not quite so predictable as the stages identified by Bradshaw, but they may be as universal. These seasons include courtship, parenting, illness, aging, loss, and socioeconomic changes. For example, the poetics of intimacy during courtship is quite different from the poetics of intimacy during a time of serious illness.

An example might be in order. Jan and Roger have been married for twenty years. They have two children in college. Jan and Roger enjoyed the typical passion and bliss of their early years of marriage. Later, they devoted themselves to their children and to both Jan's and Roger's careers. Both Jan and Roger are high-strung, independent, and success driven individuals.

Recently, Jan was diagnosed with a serious form of breast cancer. Her prognosis was not good. She went on disability as she had to undergo extensive chemotherapy and radiation treatment. Roger's desire to take charge and care for Jan in her illness did not initially sit well with Jan who, despite her illness, wanted to continue to exercise some degree of self-determination and autonomy. Roger's love had to take Jan's needs into account.

What Roger had not anticipated was a survivor instinct kicking in. He found himself thinking of life after Jan. He found it more and more difficult to sustain intimacy with Jan, to simply be with her and enjoy her warmth and love. He felt restless and detached from her.

This was clearly a new season in Jan's and Roger's relationship. Roger could have easily succumbed to his survivor mode, but he knew this was not what Jan needed at this time. He knew he needed to sustain fidelity to her by deliberately focusing on the present and enjoying the remaining time he had with her.

Each season in a relationship requires different poetic voices and devices to sustain intimacy. Sexual self-control, chastity, is simply an inadequate concept to account for the many different dispositions one needs to sustain love. One must be attentive to one's own soulful dispositions, but one must also be able to think critically about them, overriding some instinctual reactions in favor of greater attentiveness to the other.

The poetics of intimacy must give regard for the particular experience of embodiment, how each of the parties experiences sensual pleasure. Responding to the other involves learning how to pleasure him/her, knowing how to reassure him/her in the physical vulnerability of lovemaking that they are loveable and beautiful.

This means that a rich poetics of intimacy must be able to account for the specifics of gender identity, sexual orientation, and other issues associated with one's sexual identity.

Conditions Within Which Poetic Intimacy Flourishes

Are there certain types of conditions, contexts, and/or dispositions within which a rich poetics of intimacy is more likely to flourish than not? Are certain types of relationships inimical to the poetics of intimacy? Does a poetics of intimacy approach to sexual virtue legitimize a form of moral relativism which is exceedingly vague, free formed and confusing, or does it rely on some time-tested circumstances for its own flourishing? Does the abandonment of dualism validate a sexual licentiousness which is equally harmful?

First, the abandonment of dualism and chastity-based models of sexual virtue could usher in a form of sexual licentiousness if alternative models of sexual virtue are not worked out. Since the dualistic model of sexual virtue is increasingly nonpersuasive and noncompelling to Christian adults seeking to make sense of their sexuality and their relationships, it is imperative that Christianity cultivate an alternative model of sexual virtue.

Second, the poetics of intimacy is grounded in love between two people. The poetics of intimacy is not primarily a poetics of sex. It is not about finding inventive ways for coitus. It involves a commitment to share physical and emotional intimacy with another person in such a way that the rich poetic or metaphorical character of human personhood is not eclipsed by essentialistic, dualistic, rationalistic, and institutionalizing strategies for controlling existential anxiety and sexual desire. Intimacy cannot be sustained or deepened unless certain dispositions are cultivated in committed relationships. And it is the thesis of this book that chastity or control of sexual desire and sexual pleasure is alone inadequate for sustaining relationships of interpersonal intimacy and mutuality.

Third, although committed sexual relationships take many forms, there are some dispositions which are rather common to the flourishing forms of committed sexual love. The following is a representative but not exhaustive list of some of those dispositions or conditions: fidelity, commitment, fecundity (finding ways for love to be fruitful), sharing of power, thankfulness, play, honesty, courage, fortitude, respect, attentiveness, sensitivity, social support and recognition, and self-esteem or self-love.

As noted in the chapter on gay and lesbian sexuality, monogamy, or commitment to sexual exclusivity, appears to be an important condition for sustaining sexual intimacy with another. The integration of sensuality and tenderness in an intimate relationship makes it very difficult to permit sexually intimate relationships outside the committed relationship. The percentage of couples who deliberately choose to have open relationships is very small, and those who experiment with such a form often abandon it after time. Sustaining a committed intimate sexual relationship requires time, patience, forgiveness and fidelity, and the temptation of finding solace and relief in other relationships undermines the kind of attentiveness and hard work that is required to sustain intimacy.

In traditional sexual morality, monogamy was practiced in the context of patriarchal and proprietary interests. Sexual exclusivity was less a matter of fidelity to intimacy and love and more a matter of preserving reproductive interests. Women were regarded as reproductive property of men. An example of this includes the fines that men had to pay each other under Jewish moral law when they had sex with another man's wife. The violation consisted in the violation of another man's property, not a violation of emotional commitment. In contemporary society, sexual infidelity is regarded more as a violation of trust and emotional vulnerability in committed sexual relationships.

Since postindustrialized and Western societies are much more sexually integrated, with men and women working together as colleagues in all sorts of businesses, there is more opportunity for sexual attraction to occur outside marriage and other committed sexual relationships. In many traditional societies men and women were socially segregated, reducing the amount of sexual tension in the public realm.

The Poetics of Intimacy and Parenting

Traditional sexual ethics considered reproduction within stable heterosexual families an essential end or purpose of sexuality. Historically, many official codes of ethics regarded reproduction as the sole legitimate end or purpose of sexual activity and sexual pleasure. Most contemporary Christian codes of ethics have abandoned this notion in the light of increased importance given to love, affection, and intimacy between spouses. Nevertheless, most heterosexual couples marry with the expectation that they will have children. Many individuals marry because they want to raise a family.

The Roman Catholic Church will not sanction marriage for couples who deliberately intend not to procreate, nor does it officially approve the use of artificial contraceptives in marriage. Official Roman Catholic teaching regards the procreative dimension of sex to be an indispensable feature of morally legitimate sex. Therefore, it concludes that only heterosexual-marital-and-reproductively-intentional sexual acts are morally licit. All other sex is believed to be necessarily self-indulgent, even in marriage!

Other Christian denominations have not followed this line of thinking. They permit couples to marry even when they do not intend to have children, and they do not consider the use of contraceptives within marriage a violation of the moral purposefulness of sex. Thinking about procreation as part of marital life without requiring it or requiring its intention in every sexual act is to consider it a poetic dimension of marital sexuality. That is, couples express a variety of emotions in sexual intimacy. As long as sexual intimacy is loving it is morally good. The absence of an intention to procreate does not render sex less loving or less truthful. Indeed, any one particular act of sexual intimacy is incapable of embodying all of the possible intentions or emotions that could be communicated between sexual partners.

Some Roman Catholic ethicists have challenged official Church teaching by describing the procreative purposefulness of sexuality as a matter of fecundity. Sexuality should be fruitful, fecund, life giving. Some argue that fecundity is not a moral imperative of each sexual act but rather a quality or feature of covenantal love in general. In other words, love flourishes when it is fruitful, fecund, life giving. Relationships need to be life giving in order to grow, expand, and avoid solipsism.

Since the official view of the Roman Catholic Church claims that contraceptive sex in marriage is invariably selfish, couples who use contraceptives should be, on average, more selfish than those who don't. But there's no statistical or anecdotal evidence to suggest this is the case. Many couples who use contraceptives are busy raising children to whom they've already given birth. The marriage as a whole is fruitful, fecund, generous, and life giving. Often these couples make enormous sacrifices to support and nurture their children.

Couples who cannot have children or who have deliberately intended not to have children often flourish quite admirably. Their love is characterized as generous, life affirming, and often fruitful in a variety of ways (voluntarism, working with youth, teaching, coaching, or working in health care or legal advocacy). This could only be the case if fruitfulness or fecundity was something much more than merely a matter of procreation.

There are many ways to think about the poetics of intimacy and fecundity, but in this section I would like to outline or identify some challenges that couples face when they decide to parent. How might we think about the relationship between parenting and the poetics of intimacy?

The poetics of parenting within marriage. Having a child is one of the most profound and life altering experiences possible. It is a powerful expression of self-transcendence, of self-continuance, of one's values, of one's desire to leave a mark on the world and to participate in the grand cycle of life. Traditionally, having a child required cooperation with another human being and, indeed, most children are conceived jointly. Thus, children represent the way in which mutuality moves beyond itself in fruitfulness and how personal life begins as a dialogical or interpersonal event.

Parenting is related to the poetics of intimacy in at least two ways. First of all, it is impossible to have a child without facing new and heretofore unconsidered aspects of oneself such as one's vulnerabilities, fears, hopes, identity, dreams, and relationships with one's own family of origin. Second, parenting with a spouse or partner forces one to confront the poetic dimensions of that relationship as it relates to the child(ren).   Parenting partners must confront shared and conflicting values, dreams, hopes, fears, and vulnerabilities, and they must negotiate and reconcile those differences in the course of parenting. To the extent that children engage new dimensions and features of each parent, they precipitate new dynamics and complexities between the parents.

Having a child often forces parents to establish new priorities and arrange their lives in ways that support parenting responsibilities and goals. Work may become more or less important. Choices about neighborhoods, schools, church, and recreation all take on new levels of complexity and importance. These choices represent a new season in the life of parents, a new season in their own personal growth and self-awareness as well as a new season in their interpersonal love. These new considerations often draw parents closer together, consolidating and strengthening their love and shared intimacy.

But these new considerations can also be a source of enormous conflict and tension when values, perspectives, and strategies conflict. Conflict arises over questions of discipline, over issues of modeling behavior, over influence of other adult figures such as in-laws, neighbors, friends, teachers, daycare workers. These conflicts can bring up previously dormant or hidden interpersonal issues. They can bring into question the sustainability of intimacy and love.

Children challenge parents to develop new virtues, particularly selflessness, patience, unconditional love, lightheartedness, flexibility, fidelity, attentiveness, sensitivity, and responsibility. They also challenge parents to develop virtues and skills for sustaining mutuality. How, for example, does a couple move beyond the deep hurt and disillusionment that comes with discovering that one's partner has very serious differences of opinion about how to parent? How does one sustain intimacy in such a context? How does one share power with one's partner when there is fundamental disagreement over what is important to share with one's child? How does one (or can one) forgive a partner who psychologically or physically abuses one's child?

One important resource for navigating the challenges of parenting is a poetic vision of personality. If parents begin with the assumption that there is one correct way to parent and one correct set of lessons children must learn in order to be normal, they set themselves up for extreme conflict. Personality is poetic, meaning it is multifarious and multi-dimensional. There are many forms of human normalcy and well-being. Thus, there are many good ways to parent, not one. Such a view frees parents to be more flexible in listening to one another about parenting styles.

Parents should be encouraged to recognize that children appropriate lessons and events in their lives differently. Parenting is not a one-way dynamic. Children are not passive objects shaped by parenting choices. Children are active subjects who react to parents in different ways. Parents can't predict a certain outcome by making the "right" choices. The best they can do is to be themselves, love and support their children, and celebrate the personal life that the child constitutes in that love.

Spouses who look to one another as the completion and realization of their most interior hopes and dreams, who tend to eclipse one another's uniqueness by demanding unmitigated union and identity, are likely to view their children in the same way. Some parents unfairly use their children as surrogates for their own issues, requiring children to embody qualities and characteristics they wish they could possess. Or, children are often objects upon whom parents project dissatisfaction with themselves, requiring heroic achievements or harshly criticizing them for failure. Conversely, couples who deliberately preserve each other's uniqueness and poetic individuality even while desiring union are also likely to regard their children as real individuals, as real subjects whose reason for existence is not to complete their parents but to become subjects-in-relationship.

It is ironic that much of the contemporary Christian ethical concern about reproductive technologies and genetic therapy centers around how such processes could lead us to think about the child as a product of our technological power, an object to be shaped and formed by our limited ideals of normalcy. It is ironic because so much of the contemporary rhetoric about so-called traditional family values centers around narrow definitions of what constitutes normalcy and human excellence. The same dynamic which seeks to manipulate the genetic outcome of reproduction is at work in the attempt to control the form and outcome of parenting through narrowly defined models of gender, personal identity, and family life.

Another way of putting this is to suggest that some parenting conflict stems from a lack of appreciation for the poetic form of personality. Some parents have not yet arrived at an ability to value or celebrate their own diversity, so they still strive for unanimity as parents and conformity in their children. To the extent that parents demand a united front of themselves, children grow to think that diversity and love, difference and affection, goodness and plurality are incompatible.

Imagine how much easier it would be for a child to think of people and relationships poetically if he/she witnessed parents celebrating and honoring differences between themselves. Conventional wisdom suggests that children will be confused and will have greater difficulty developing their own identity if they witness disagreement and substantial differences between parents. Children who grow up in families where parents celebrate differences not as threats but as richness are likely to have an easier time sustaining adult poetic intimacy.

Obviously, there are differences which are so great that intimacy and mutuality are not sustainable. I do not want to suggest that reconciling different perspectives is undesirable. I simply want to encourage people to become more comfortable with a model of excellence and flourishing which is more poetically rich and less essentiallistically defined.

Let's consider an example. Jorge and Alice have been married five years. They have a four-year-old son, Miguel. Jorge is Puerto Rican. Alice is of Irish and German heritage. Alice belongs to the United Church of Christ (Congregational) and Jorge is a Roman Catholic. Although Jorge and Alice were able to reconcile their religious differences by respecting each others' traditions and beliefs, questions about Miguel's religious education challenge the established equilibrium. Jorge would like to raise Miguel Catholic. Alice strongly objects since she believes Catholicism is sexist and doesn't want her son to grow up in that environment.

Although Alice expressed concern about sexism in the Catholic Church when they dated, the issue was eclipsed by more pressing concerns like finding stable employment, finishing college, and taking care of Miguel when he was an infant. Jorge always knew his wife was progressive on such issues, and Alice always suspected Jorge was more traditional, but neither considered it very important. Now that issues surrounding Miguel's participation in religion have become pressing, so, too, have their differences.

Alice has begun to look at Jorge more in the light of his traditional religious and sexual views, and she feels a growing resentment and disaffection over them. She believes that their marriage, built on principles of equality and mutuality, is now more fragile since she does not believe that Jorge really regards her as a partner. She finds it more difficult to be intimate and affectionate with Jorge.

Jorge is surprised at his wife's increasing hostility and alienation and wonders what he did to precipitate those feelings. He thinks she's being too critical of the Church. He doesn't see her point. He, too, is finding it more difficult to be affectionate and playful with her.

Religion brings up deeply held beliefs about what is right, normal, good, and noble. Conflicts about religion force couples to deal with issues that are very personal and intimate. And when these are identified as conflictual, couples may find it more difficult to be intimate with each other. Parenting frequently forces couples to face issues they would often rather leave buried!

Jorge and Alice face a lot of opportunities for growth around this matter. Their differences about gender and sexism may stem from family of origin issues. Jorge may believe that to be a true man he has to be in control and assume responsibility. His father may have impressed that upon him. Alice may have witnessed the psychological abuse of her mother by her father. She may be very sensitive to such matters in her own marriage, and the differences with Jorge provide her an opportunity to share those experiences and traumas with him. If they are willing to listen to each other's stories, they might come to appreciate how their differences emerged and what kinds of ways they could sustain intimacy with those differences present.

By listening to Alice's story, Jorge might come to appreciate how male responsibility and control can appear abusive and infantalizing of women. Conversely, by listening to Jorge, Alice might come to see that men are not necessarily malicious in their dominance but are attempting to fulfill deeply held beliefs about what they believe they are supposed to do. This is not an easy process, but it illustrates the manner in which parenting precipitates crises which can become poetically enriching events in the life of a relationship.

It might be interesting to imagine Miguel participating in two religious traditions. As he gets older, he might ask why Mommy and Daddy don't share the same beliefs. Imagine Jorge telling Miguel that he loves Catholic ritual and Catholic history but shares his wife's concern about institutionalized sexism and wants him (Miguel) to be exposed to those beliefs as well as his own. Imagine Alice telling Miguel how proud she is that the United Church of Christ ordains women and openly gay men and lesbians but how she also appreciates Catholic ritual and wants Miguel to have that experience. Miguel then has the possibility of appreciating the ambiguity of religious traditions, of learning an important lesson about how adults can disagree but still sustain intimacy, and how his own identity can be poetically rich by embracing multiple perspectives.

This is not necessarily how all parenting crises will be resolved. Sometimes differences are more intransigent and irreconcilable. Sometimes conflicts have less poetic complementariness. For example, differences over corporal punishment are less easy to reconcile than those over religious practice. Parenting conflicts are often the occasion when couples recognize they cannot remain together. This, in turn, raises questions about whether sustaining a marriage for the sake of the children is good or not.

The poetics of parenting outside traditional marriage. Often, contemporary parenting takes place outside traditional marriage. Many parents have divorced and remarried. Their children often live in two households. These children face formidable challenges. Their world of love, nurture, security, and order are dissembled. Parents, in turn, face dilemmas between honoring prior commitments which may be personally harmful and sustaining commitments out of concern for their children.

There are no well-defined formulas for resolving these dilemmas. Children raised in intact families where strife and discord are the norm will not necessarily fare better than those who must undergo the ordeal of their parents' divorce. It is also not easy to predict how a child will navigate or respond to a divorce. Sometimes it is devastating; in other instances they may understand and appreciate divorce as part of the risk and fragility of committed relationships.

It is clear, however, that when children are used as pawns or surrogates for fighting between spouses or former spouses, their own personal development and sense of self are deeply and pejoratively affected. As in intact relationships, disagreements need not be glossed over, but neither should children be the agents of communicating those disagreements. Parenting also occurs in single-parent families, in gay and lesbian families, and in adoptive and foster families.

Several questions need to be raised in terms of the poetics of parenting outside traditional marriage commitments. First, with respect to post-divorce parenting, how does living in two households affect the process of developing a healthy self-concept? Does living in two households nurture a greater appreciation for poetic diversity or does it thwart the development of a healthy sense of self? Some societies have a greater network of extended family where children spend significant time in the homes of grandparents, aunts, uncles, and cousins. Some children are co-parented by these extended families. The contemporary North American and European nuclear family places enormous pressure on its members to fulfill the relational needs of one another. Is this healthy? Much more thought and study need to be done on this.

Second, children raised in single-parent families do not ordinarily fare as well as those raised in two-parent families. But when controls are made for economic resources, these differences evaporate. In other words, the most significant harm resulting from single-parent families is the likelihood that children will have less economic resources with which to benefit in terms of education and socioeconomic advantages.[19]

Children raised in gay and lesbian families show no significant differences from children raised in heterosexual families, according to recent studies.[20] They are not statistically more prone to be gay nor do they demonstrate any greater difficulties in terms of personal identity, gender identity, or social/relational skills. Some children undoubtedly have difficulty facing prejudices at school and in the neighborhood, but studies show that gay/lesbian parents, when they are comfortable with their family, engender similar confidence in their children.

Many people wonder if children raised in single-parent families or in gay and lesbian families will have adequate gender role models (from adults of the complementary gender). If a child is raised by a mother only or by two mothers, will he/she have adequate contact with male parenting figures?This would be arguably more problematic when parenting takes place in restricted nuclear family configurations where a child has little or no contact with adults other than one's parent(s). But children have contact with adults in a variety of contexts including the extended family, daycare centers, schools, sports teams, neighborhoods, and with the personal friends and social network of the parent(s). Indeed, some single parents and gay and lesbian parents make a special point to include a variety of gender models for their children.

As noted earlier, if personality and relationships are poetic, then strictly defined gender roles can hinder the achievement of excellence and personal well-being, particularly if one's personal constitution does not readily correspond to socially prescribed gender identity. Moreover, a society which attempts to impose strictly defined gender roles is more likely to eclipse the poetic character of personality and mutuality. This is an impoverishment, notwithstanding the social conformity and coherence it might afford.

It is beyond the scope of this chapter to explore the many new types of families and parenting arrangements that are arising in North American and European societies. Many of these raise interesting questions about the poetics of parenting. For example, when two lesbians make an agreement with a male friend to provide sperm for artificial insemination, there are a number of poetic forms that could be imagined in terms of his relationship with the child and with the lesbian mothers. There are arrangements in which he is merely a donor and has no subsequent relationship. In other instances, he might play a very active fathering role. In some cases, he may be an uncle figure. These co-parents discover unanticipated challenges and graces, as do all parents, when they have to make joint decisions about education, health care, home environment, discipline, and values.

From the perspective of an essentialistic model of human sexuality, where the only normal way to be sexual is in patriarchal-heterosexual-marital-and-reproductively-centered relationships, diverse family forms and diverse models of gender are considered immoral because they are thought to encourage the development of sexual identities which are unfavorable to patriarchal heterosexuality. This assumes, however, that personal flourishing and well-being are only possible when one attempts to conform to patriarchal heterosexuality. But this is not the case. People of very diverse sexual identities flourish quite admirably, at least as measured by conventional standards of psychological and sociological well-being.

What is absolutely critical to personal well-being and healthy psychological development is that one experience covenantal love from one's parent(s).[21] Covenantal love is nonutilitarian love. It is the kind of love which affirms another's importance and loveableness because they belong, because their very being and presence are considered a grace, a gift. Children's personal development is not threatened by different parenting forms but by the absence of love. When a child knows he/she is loved and supported, it matters little whether the love comes from a mother and father, a single father, a single mother, divorced parents, gay parents or lesbian parents. Conversely, traditional intact heterosexual families do not guarantee such love nor do they possess any advantage simply because of form.

If the object of parenting is the nurture and education of children, then parenting ethics is poetic. That is, since the kinds of people we are and the kinds of relationships we form are at root poetic, not essentialistic, the form of parenting must be thought of poetically rather than essentialistically. There is an essential core to parenting: lifelong covenantal advocacy.[22] That is, parents make a lifelong commitment to advocate the well-being of their children through covenantal love. But the form that lifelong covenantal advocacy takes is poetically rich!

The poetics of infertility. Many individuals and couples face enormous challenges when they discover they are infertile. Typically, infertility precipitates a sense of inadequacy, powerlessness, depression, emptiness, unloveableness, shame and guilt. Although today we know more about the biological and physiological causes of infertility, individuals still internalize them as if they were personal failures.

The anguish associated with infertility may stem from two sources. First, the desire to have children is most likely a profound biologically and psychologically reinforced urge. When one cannot fulfill that urge, it produces great disappointment, sadness, and disillusionment. Second, society reinforces this urge with its heterosexual-marital-and-reproductively-centered value system. Many activities and social institutions center around having families and raising children. The individual who foregoes that or the couple who cannot manage to achieve pregnancy often feels socially marginalized, even if there are no direct or explicit statements to the effect.

Historically, women suffered enormous shame and alienation when marriage failed to produce offspring. Today we know that the causes of infertility are equally divided between men and women. When couples discover they are infertile, there is enormous anxiety about "who" is the cause. Neither partner wants to "disappoint" the other over something as important as having children. Infertility is another challenge and opportunity in the process of learning to love poetically. Let me outline a few of these challenges and opportunities.

First, many causes of infertility can be overcome with modern medicine and technology. But fertility treatment is a personally invasive and humiliating experience. If the tests, measurements, and probes are not invasive enough, the roller coaster of emotions around hopes and disappointments will challenge even the most psychologically adjusted individual or couple. The process can solidify a companionate form of poetic love as spouses support one another through it, or it can further erode and weaken intimacy, self-esteem, and lightheartedness.

Second, to whatever extent the biological or physical cause of infertility rests with one rather than both partners, that one individual is prone to feel increased shame, guilt, or responsibility for the success or failure of the marriage as a whole. This is a challenge, but it is also an opportunity for couples to develop and accentuate other poetic aspects of their love. This is not easy when couples are intensely attempting to overcome infertility. But, to the extent possible, couples should be encouraged to celebrate and be grateful for other poetic riches of their relationship.

This leads to a third challenge/opportunity. If fertility treatment fails or if the process presents risks/harms/costs which a couple is unwilling to endure, infertility can be the occasion to discover other poetic forms of fecundity. Adoption is one of these. But other forms of fecundity include voluntarism (for the community, environment, social justice), coaching children's sports, getting involved in educational programs/activities, and offering to help siblings and friends parent.

Each of these approaches—support through fertility treatment, accentuating other poetic features of love, and developing diverse ways to express and realize the fecund nature of love—requires a poetic sensibility. For those who cannot think of their relationship poetically, infertility can be an almost insurmountable obstacle to intimacy. For those who develop a richer poetic appreciation of their relationship and its fecund orientation, infertility can be an intense opportunity for personal and coupled transformation.

New challenges are just around the corner as we unravel the relationship between DNA and one's physical and psychological makeup. Couples will face daunting decisions about risks of passing on defects, whether to test fetuses or not, whether to access assisted reproduction and/or genetic engineering, and how all of this impacts their ability to love and accept their children covenantally. A poetic model of personal excellence could enable us to be more accepting of personal diversity, thus avoiding the seduction of using reproductive technologies to create perfect children!

Ending Committed Sexual Relationships

Traditional Christian morality considered heterosexual-household-management-and-reproductively-centered marriages indissoluble. In contrast to Jewish law, which permitted a man to divorce his wife and remarry (but not she him), and Roman law, which permitted divorce and remarriage for both men and women, Christians did not ordinarily permit divorce and remarriage. Appealing to Jesus' statements in the synoptic Gospels that God intended for man and woman to become one flesh, Christians traditionally considered marriage a permanent reality and, hence, remarriage a form of adultery.

Many scholars believe that Jesus' statements about marriage were motivated out of a concern for the plight of women who lost social legitimacy through divorce. The Jewish emphasis on the mitzvah (obligation) to have children encouraged men to dismiss barren wives. They could also dismiss women they found disagreeable in any way. Since women had little independent status apart from their fathers or husbands, and since a divorced woman was not likely to be remarried, the Jewish practice of divorce left them socially disenfranchised.[23]

The context of Jesus' statements becomes clearer when we consider what, to us, appears to be a very cryptic statement: "Not everyone can accept this teaching, but only those to whom it is given. Some there are who are eunuchs from their mother's womb; some have been made so by men; and some have made themselves so for the kingdom of God. Let him accept this teaching who can." (Matthew 19:12) This follows Jesus' statement about the indissolubility of marriage. It only makes sense when we understand that the term eunuch can refer to someone born without complete male genitalia, men who have been castrated, or a man who has no children.[24] The willingness of a man to remain committed to his wife despite the absence of children is an expression of the way God loves, it is a form of covenantal love. Covenantal love contrasts with the economic and reproductive interests that often characterized marriage at the time of Jesus.

Jesus was essentially describing marriage as a form of covenantal love. He was encouraging his followers to think of the relationship between a man and woman as one of a deep intimacy and sharing of life, of a union which, grounded in mutuality, is not to be dismissed when it does not serve economic or reproductive interests. We now face a different social context. Men and women both initiate divorce, and they do so most often because they are not able to sustain covenantal love.

The consequences of divorce are serious, as they must have been in Jesus' time. Children are severed from the security and stability of their original family, all parties are vulnerable to economic and social losses, the social network of in-laws and friends is often torn asunder, and both husband and wife suffer deep emotional and physical loss.

But despite these consequences, nearly fifty percent of all marriages in the United States end in divorce. Some argue that marriage is no longer taken seriously and that the divorce problem is symptomatic of an erosion of family values. But this is not a fair assessment. Most couples do not take the dissolution of their marriage lightly. They agonize for months or even years before making a decsion. Many undergo extensive couple counseling. Many couples stay together in the face of great alienation and hostility for the sake of their children. Even with couples who have financial resources to live separately, divorce is difficult and traumatic. And even religious prohibition of remarriage (particularly in the Roman Catholic Church) has not been a significant deterrent against divorce.

Most Christian denominations have made accommodations to this sociological trend by permitting remarriage. There is some evidence that the early Church permitted remarriage in some select circumstances. Tertullian, Basil the Great, and Pope Gregory II all permitted remarriage. Eastern Christians permitted divorce and remarriage not only for the exception Jesus mentioned in Matthew (infidelity) but also for attempted murder, abortion, a married priest's elevation to episcopacy, lapse of one of the spouses into heresy, "a wife's fraudulently concealing a physical defect from before the marriage vows; the wife's hatred for her husband brought on by his cruelty or his forcing her into sodomy; (and) irreconcilable discord of spouse from spouse."[25] Luther, appealing to Paul's concern about the dangers of errant sexual desire in 1 Corinthians, believed it was better to permit remarriage even though he did not encourage divorce. Many Protestant denominations have followed this line of thinking in recent years. A notable exception was the Anglican Communion which had neither provisions for annulment (as did the Roman Catholic Church) nor remarriage. But a study commissioned by the Archbishop of Canterbury in the 1970's reported that "marriage is the normal means for the maturing of adult sexuality," that it "is also one of the central means through which the continuation of the development of personality occurs," and that marriage often heals "childhood traumas and alienation."[26]

> Marriage, considered not merely sexually, but also in its psychological aspects, can meet the deepest human needs, because it contains the basic ingredients of a relationship within which each partner can discover himself or herself through the other, and each can offer to the other the opportunity for healing and growth on the basis of progressive mutual completion.[27]

These statements implicitly suggest that those who are denied access to marital love through the prohibition of remarriage after divorce are denied access to the resources by which human beings normally mature and achieve personal well-being. Unless equally compelling reasons could be given for sustaining the prohibition of remarriage after divorce, the Commission constituted by the Archbishop of Canterbury did not feel that sustaining the old canons served the Church or its people. It noted that, despite the prohibition of remarriage, divorce rates continued to increase, that remarriage would probably not cause scandal, and that Scriptural texts gave some precedent for remarriage (Matthew's exception clause) and most certainly for compassion.

The Roman Catholic Church has approached the contemporary problem of divorce and remarriage by amplifying grounds for annulment. Traditionally, unions were considered invalid (nonexistent) when they were attempted without the proper ceremony (for example, civil ceremonies did not constitute a valid marriage for Catholics), when consent was defective (for example, if conditional, coercive, or for a limited duration), or when not consummated. With Vatican II's retrieval of covenantal language to describe marriage, canonists began to identify a broader range of attitudes, dispositions, abilities, and practices which constitute genuine marriage.

In the Roman Catholic Church, if a man and woman divorce and if they want to remarry, they must seek a declaration of nullity for their union. They must convince a Church court that something essential to marriage was lacking in their union and that its absence was the reason why their "marriage" failed. In this way, the Church both preserves the notion of the indissolubility of marriage and yet provides a way for some to remarry.

But there remains a good deal of tension in Roman Catholicism between juridical and covenantal models of marriage. Traditional canon law considered marriage a juridical institution which, once validly established, could not be dissolved. Even if love and mutuality were absent, marriage still existed. Traditional theology placed the importance of this indissolubility on the responsibilities parents had for children, the primary purpose of marriage.

In Vatican II, marriage was described as an "intimate partnership of life and love," "a mutual giving of two persons," "an affection between two persons rooted in the will," and "a free and mutual giving of the self, experienced in tenderness and action, and permeat(ing) their whole lives . . ."[28] Consequently, some scholars began to wonder how a marriage could actually exist where there is not mutuality, affection, or love.

Theodore Mackin suggests that Vatican II comes very close to placing the importance of indissolubility on the very nature of this mutual self-surrender. He refers to a line in paragraph 48 of Gaudium et Spes (Vataican II): "The intimate union of marriage, as a mutual giving of two persons, and the good of the children demand total fidelity from the spouses and require an unbreakable unity between them." For example, how can one surrender oneself to another in order to share life and intimacy only temporarily? And if it is the nature of the self-surrender that creates the importance of permanency and fidelity, would the revoking of that self-surrender effectively dissolve the marriage?[29]

Pope Paul VI responded to these considerations by describing the bond between husband and wife to be an irrevocable one. Theodore Mackin describes Pope Paul's position thusly:

The spouses' marriage, being the juridical bond, is a thing of the objective order. Their marriage is not something in them or of them. It is not a condition of their wills, of their intentions, of their minds or souls. Therefore it is not a real relationship of their persons to one another. Therefore, too, once they have created this bond by their acts of will, it exists apart from their control . . .[30]

Few people today are able to make sense of such a juridical notion of marriage. While most believe the commitment to marriage should not be intentionally temporary, they cannot understand how a relationship really continues or endures when the two who constitute it are unable to be mutual, loving, intimate, or affectionate.

The Roman Catholic response to this concern includes an appeal to the sacramental character of marriage. In Ephesians, Paul writes:

> For no one hates his own flesh but rather nourishes and cherishes it, even as Christ does the church, because we are members of his body. 'For this reason a man shall leave [his] father and [his] mother and be joined to his wife, and the two shall become one flesh.' This is a great mystery, but I speak in reference to Christ and the church. In any case, each one of you should love his wife as himself, and the wife should respect her husband.[31]

Sacramental marriage, accordingly, "is" or "ought to" image the faithful love of Christ for the Church. Mackin questions whether Paul's thinking is a deontological comparison (marriage "ought to" image Christ's faithful love) or an ontological comparison (marriage "does" image Christ's faithful love).

But then the contradictions seem even more apparent. If Paul's thought is ontological, as the Roman Catholic juridical position suggests, then sacramental marriages are indissoluble because they do image Christ's love, and they do so necessarily, even if the baptized no longer practice their faith and even if the marriage does not indeed image faithful love! But how can a sign be a sign if it doesn't sign or image that which it signifies/images? If Paul meant that marriages "ought" to image the faithful love of Christ, then those that don't have failed. The Church might appropriately deal with such failure in moral rather than juridical terms. Thus, remarriage might fall short of the ideal of a permanent covenant of mutual love, but it would not be invalid.[32]

More to the point of the poetics of intimacy and the harm of long-term sexual abstinence, Mackin points out that the practice of the early Church to permit remarriage for the good of Christian spouses abandoned by their non-Christian spouses, or the medieval practice of permitting remarriage in unconsummated marriage when one of the spouses entered monastic life, is inconsistent with the unwillingness of current authorities to consider the well-being of those spouses who, sometimes through no fault of their own, are now condemned to lifelong sexual abstinence. Mackin hits it right on the head when he insinuates that some of these earlier Church practices (as well as the general approach taken in the Eastern Churches) were concerned about the harm that would be caused to someone who, though not called to a life of celibacy, would be forced to do so by the unforeseen end of their marriage.[33] At least implicitly, there is some sense here that long-term sexual abstinence for adults can be personally disintegrating, even devastating!

Bracketing canonical and sacramental considerations, are there any other reasons to hold spouses to their marital commitments? If not, why make commitments? Why make vows to one another if they aren't binding?

In what, precisely, does a commitment to marriage or other covenantal sexual relationship consist? What is it that we commit to? Margaret Farley makes the following point:

> Like any other commitment, a commitment to love is not a prediction, not just a resolution. It is the yield of a claim, the giving of my word, to the one I love—promising what? It can only be promising that I will do all that is possible to keep alive my love and to act faithfully in accordance with it. Like any other commitment, its purpose is to assure the one I love of my ongoing love and to strengthen me in actually loving.[34]

The commitment creates an obligation, but an obligation which Farley suggests corresponds to love itself. Even so, love can sometimes "cease to want its own law. The law of commitment may become, then, a burden to love, a structure of fear and violence, a destroyer of love."[35]

Commitment is a way of serving, supporting and sustaining covenantal sexual relationships. But we also know that even with that support, these relationships sometimes become unsustainable. Farley outlines four categories wherein commitments either cease to be binding or where a just release from them seems reasonable. First, the original meaning of the commitment may foretell situations where release is just. Both the one making the commitment, the matter and manner in which it was made, and the limits of its making might all impact its enforceability.[36] We might envision limits to the enforceability of vows if the original parties were not free, were not in possession of their faculties, were not mutual in what they committed to (different notions of what such a relationship should entail), or encountered behavior in each other which was either explicitly or implicitly excluded from the original commitment (like psychological or physical abuse or infidelity).

Second, if the promisee releases the promisor, he/she is no longer obligated.[37] In committed sexual relationships, one cannot really have an obligation to love and share intimacy with another if the other has either released one from one's promise or, indeed, asks that the original commitment not be honored.

Third, if the commitment cannot be fulfilled, it is no longer binding.[38] There are any number of reasons why individuals might find themselves unable to fulfill commitments made to sexual covenantal relationships including irreconcilable aversion to one another, insurmountable conflicts, psychological incapacity due to acute and chronic psychosis and/or addictions, or physical limitations. Farley describes this as follows:

> Growing intractable and all-consuming irritation; moods endlessly whirling us away from each other; radical and comprehensive misunderstandings of deepest intentions; disagreement regarding the fundamental requirements of our commitment and its way of fidelity; vicious, active attacks mutually launched or with one the aggressor and the other the victim—at some point these aspects of our experience resist all "conflict resolution" and render our continuation in the relationship impossible.[39]

The impossibility of fulfilling an obligation or commitment might also rest with the other's actions or responses to efforts of fulfillment.[40] How can one sustain faithfulness, vulnerability or intimacy with someone who consistently violates one's vulnerability and trust or who is closed to the sharing of power and intimacy as originally promised?

Fourth, if there are competing and more serious obligations, the original commitment may be no longer binding.[41] Farley refers to both the loss of meaning or purpose the original commitment was meant to serve and superseding or competing obligations.[42] If one had made a commitment to a household-management-and-reproductively-centered marriage and found that it was difficult to be affectionate or intimate, it is likely that the original meaning or purpose of the commitment is still viable and sustainable. But if one had made a commitment to a relationship centered in covenantal mutuality where sharing of power, intimacy and affection are central and found that it was impossible to be intimate, affectionate or mutual, to what purpose would the sustaining of that obligation serve?

Commitments to covenantal sexual relationships are made in the context of other commitments. Ideally, we envision balancing and integrating these various commitments, but sometimes we find that they compete for our attention and allegiance. One can imagine situations where obligations to one's children may compete with commitments and obligations to one's sexual companion. In the best of situations, these are balanced and integrated. But sometimes the committed sexual relationship threatens the well-being of one's child, particularly a young one.

Obligations to oneself also compete with commitments to others. When a committed relationship seriously threatens one's physical or psychological well-being, one's commitment to oneself would ordinarily take precedence. Although we have obligations to ourselves, it is not always clear when a committed sexual relationship threatens that obligation. Let me propose an example to illustrate.

Lucy and Darrell have been married for ten years. They have two children. Lucy and Darrell are both successful professionals and enjoy a secure upper middle class life. Lucy enjoys Darrell's companionship. It is easy to communicate with Darrell, and they both have a lot of shared interests and values. But Lucy feels dissatisfied with the relationship, not because there is anything particularly problematic about it but because it isn't particularly fulfilling. She has grown to believe she could have done better. The commitment she made to Darrell competes with an obligation to her own well-being.

But does her relationship with Darrell really threaten her well-being or just it's optimal flourishing? How does one decide when the harm to one's well-being is serious enough to warrant the compromise of another's well-being and commitments made? This is a delicate matter, one requiring a poetic sensitivity to the seasons of love and to the dynamics of sexual relationships. Does Lucy's dissatisfaction stem from Darrell or from her own resistance to intimacy? Is the relationship passing through an unusually dry season but otherwise able to be lived at a much greater intensity of mutual satisfaction? Does Lucy need a richer constellation of friendships to complement the one with Darrell? Can she develop a deeper appreciation for Darrell or is she increasingly resentful and disillusioned?

Ending such a relationship may be less problematic if Darrell is also dissatisfied or if he is able to recognize that the relationship, while generally good for him, is not particularly good for Lucy. He may be willing to release Lucy from her commitment out of a concern for her happiness. This might be more complicated if children are involved, but not necessarily. Other mutual attachments (to friends, in-laws, or common social involvements) may also make it more difficult to end the relationship.

We must take the poetic character of relationships and the poetic subjectivity of the committed parties into account when we describe the morality of ending committed sexual relationships. Our contemporary model of committed sexual covenantal love is less institutional and more interpersonal and poetic. Thus, grounds for a just or right ending of these relationships are much broader than for ending household-management-and-reproductively-centered ones. But these grounds are no less moral or serious. They are different and they require a different set of sensitivities.

A juridical model of assessing the validity/invalidity of marriage in Catholic tribunals does not match the more complex set of dispositions we assume are necessary for mutuality-based marriages to succeed. Constituting a relationship of genuine mutuality requires more than promises and consummation. When we describe the moral imperatives of committed relationships of mutuality, we must actually amplify them rather than diminish them. Thus, the movement from a juridical model to a poetic one is an enriching vision, not a cheapened one.

A juridical model of assessing the validity/invalidity of marriage is unsuitable for affirming the dynamic and historical nature of mutual relationships. Marriages might be initially valid but become nonsustainable through choices and decisions couples make over the course of their relationship. If we are to take the historical and poetic character of people and relationships seriously, then we have to acknowledge that people and relationships change. But the Catholic approach to marriage suggests that once validly contracted a marriage can only be dissolved upon the death of one of the parties. Thus, according to the Catholic approach to marriage, even when a couple suffers irreconcilable conflicts, hostility, or alienation, we accurately describe their relationship as marriage, as a sign and instance of God's love.

When we shift to looking at relationships in terms of a poetics of intimacy, this need not involve a lowering of standards making divorce and remarriage a casual matter. Challenging companioned partners to be attentive to the various dynamics that may be at work in the waxing and waning of affection or to the enriching possibilities of facing difficulties with poetic imagination is a way of enabling them to sustain intimacy and love where possible. However, when intimacy and love are not possible, we neither serve the individuals nor the ideal of committed covenantal love by forcing people to remain together or by prohibiting them from remarrying once divorced.

The Poetics of Intimacy After the End of Committed Sexual Relationships

Traditional sexual ethics, at least in its Christian form, expected the divorced to practice sexual abstinence for the remainder of their lives. We have already noted that this was not universally practiced nor endorsed, with exceptions existing in both Roman Catholic and Orthodox Churches. Since Jesus' prohibition of divorce and remarriage was probably linked to its adverse impact on women regarded as the reproductive property of men, it is not inconsistent with the Christian tradition to look at current forms of marriage, divorce, and remarriage and ask whether the traditional (and current in the Roman Catholic Church) prohibition of remarriage really helps men and women flourish.

As already noted, the contemporary context for this consideration is decidedly different from the time of Jesus and/or from times in which the current canonical norms prohibiting remarriage in the Roman Catholic Church were elaborated. Contemporary marriage, both socially and ecclesially considered, is a more love-centered institution. As such, it is more fragile and difficult to sustain. Divorce rates are not necessarily a symptom of moral decay and disrespect for marriage but are more likely evidence that love-based relationships, built as they are on intimacy, mutual vulnerability, and sharing power, require a much more developed set of skills and virtues. Prohibiting remarriage does not make Roman Catholics any less likely to divorce than their Protestant or secular counterparts.

In addition, the contemporary situation is different from former ages in that life expectancy is longer. A person who marries in his/her mid to late twenties and divorces in his/her mid to late thirties can look forward to at least another forty years of life. In previous ages, a similar individual would have had between ten to twenty years more of life. While Luther and others argued that divorce without remarriage was a burden for these individuals, how much more so for one who has double the life expectancy!

As already noted, marriage (and other types of committed sexual relationships) encompasses various kinds of goods including companionship, intimacy, touch, social connectedness, support in parenting, and the context within which personal and psychological growth and integration enable one to love with greater depth, integrity and generosity. These are not superficial or ancillary goods. While some are able to be accessed in other kinds of relationships or contexts, many are not.

The divorced experience extraordinary burdens and challenges for which these goods may be even more important. Individuals accustomed to the intimacy and sensual touch of marriage often find that divorce is a time of intense loneliness and physical isolation. The hopes and dreams associated with marriage are broken. This leaves many disillusioned, feeling both hopeless and powerless. For those who were betrayed or left, there is often the associated feeling of unloveableness. The resources for rebuilding one's life, for reclaiming the physical benefits of touch and intimacy, for loving and being loved, and for imagining new hopes and dreams are frequently enabled in new sexual relationships.

The importance of new sexual relationships is particularly acute for integrating and solidifying lessons learned through the dissolution of one's marriage. Sexually intimate relationships normally force us to confront aspects of ourselves which need healing and transformation. The poetics of divorce and remarriage center on these lessons. Divorce can teach us a lot about illusions we may bring to relationships, virtues we still need to develop to sustain love, obstacles to intimacy we carry with us, and self-esteem issues which either undermine our expectations or diminish our ability to love generously and gracefully.

These are important lessons which can enable an individual to form more stable and graceful relationships. Indeed, a new committed sexual relationship becomes the context within which these insights are integrated and effected. And this, in turn, has implications for one's spiritual journey. If the Christian vocation is to love, these lessons and their integration become important foundations for Christian maturity! It is difficult to see how the prohibition of remarriage enhances Christian maturity when it distances individuals from the context in which certain graces are strengthened!

Obviously, there are some caveats! Some individuals are so over-whelmed by the disorientation, darkness and loneliness of divorce that they enter hastily and unreflectively into new relationships. This is not necessarily wise but, from a poetic point of view, might be graceful nevertheless. The Church could be of great service to individuals if it were to approach divorce and remarriage as part of one's spiritual journey and provide the kind of support and fellowship which might mitigate against the alienation and isolation many divorced people feel.

Some divorces occur because one or both of the individuals have succumbed to conflicting sexual passions. Sexual infidelity is not rare, and many marriages do not survive it. Indeed, love or romance-based relationships are more likely to fail when infidelity is discovered. Household-management-and-reproductively-centered relationships were concerned about infidelity because it jeopardized proprietary reproductive interests. But in love-based relationships, one's trust, vulnerability and intimacy are at issue. It is not clear that the prohibition of remarriage is a useful or effective strategy for preventing sexual infidelity, nor is it clear that couples are served when they must remain in relationships where trust and intimacy are impossible.

Conversely, the Church does not want to encourage a less-than-serious respect for the kind of commitment and fidelity required of marriage. It would appear, however, that as marriage becomes more love-based its seriousness intensifies. Indeed, the current trend among married couples is toward a greater commitment to and regard for sexual fidelity. The Church's pastoral approach might be to help couples understand the poetic seasons of their affection so they can weather the storms and conflicting passions which invariably accompany love!

Paradoxically, some divorced individuals may find that not remarrying is an important move toward personal maturity and serves the poetics of intimacy. Some committed sexual relationships are characterized by union which eclipses individuality or by relationships where one party dominates the subjectivity of the other. An individual who works hard to please his/her companion, even when it means compromising important personal gifts, insights, preferences, or beliefs, may find that it is important to recover and reclaim his/her own autonomy. Developing skills for self-reliance and self-constitution could be enabled by a significant period of singleness. Where the domination of one's subjectivity by another was more abusive, a good deal of healing is necessary. Sometimes singleness is an important season in preparing one to enter future committed relationships with more autonomy.

Whether an individual chooses a long or short period of singleness is not a matter for moral judgment. Indeed, some might choose to remain single for the rest of their lives. This need not be viewed as a contradiction of the thesis that long-term and lifelong sexual abstinence is problematic. Older individuals may draw upon the lessons and graces of committed sexual relationships for many years after the relationships have ended. The length of time it takes to heal from an abusive relationship may be long. Some individuals have networks of close friends or companions with whom significant intimacy is possible. Some of these relationships might include cohabitation or communal life. Some might include occasional opportunities for sexual intimacy.

In summary, there are two fundamental considerations for a poetics of remarriage or a poetics of intimacy after the ending of a committed sexual relationship. First of all, it is harmful to institutionally deprive people of the kinds of relationships which have the greatest potential for enabling them to grow, heal, and have access to the resources for physical, psychological, and spiritual well-being. Committed sexual relationships are normally the context for this, and remarriage after divorce should be a prima facie right.

Second of all, it is important for people to think poetically and creatively about the season of love and life that follows the ending of a relationship. What lessons is one being challenged to learn? What graces and abilities is one being challenged to acquire, embody, and solidify? The challenges and opportunities people face after the ending of a committed sexual relationship are varied and require poetic imagination. Remarriage and long-term sexual abstinence are not the only options available. Hopefully, we can imagine paradigms of sexual morality which transcend dualism and, instead, think poetically about ways to enable a rich and graceful life of love.

Notes

[1]   Carter Heyward, Op. cit., p. 99

[2]   Thomas Moore, *The Soul of Sex*. Op. cit., p. 20.

[3]   Wallerstein and Blakeslee, Op. cit.

[4]   Vacek, Op. cit., p.45.

[5]   Mary Ann Lamanna and Agnes Riedmann, *Marriages and Families: Making Choices and Facing Change* (Belmont, CA: Wadsworth, 1994) p. 223.

[6]   Ibid., p. 223.

[7]   Vacek, Op. cit.,and Farley, M., *Personal Commitments,* Op. cit.

[8]   Margaret Farley, *Commitments*, Op. cit., p. 34.

[9]   Vacek, Op. cit., p. 23.

[10] Ibid., p. 23.

[11] Keenan, Op. cit. pp. 58–75.

[12] Wallerstein and Blakeslee, Op. cit. pp. 19-29.

[13] Ibid., pp. 91–101

[14] Ibid., pp. 211–247

[15] Scott Peck, *A World Waiting to be Born* (New York: Bantam Book, 1993).

[16] Martin Buber, *I and Thou*, Op. cit.

[17] James Keenan, Op. cit. pp. 58–75.

[18] Ibid., pp. 78–79.

[19] Michael J. Hartwig, "Parening Ethics and Reproductive Technologies," *Journal of Social Philosophy* vol. XXVI, no. 1, Spring 1995, 183–202.

[20] Ibid., pp. 195–196.

[21] Ibid., pp. 196–198.

[22] Ibid., pp. 196–198.

[23] Theodore Mackin, *Divorce and Remarriage* (New York: Paulist Press, 1984). p. 272.

[24] Mackin, Op. cit. p. 300.

[25]   Op. cit., pp. 373–374.

[26]   "Marriage, Divorce and the Church: The Report of a Commission Appointed by the Archbishop of Cantebury to Prepare a Statement on the Christian Doctrine of Marriage," (London: SPCK, 1972) paragraphs 27, 36 and 38.

[27]   Ibid., paragraph 40.

[28]   *Gaudium et Spes*, paragraphs 48 and 49.

[29]   Mackin, Op. cit., pp. 478ff.

[30]   Mackin, Op. cit., p. 514.

[31]   Ephesians 5:29–33.

[32]   Mackin, pp. 515–537.

[33]   Mackin, pp. 515–537.

[34]   Margaret Farley, *Personal Commitments*, Op. cit., p. 34.

[35]   Ibid., pp. 35-36.

[36]   Margaret Farley, *Personal Commitments*, Op. cit., p..74–75.

[37]   Ibid., pp. 75–76.

[38]   Ibid., p. 76.

[39]   Ibid., p. 87.

[40]   Ibid., pp. 88–89.

[41]   Ibid., p.76.

[42]   Ibid., pp. 92ff.

❖ Chapter Seven

The Poetics of Intimacy for Gay Men and Lesbians

Changing Perceptions

Traditional Western/Christian sexual morality considers sex between two men or two women to lack moral finality, that is, moral purpose and, thus, to be nothing more than sexual self-indulgence. Under the influence of Stoic philosophy, sexual passion was considered inherently dangerous and irrational and could only be redeemed if directed to something greater than itself—reproduction in marriage. Even nonreproductive sexual activity in marriage was considered self-indulgent. Although Christian morality now considers sex between married persons to be an important expression and cultivation of emotional bonds even when it is not procreative, most mainstream Christian churches have had difficulty extending such recognition to sex between persons of the same gender.

Traditional Christian moral attitudes about homosexuality have been challenged in recent decades due to the large number of people who have "come out." Social perceptions of gay men and lesbians have changed. People have discovered that their physicians, teachers, bankers, ministers, counselors, artists, sons, daughters, parents and grandparents are gay. Thus, previous vilification of homosexuality has not generally resonated with personal experiences of particular gay men and lesbians. "In 1985, a *Newsweek* poll found that twenty-two percent of Americans had a friend or acquaintance whom they knew to be homosexual. Today the statistic is fifty-sex percent."[1] Many have watched their gay relatives, friends, and business associates achieve new levels of self-esteem, in-tegrity and well-being as a result of new honesty and personal accept-ance. Since Christianity claims to offer good news to human beings and a morality that fosters growth, integrity, and well-being, it is increasingly difficult to sustain claims that being gay and/or forming sexually intimate relationships between persons of the same gender is evil. Consequently, many Christian groups have undertaken efforts to rethink traditional condemnation of homosexuality.

However, efforts to reform mainstream Christian attitudes about same gender sex have been generally disappointing. Over the past twenty years, Presbyterians, Lutherans, Methodists, and Episcopalians raised the issue at their national conventions.[2] Subcommittees were formed to conduct studies and to draft proposals for changes. Initial reports included emerging sociological, psychological and biological evidence which brought into question stereotypes and unfounded assumptions about the pathology and dysfunctionality of homosexual persons and gay and lesbian relationships. Biblical scholars made reports about why it is not conclusive that the Bible condemns consensual gay and lesbian relationships. Testimonies of gay clergy and gay and lesbian couples helped many delegates develop a new appreciation for the unjust suffering and discrimination of gay men and lesbians in Christian churches and society. But conservative reaction to these reports and proposals brought the threat and fear of division and the disaffection of many members. Ultimately, these institutions voted to continue to study the issue but not to take a strong stand in favor of moral reform. A most recent exception may involve the U.S. Episcopal Church's vote to apologize to gay men and lesbians and to draft proposals for same-sex commitment ceremonies for the convention in the year 2000.[3] However, this move was undermined by the 1998 Lambdeth Conference's (world-wide conference of Anglican Churches) decision to go on record opposing the moral affirmation of same gender sexual relationships.

The practice of contemporary Roman Catholicism does not generally offer its members formal opportunities for dialogue and discussion of doctrinal or moral issues nor to share in the administration of the institution. But Roman Catholic scholars have been active in studying the issue from historical, Biblical and social scientific perspectives. The potential impact of their efforts can be insinuated by increased efforts of the Vatican to suppress the activities of Dignity, an organization of gay and lesbian Roman Catholics, and to censure theologians and clerics who propose positions contrary to official Church doctrine, most notably John McNeil, Charles Curran, Robert Nugent, Janine Grammick, and Bishops Hunthausen and Galot. The U.S. Conference of Catholic Bishops issued a document in 1997 entitled: "Always Our Children." The document made a number of important points toward the affirmation of gay people, namely, that sexual orientation is not chosen, that it is normally unchangeable, and that, therefore, sexual orientation itself is not a moral question. This conclusion leads the Bishops to call for better under-standing and affirmation of the rights of gay men and lesbians in society and in the Church. Each human being is of incalculable dignity and value, and being gay or lesbian does not diminish that dignity.

The United States Catholic Conference/National Conference of Catholic Bishops did not, however, endorse gay and lesbian sexual relationships. Although the Bishops encourage parents to love their children, listen to them, and support them, they implicitly reaffirmed traditional sexual morality by stating that gay men and lesbians who live chaste lives (i.e., sexually abstinent) should be invited to exercise ministry and leadership within the Church.

Cultural Poetics

It might be helpful to put much of this in historical and cultural perspective. And this is difficult because language and poetical identity change. In the light of post-modern philosophical insights, we know that personal identity is not a matter of essentialistic determination. That is, identity is not determined by a fixed essential nature (be it genetic, spiritual, or other). Rather, personal identity is a dialectical process involving personal, social, genetic, and cultural/linguistic resources.

The search for a genetic cause of homoerotic desire does not solve the issue of sexual orientation or sexual identity. It is probable that homoerotic desire includes some genetic features, but how an individual incorporates sexual desires into an identity is largely a matter of both personal and cultural dynamics as well. Some, for example, will disregard such impulses with indifference or scorn. They might be thought of as aberrant emotions, peripheral to one's other emotions and desires. For others, such desires may be more important, particularly if they are associated with significant experiences or relationships. But the process of affirming or disregarding certain impulses is, itself, influenced by social and cultural systems of meaning.

An individual's identity is circumscribed by cultural language and possibility. Forty years ago, few American adolescents could have developed a gay or lesbian identity. There were simply few if any cultural names or examples with which to identify. Today, adolescents know gay and lesbian relatives, friends, professionals. Some of these are more self-identifiably gay, others not. Some have formed committed sexual relationships, others not. Some develop an identity which is more of a protest to conventional norms, others assimilate to the so-called dominant culture. Today, adolescents see gay characters portrayed positively in the media. There are gay and lesbian athletic, religious, cultural, and recreational associations which provide a wide spectrum of gay and lesbian identity, associations which were unheard of forty years ago! Thus, the possibility of developing or constituting a gay or lesbian identity is significantly different for contemporary adolescents than for those of previous ages.

When we attempt to gain an historical perspective on the poetics of gay and lesbian sexuality, what we find are different cultural systems of meaning within which people who experienced homoerotic desires could claim an identity or not. In other words, different cultural and historical epochs provided different resources and/or possibilities for an identity which included homoerotic desire.

This is analogous to the manner in which a personal identity associated with heterosexual marriage has changed from classical culture to our own. If one asked a married man in classical Rome to describe his identity as a married man, it would be strikingly different from the kind of description a contemporary North American man might give of his marital identity. Classical culture provided very few resources by which a married man could develop an identity around mutual affection, emotional vulnerability, shared intimacy, shared power, and marital romance. That is not to say that married men never experienced those features of married life, but, if they did, it would have been difficult to describe since there were few cultural linguistic resources with which to do so. These were concepts almost entirely foreign to their notion of heterosexual marriage.

The following historical analysis will illustrate that, while there have always been individuals who experienced homoerotic desire, cultural systems of meaning greatly determined what kind of identity could or could not be developed around those feelings.

And this raises several moral questions: given that sexual identity is partly influenced by cultural resources or systems of meaning, what responsibility does a religious group or society have for encouraging or discouraging certain forms of sexual identity? Against what standard would we decide which forms are "good" and which are "harmful"? Is the exclusion of certain sexual identities harmful? If so, in what sense?

Historical Perspectives

John Boswell, an internationally acclaimed historian, published two groundbreaking books on the history of Christian attitudes about homosexuality, *Christianity, Social Tolerance and Homosexuality* and *Same-Sex Unions in Premodern Europe.*[4] Boswell claims that the intolerance of homosexuality is a more recent phenomenon not universal in the earliest life of the Church. Moreover, social attitudes about gay relationships were much different in the classical world and need to be recalled when harbingers of doom predict the collapse of civilization if society begins to affirm gay relationships.

Boswell notes that there were different kinds of gay relationships in the ancient world, particularly in ancient Greek society. One type involved male slaves kept and used by male masters for sexual favors. Another involved male concubinage, parallel to heterosexual concubinage, but less common. A man would live with and maintain a male sexual companion until he married, at which time the *"concubinus"* would be dismissed. Boswell cites references in Juvenal and Seneca to such arrangements.[5]

However, according to Boswell, the most common type of gay relationship was that of "lovers." It is easy to appreciate the commonality of emotional bonding between persons of the same gender in a more sexually segregated society like the classical Greco-Roman world. Men and women moved in homosocial environments. Men spent much of their time working and socializing with men and women with women. Since marriage was not necessarily romantically oriented, emotional friendship often developed between persons of the same gender. Obviously, it is important to distinguish between same gender friendship and same gender sexual intimacy.

There is ample evidence in classical literature of the existence and celebration of romantic and sexually intimate relationships between persons of the same gender. Plato notes in the *Symposium* that sexual attraction derives from the search for one's other half. But in primeval history, there were three types of beings: double men, double women and androgynes (half man and half woman). The androgynes were split and resulted in heterosexual attraction. When the double men and double women were split, they sought out persons of the same gender as their other half. Plato's biology of sexual attraction is certainly primitive, but it illustrates a budding sensitivity to the reality of same gender sexual attraction. Homoeroticism was not considered a perversion of sexual nature but an expression of its variety.

Both Plato and Aristotle refer to famous homosexual couples who were lifelong sexual companions and who, for all intents and purposes, paralleled heterosexual bonds. Plato refers to Achilles and Patroclus, both warriors, who loved each other with the same intensity as husband and wife,[6] and Aristotle refers to Thebes (a lawgiver) and Dioclese (an Olympic athlete) who "spent their whole lives together, maintaining a single household, and arranged to be buried beside each other."[7]

Boswell cites famous examples of male couples in Roman literature, notably Catiline's lover, a consul, who approaches Cicero repeatedly in his behalf, the male couple in Petronius's *Satyricon*, Giton and Encolpius, the Emperor Hadrian and his lover Antinous, and Plutarch's admonition to heterosexual couples to emulate the fidelity of homosexual ones.[8]

Plutarch's statement is characteristic of an overall lack of concern about homosexual lovers threatening the institution of heterosexual marriage. While classical society clearly regarded heterosexual marriage as a socially sustaining institution, there seemed to be little evidence or sense that homosexuality would ever constitute a threat to marriage or society. Boswell relates the relative indifference of Romans to "sexuality." He states:

Sexual (as opposed to romantic) issues for Romans were primarily proprietary: Romans were concerned to see that their rights over their spouses and children (of either sex) were not violated, that their offspring married into situations which enhanced their prestige (or wealth), and that they themselves avoided any overt violations of the rights of others which might be unjust (or incur retribution). Apart from these simple, if compelling, interests, Roman sexuality was virtually untrammeled. Proven adultery was theoretically a hazard even for the powerful, but Latin literature abounds with accounts and accusations of infidelity. ... Marriage for the upper classes was largely dynastic, political, and economically arranged, at least for females, by the father and often could be dissolved by him. Amicable divorce was common. For the lower classes practical considerations also constituted the principle issue in deciding upon marriage: propinquity, financial feasibility, family wishes, etc., were paramount. Among no group of people would considerations of romantic "love" parallel to those common today have been the operative factors in arranging marriage: "love" between husband and wife was something expected to develop as a consequence of marriage, not to occasion it. It consisted of fair treatment, respect, and mutual consideration and often corresponded more to paternal affections in the modern world. . . For males of any social class sexual morality was largely personal and ranged from severe asceticism to extreme promiscuity.[9]

In the classical world, there would have been more concern about patterns of sexual self-indulgence, heterosexual or homosexual, than with whether the institution of heterosexual marriage might be undermined by the presence of same-sex couples.

It is difficult to determine whether the prevalence of homosexual people in the classical world was roughly similar to our own. It was only with the Kinsey report in the 1940's and 1950's that any effort to quantify or measure sexual expression took place. Kinsey developed a scale of seven categories representing different levels of same gender attraction/activity and opposite gender attraction/activity. Definitions were and remain problematic. Is sexual orientation a matter of activity or erotic attraction? Does someone who engages in sexual activity with someone of the same gender but who does not experience erotic attraction for members of the same gender constitute a homosexual? Is someone primarily erotically attracted to persons of the same gender, but who engages exclusively in heterosexual sex, a homosexual or heterosexual? Kinsey's conclusions about the percentage of people who are homosexual were and are controversial. More recent studies estimate that from two to five to ten percent of the population have a primary erotic attraction to persons of the same gender.

Boswell cites several references to same gender sex in Greek and Roman sources. They seem to suggest that the "practice" was so widespread as to be considered commonplace.[10] Indeed, for much of the Greco-Roman world, the gender of one's lover was relatively insignificant.[11] Boswell refers to a popular romantic novel from the third century that remained popular for several centuries, even among Christian monks, *Clitophon and Leucippe*. According to Boswell, hetero-sexual and homosexual romantic love "appear as absolutely indistin-guishable except for the accident of gender."[12] It seems that few Greeks or Romans considered same gender romantic love a threat to the sustenance or integrity of their civilization.[13]

It is interesting to compare the relative absence of concern about the stability of heterosexual marriage in the classical world with contemporary social/political rhetoric that gay unions represent the unraveling of heterosexual marriage. Heterosexual marriage was a strong institution in the classical world. The presence and success of homosexual relationships, even among soldiers, politicians and emperors, were not perceived to undermine the strength of heterosexual marriage.

Heterosexual marriage is besieged in contemporary society, but not by the presence and success of homosexual relationships. Two phenomena seem most stressful for traditional heterosexual family life: the economy and the erosion of patriarchy and sexism. Economic forces have made sustaining the traditional heterosexual family more difficult. Many poor and middle class families require two adult incomes. Even this is often insufficient to meet increased living and educational costs associated with modern life. Heterosexual couples, consequently, suffer enormously through the demands on energy and leisure needed to cultivate and attend to their emotional lives. Moreover, increased economic opportunity and equality for women have encouraged many to leave abusive and intolerable husbands. This threatens patriarchal and sexist models of male-female relationships. Marriage is increasingly regarded as a consensual relationship that involves a sharing of power. In the past, the relatively unchallenged authority of male heads of households created a more stable family system. Since contemporary society seems committed to a model of gender equality, it will have to expect that marriages will be more vulnerable to dissolution.

Gay men and lesbians are symbolic of the collapse of patriarchalism since they do not conform to traditional gender models of males dominating women and women being dependent on men. It may be this association that makes hatred of gay men and lesbians so prominent during the contemporary cultural transition from patriarchalism to a more gender equitous society. Since that shift was not occurring during the classical age, hatred and intolerance toward gay men and lesbians was relatively mild.

According to John Boswell's research, early Christianity showed a good deal of tolerance toward people who engaged in same gender sex. His scholarship suggests that with the collapse of urban populations at the end of the Roman Empire, a more rural and, hence, less tolerant morality ensued. The first civil laws legislated against same gender sex occurred in 533, a full two centuries after Christianity had become the official state religion.[14]Boswell concludes that Church injunctions against homosexuality were no harsher than those against other common sexual sins but that civil authorities, attempting to regain political control over the populace, enacted harsher restrictions.[15] In fact, civil authorities were scandalized by both the lack of ecclesiastical concern and the apparent commonality of same gender sex among clerics.[16] And with the revival of urban life in the thirteenth century, a revival of literature about gay love emerged, most notably from within clerical circles.[17]

Why did Western civilization become more intolerant of gay people? Boswell speculates that it occurred simultaneously with late medieval attempts to consolidate civil and intellectual unity. Intolerance toward Jews, Muslims, gays and other social minorities were part of a European-wide effort to consolidate civil power and intellectual unity. The effort to consolidate power was evident not only in civil authorities but in the Church with the Inquisition. Emergence of "summas" and "encyclopedias" were evidence of the effort to unify knowledge and science.[18] Reference to "natural law" was a way of enforcing uniform law over diverse peoples by arguing that all are bound by the same "nature" and "laws inherent to that nature." Thus, theories about natural law served political and ecclesiastical interests in consolidating power. All minorities, including homosexual persons, suffered accordingly.

Elaboration of theories about human nature was common to Stoic moral paradigms where efforts to conform to reason and to a rational providential order were central. The idea of a universal essential human nature was appealing to Christianity when it began to emerge as a candidate for a world-class religion. Not only did this give Christianity a universal applicability, but it became increasingly apparent (perhaps as early as the time of Constantine) that a universal religious system like Christianity might provide a unifying force for an increasingly fragmented empire.

Stoic/Christian models of sexuality became increasingly essentialistic. Human nature was regarded as universally heterosexual and oriented toward procreation in marriage. Thus, a person engaging in same gender sex was performing an act discordant with his/her nature. Since it lacked an inherent human rational purpose, it was deemed irrational and, hence, immoral.

Modern Insights

While earlier Greek and Roman civilizations supported a plural model of sexual romantic attraction, under the influence of later Roman and Christian Stoicism an essentially heterosexual concept of human nature was imposed. Not until 1864 did the idea of same gender sexual orientation reemerge with the work of the German jurist Karl Heinrich Ulrichs (1825-1895) who argued that the human embryo has the potential to develop in either a female or male direction. In some fetuses, however, bodily development is male while mental development is female. These individuals constitute a "third sex," which he called "urnings" (gay men). There were also "urningins" (gay women), whose bodily development was female but whose mental development was male.[19]

Ulrichs' statements were intended to effect a change in society's attitude about the criminality of same gender sex. "As long as homosexuality was inborn, Ulrichs felt he could justly claim that homosexual behavior was natural for homosexual people and, therefore, should not be criminalized or viewed as sinful."[20] Another German, Magnus Hirschfeld, took the cause of gay liberation a step further. He elaborated theories about prenatal formation of sexual orientation and founded the *Wissenschaftlich-humanitares Komitee* (Scientific-Humanitarian Committee) which presented petitions to the German government to repeal laws against homosexual persons. He also founded the *Institut fur Sexualwissenschaft*, the first world institute for sexual research. Unfortunately, Hirschfeld compared homosexuality with other congenital pathologies. Although progressive in calling for a repeal of discriminatory laws, his theories did not rehabilitate public opinion about the "normalcy" of homosexual persons.

Hirschfeld's scientific approach influenced, most notably, Sigmund Freud (1895-1939), who took a different direction with respect to sexual orientation. Ulrichs and Hirschfeld had hypothesized that sexual orientation was constituted during fetal development. Freud theorized that it occurred during early childhood formation, most notably during an arrest in normal psychosexual development. Freud's psychoanalytic approach called for more compassion and understanding of homosexual persons, but also led to various attempts to "cure" them through psychoanalysis.

The influence of Ulrichs, Hirschfeld, and Freud can be noted in recent Christian pronouncements about homosexuality. Contemporary institutional statements about homosexuality include distinctions between orientation and sexual activity. Since it is currently assumed that homosexual orientation is not usually a thought out, deliberate choice, it is considered inappropriate to condemn a person for "being" homosexual. Thus, many Christian churches call for more understanding and compassion of gay people. Only a few Christian denominations have been able to take the step of approving the morality of same gender sexual activity. For most, it falls outside the traditional heterosexual-marital-reproductively-oriented ethic. And, since it is assumed that sexual abstinence is not harmful, these churches do not consider their moral pronouncements unjust or inhumane! It may be difficult for homosexual persons to practice lifelong sexual abstinence, but it is considered the only moral way for them to live out their sexuality. Some are even inclined to encourage psychotherapy and prayer, hanging on to the idea that sexual orientation could be altered. But the "cure" strategy is increasingly rare.

Freud's theories were persuasive until some of his own disciples began to question the applicability of the Oedipal theory to all forms of neurosis. Consequently, a number of psychologists began to question the "neurotic" character of homosexual persons. One of the most influential of this group was Evelyn Hooker. Hooker became acquainted with a gay neighbor in the 1940's and thought it strange that no one had conducted a study of homosexual men outside clinical contexts. She conducted a longitudinal study comparing homosexual men with heterosexual men in a blind administration of various standard tests for intelligence and developmental adjustment. She concluded that homosexual men were indistinguishable from heterosexual men as a clinical category. In other words, they did not represent a psychopathological group.[21] Others conducted similar kinds of studies which led the American Psychiatric Association and the American Psychological Association to eliminate homosexuality from the list of diagnostic pathologies.

Accordingly, homosexual persons do not represent a special kind of pathology or neurosis. When biases and prejudices are removed, homosexual persons represent the same kind of diversity and "normalcy" as heterosexual persons do. They do not need to be "cured" of their condition and, indeed, current research suggests that attempts to alter sexual orientation are ineffective.[22]

Scientific research about sexual orientation poses a problem for traditional Western/Christian condemnation of homosexuality. It challenges two assumptions. First, it challenges the belief that all human beings are by nature heterosexual. Some of the strongest evidence to date suggests that sexual orientation is constituted either prenatally or in early childhood and that it is diverse. If human beings are not universally naturally heterosexual, it would be difficult to argue that heterosexuality is morally normative (unless one could show that same gender sexual intimacy is inherently personally destructive).

Second, and most important, there is no evidence to suggest that homosexuality represents a distinct class of pathology. When social biases and prejudices are removed, homosexual persons who engage in sexual intimacy with people of the same gender are capable of securing the same degree of personal and social well-being as heterosexual persons do. Thus, even if sexual orientation was a choice, it could not be portrayed as one that leads to personal dissolution and perversion. Whatever examples detractors point out about the perversion of homosexual persons, those same examples are equally common among heterosexuals. There is no significant scientific evidence suggesting that homosexuality invariably or inevitably leads to personally or socially degenerative life.

Traditional Western/Christian moral condemnations of homosexuality assume that same gender sex is the fruit of a perverted choice, one that both contradicts one's sexual nature and one that thwarts healthy psychological sexual life. Neither of these assumptions is born out by scientific research. If Christianity intends to remain faithful to its own methodological principles, it cannot propose a moral teaching that contradicts clear and certain reason. Thus, it cannot continue to claim that homosexuality is morally wrong. If same gender sex is not morally wrong, and if sexual intimacy is normally integral to people's well-being, it is unjust to expect gay men and lesbians to practice lifelong sexual abstinence.

Reconsidering Biblical Teachings

Notwithstanding arguments that Christian morality is ideally non-sectarian, many mainstream Christian churches continue to insist that the Bible is morally authoritative and that its moral norms cannot be altered. Some of these same churches have diverged from explicit Biblical statements about the nonpermissibility of divorce and remarriage but claim no authority to change the tradition with respect to homosexuality. Many of these appeal to the "word of God in Scripture" as the moral authority from which they cannot deviate.

Unfortunately, in societies where the Bible is used to vilify gay men and lesbians, Biblical texts and language must be addressed. If a rich and graceful poetics of intimacy is to be possible for gay men and lesbians, it will require a shift in Biblical/moral language about same gender sexual intimacy. The following is a summary of some of the ways that contemporary scholars have sought to accomplish such a shift. One approach includes a rejection of Biblical texts as sufficient for determining moral obligation; the other includes rereading texts in the light of historical critical insights, illustrating the inconclusiveness of their relevance in condemning same gender sexual intimacy.

Patricia Beattie Jung and Ralph F. Smith make a strong argument for the importance of seeking wisdom about Christian teaching on heterosexism and homosexuality outside the Bible.[23] They cite four principle problems with using the Bible as the sole moral authority. In some cases, the Bible is silent about contemporary moral problems. In other cases, the Bible's texts are "suspicious" or even "mistaken." By this they mean that they make statements that are so out of line with common Christian belief that we could not take them literally. They have in mind certain passages that encourage revenge or hate. Some texts are not applicable to contemporary situations, largely because of changed social practices. And most importantly, there are moral positions taken in the Bible which seem to be diverse and/or contradictory.[24]

They highlight three traditional Bible-oriented attempts to solve these problems. One approach is to assume that the Bible does have substantive integrity, notwithstanding apparent contradictions. To do this, one would have to gloss over contradictions. Another is to assume the Bible has a formal integrity. In other words, certain formal structures of interpretation and organization are held to unify and integrate Biblical teaching. Another related strategy is to seek a canon within the canon, a set of interpretive principles that is privileged within the Bible.[25] None of these, according to Jung and Smith, prove ultimately satisfactory. Thus, we must, according to them, reframe the question of Biblical authority. It is only by seeking wisdom in sources outside the Bible that we can hope to understand and interpret the wisdom in the Bible.

> Such external sources include all that might be grouped under the broad categories of experience and reason, including historical, literary, and scientific accounts both normative and descriptive of the human. These other sources of moral wisdom are in themselves never the final arbiter of what constitutes authority for Christians. Instead, listening to their voices enables the faithful to hear Scripture anew and to test their interpretive traditions in light of that fresh Word. These nontraditional sources of wisdom do not replace or usurp the authority of Scripture. They are conversation partners that open our hearts to God's Word, inviting either the affirmation or reformation of our tradition.[26]

Of course, within the Roman Catholic tradition, the appeal to reason as a source of moral authority has more formal and long-standing examples. Paradoxically, however, the Roman Catholic Church has tended to place more emphasis on the so-called "magisterium," the teaching authority of the Church itself (notably located within hierarchical structures).

Victor Furnish, a Methodist Biblical scholar, offers another set of helpful insights. He notes that the Bible never claims that God's word is strictly identified with the words of Scripture.[27] Moreover, "the subject matter of the Bible is the history of salvation," not some deposited set of revealed teachings. What is revealed is an event, a process, a relationship.[28] The authority of the Bible, for Furnish, derives from its historical, not superhistorical, character. This means that the Bible only makes sense in the actual historical context of God's self-disclosure and its graceful reception in an historical community. The event of salvation requires the active cultivation of a faith community within which the "searching out of God's will" takes place as a reasoned interpretive process.[29] This would not occur if the Bible were taken as literally and superhistorically authoritative as such!

So, how does the contemporary faith community make sense of a new situation? We are confronted with scientific evidence about sexual orientation which suggests that it is diverse. We are confronted with sociological evidence that gay men and lesbians are capable of achieving the same levels of personal, relational, parental, and professional integrity and excellence as heterosexuals. It is intellectually dishonest to continue to vilify homosexual persons. It makes no sense to continue to condemn homosexual activity. So how do we reconcile this with our Biblical heritage? As Pope John Paul II suggested, citing Augustine, when there is an apparent contradiction between clear and certain reason and the teaching of Scripture, interpreters of Scripture must find new ways of understanding the meaning of the texts in compatibility with the findings of reason![30] Thus shall we proceed!

There are several passages in the Bible that have been traditionally used to condemn homosexual activity. But as Furnish notes, there is no concept in the Bible that refers to "homosexuality" as a condition or orientation. "It was universally presupposed that everyone was "heterosexual," in the sense of being inherently ("naturally") constituted for physical union with the opposite sex."[31] This is very significant. It raises serious questions about what these authors really condemned and how they might respond to the information at hand today!

Genesis 19:1-25: Lot offers hospitality to two travelers (who are angels in disguise). The men of the town of Sodom attempt to rape them. Lot, fearing a compromise of his duties as one who offers hospitality, attempts to thwart the violence by offering his virgin daughters to the crowd. God destroys Sodom for its wickedness, but the wickedness does not consist in consensual gay sexual intimacy but same gender sexual violence and, most importantly, inhospitality! References to Sodom in other Biblical passages confirm the absence of concern about consensual gay sexual intimacy. "This was the guilt of your sister Sodom: she and her daughters had pride, excess of food, and prosperous ease, but did not aid the poor and needy." (Ezekiel 16:49) Jude's reference to the unnatural vice of Sodom, as both Furnish and the commentator in *The Personal Study Edition* of the New American Bible mention, refers literally to "went after alien flesh." The passage condemns the violation of hospitality rules and sexual violence toward angels.[32]

It is unfortunate that the term "sodomy" and "sodomite" were applied to anal sex (and sometimes to other forms of same gender sex) and/or to gay men. Mark Johnson's recent book argues that the misapplication of this term to the story of Sodom is a Christian contrivance.[33] Johnson's analysis illustrates how the consolidation of all homoerotic desire and affection under one concept, "sodomy," reflects a cultural effort to identify and then circumscribe a phenomenon. Reducing homoeroticism to a defined entity, particularly one which is evil, impoverishes its poetic richness. Consequently, in such a cultural context, any positive affirmation of one's sexual desire for persons of the same gender renders one a "sodomite" and, hence, a seriously flawed individual.

Leviticus 18:22 and 20:13: Leviticus 18 states: "You shall not lie with a male as with a woman; such a thing is an abomination." And Leviticus 20 states: "If a man lies with a male as with a woman, both of them shall be put to death for their abominable deed." Several points are worthy of note. These are the only statements that explicitly condemn same gender sex within the entire Torah. The subject is not given extensive attention. There is no mention of women having sex with women in the entire Torah. The penalty of death is associated with other sins as well: cursing one's father or mother (Lev. 20:9), adultery (Lev. 20:10), incest, marrying your wife's mother (Lev. 20:14), and if a man has sex with his menstruating wife, they are to be cut off from their people (Lev. 20:18).

Several commentators show that these passages are part of an overall code of "purity." Furnish puts it best:

> To be "pure" meant to be an unblemished specimen of one's kind, whole in oneself and unmixed with any other kind (which would be

pollution). Within this context, "defilement" does not mean moral defilement, but pollution in a literal, physical sense. This is why, according to the Holiness Code, animals must not be allowed to "breed with a different kind," a field must not be sown "with two kinds of seed," and one must not wear any clothing "made of two different materials." (Lev. 19:19). Similarly, a male must not have sex with another male, since that would mean—as the Hebrew text literally says—that one of the partners must "lie the lyings of a woman." Because his maleness is thereby violated, he is no longer an unblemished specimen of his kind.[34]

The term "toevah" (translated abomination) is a purity term, not a moral one. Boswell notes a distinction between something that is "intrinsically wrong" and something "ritualistically impure."[35] Proscriptions of homosexual behavior are associated with the latter category. And Boswell notes that, since early Christians increasingly rejected the ritual purity orientation of the Torah, the Levitical text was not usually cited as grounds for Christian moral condemnation of homosexuality.[36]

Fundamentalist Christians will usually concur that the Jewish Torah is not binding for Christians who have been liberated from the Law by Jesus. But they will cite passages from Pauline writings which they claim are a Christian condemnation of homosexuality. The most frequently cited passages are: I Corinthians 6:9, I Timothy 1:10 and Romans 1:26-27.

I Corinthians 6:9 and I Timothy 1:10: Most commentators address the Corinthian and Timothian texts as a problem of terminology. I Timothy states:

> We know that the law is good, provided that one uses it as law, with the understanding that law is meant not for a righteous person but for the lawless and unruly, the godless and sinful, the unholy and profane, those who kill their fathers and mothers, murderers, the unchaste, sodomites, kidnapers, liars, perjurers, and whatever else is opposed to sound teaching... (I Tim. 1:8-10) (New American Bible version)

I Corinthians reads:

> Do you not know that the unjust will not inherit the kingdom of God? Do not be deceived; neither fornicators nor idolaters nor adulterers nor

boy prostitutes nor sodomites nor thieves nor the greedy nor drunkards nor slanderers nor robbers will inherit the kingdom of God. (I Cor. 6:9-10) (New American Bible version)

The texts reiterate common Greco-Roman lists of moral evils. There is nothing uniquely "Christian" about these lists. They assume basic communal values about what is right and wrong. But, more problematic is that of understanding to what is referred by the terms. The first term in I Corinthians is "malakos" meaning "soft" or "effeminate." It can, according to Boswell, refer to someone who is "licentious" or "loose" or "wanting in self-control"[37] since these were unmanly (womanish) characteristics. Translating it with the word "sodomite" is simply erroneous since it unduly associates it with homosexuality (which the term does not, in fact, do) and since the term "sodomy" is a misapplication of the point of the story in Genesis.

The other term used in I Corinthians and in I Timothy, "arsenokoitai" is a combination of two words meaning something like men who lie with men. Furnish notes that it is difficult to understand how Paul is using this term. It could mean pederasty, male prostitution or consensual loving same gender sexual relationships.[38] Boswell suggests that its most common meaning and use was to refer to male prostitution.[39] This being the case, the passage cannot be conclusively used to condemn consensual, loving and committed sexual intimacy between two gay men or two lesbian women. We simply do not know to what Paul is referring; the passage is too ambiguous.

Romans 1:18-31: A more serious ethical challenge arises in Paul's let-ter to the Romans. Since the context of this passage is critical, I will cite it more extensively here. It reads:

The wrath of God is indeed being revealed from heaven against every impiety and wickedness of those who suppress the truth by their wickedness. For what can be known about God is evident to them, because God made it evident to them. Ever since the creation of the world, his invisible attributes of eternal power and divinity have been able to be understood and perceived in what he has made. As a result, they have no excuse; for although they knew God they did not accord him glory as God or give him thanks. Instead, they became vain in their reasoning, and their senseless minds were darkened. While claiming to be wise, they became fools and exchanged the glory of the immortal

God for the likeness of an image of mortal man or of birds or of four-legged animals or of snakes. Therefore, God handed them over to impurity through the lusts of their hearts for the mutual degradation of their bodies. They exchanged the truth of God for a lie and revered and worshipped the creature rather than the creator, who is blessed forever. Amen. Therefore, God handed them over to degrading passions. Their females exchanged natural relations for unnatural, and the males likewise gave up natural relations with females and burned with lust for one another. Males did shameful things with males and thus received in their own persons the due penalty for their perversity. And since they did not see fit to acknowledge God, God handed them over to their undiscerning mind to do what is improper. They are filled with every form of wickedness, evil, greed, and malice; full of envy, murder, rivalry, treachery, and spite. They are gossips and scandalmongers and they hate God. They are insolent, haughty, boastful, ingenious in their wickedness, and rebellious toward their parents. They are senseless, faithless, heartless, ruthless. (Romans 1:18-31) (New American Bible version)

Paul obviously considers the sinfulness of those who are not Christians to be inexcusable. Awareness of right and wrong is not the privilege of a sectarian revelation. God's being and will are manifest in creation at large. Thus, we are not dealing here with a morality that is unique to Christianity. Paul assumes all human beings are held accountable to this moral standard.

Paul shares other Greco-Roman philosophical assumptions about how sin is a symptom of perverted reason. In this case, failure to worship the true God causes a perversion of reason, weakening one's ability to perceive what is right and wrong. Without a proper moral orientation (direction to the true God and/or the supreme Good), one's desires are likely to become perverted or disoriented. Paul obviously considers same gender sexual desire to be a perversion.

Furnish notes that Paul's assumptions are understood against other common Greco-Roman beliefs about homosexual practice. First, homosexuality was considered a matter of choice. Thus, Paul could not have anticipated contemporary psychological, biological and sociological evidence about predisposition to homosexual orientation. Second, there was little evidence of cultural confidence in enduring committed homosexual relationships. They were assumed to be passing lustful relationships. Third, same gender sexual relationships violated an assumed sexual order, namely the normal procreative orientation of sex and the superiority of males over women (undermined by men becoming passive to other men or women becoming active toward other women).[40]

Most importantly, Paul's passage suggests that a constellation of practices ensues from impiety. According to Jung and Smith, the entire passage is a condemnation of idolatry. Disordered sexual desire is a consequence of idolatry, not the cause of it.[41] The perversion of reason that leads to degrading sexual passion also leads to malice, greed, envy, and murder (as well as other vices). Gay men and lesbians are not any more prone to these activities than are heterosexuals. Current sociological profiles of homosexual persons must lead us to a new assessment of Paul's description.

For Jung and Smith, this passage raises the problem of how sexual desire in general has been disordered by sin. Sexual passion is a blessing of creation, but it has been disordered by sin. But the disordering of sexual desire is not a matter of disordering orientation. "Concupiscence is a reality for both homosexual and heterosexual people."[42] There are many Christians, however, who believe that God created a sexual order and that that order is heterosexual. They argue that homosexuality is not only a matter of concupiscence but also a matter of a perversion of an original heterosexual order. Let's examine the assumed Biblical grounds for that order, the stories of creation in Genesis.

Genesis 1:26-28 and Genesis 2:18 and 21-24: There   are   two stories of creation in the first book of the Torah, Genesis. The first reads:

> "Then God said, 'Let us make man in our own image, after our likeness. Let them have dominion over the fish of the sea, the birds of the air, and the cattle, and over all the wild animals and all the creatures that crawl on the ground.' God created man in his image; in the divine image he created him; male and female he created them. God blessed them, saying, 'Be fertile and multiply; fill the earth and subdue it...' (Genesis 1:26-28) (New American Bible version)

The second reads:

> Then the Lord God said, 'It is not good for the man to be alone. I will make a suitable partner for him.' ... So the Lord God cast a deep sleep on the man, and while he was asleep, he took out one of his ribs and closed up its place with flesh. The Lord God then built up into a woman

the rib that he had taken from the man. When he brought her to the man, the man said: 'This one, at last, is bone of my bones and flesh of my flesh;' …That is why a man leaves his father and mother and clings to his wife, and the two of them become one body. (Genesis 2:18 and 21-24) (New American Bible version)

With respect to the first account, many interpreters of Scripture argue that God intended to create a heterosexual order, male and female sexual complementarity. Since the passage refers to God's creation of human beings in God's image, some conclude that homosexuality violates the inherently heterosexual character of God. But, if taken literally, this would mean that God must be quite different than we imagine God to be!

Furnish argues that the context of this passage is extremely important for understanding its meaning. This passage is an explanation of why things "are" as they are, not an explanation of what or how they "ought" to be. He states: ". . . in this account the Priestly writers are intent on explaining why species and kinds are properly kept separated (the basis of the Priestly system of ritual purity—because they were created separate; and in particular why the sabbath day is special—because on the seventh day God had rested)."[43]

The creation of human beings in God's image is meant to emphasize the distinctiveness of human beings with respect to the rest of creation. Nothing in this passage suggests "how" humankind is the image of God. But Furnish notes that sexual differentiation and reproduction are precisely how humankind is like the rest of creation. And he notes, of all religions in the Ancient Near East, only Israel's God was regarded as "asexual."[44]

Similarly, with respect to the second account, Furnish notes that the passage is an explanation of why marriage bonds are as they are (the shifting of kinship in marriage), not a treatise on the normativeness of heterosexuality. In a sense, the passage doesn't command hetero-sexuality, it merely explains it.[45]

More importantly, the second passage begins with the idea that "it is not good for man to be alone." Sexual companionship appears to be one of the blessings of God's creation. Its absence, conversely, is an impoverishment. If this is the case, then Judaism and Christianity must be concerned about those who are not suited for heterosexual union. Prior to recent scientific research on sexual orientation, it was assumed that human beings were universally suited for heterosexual union. With new information at hand, we must find ways of understanding these texts that will enable gay men and lesbians to flourish as those who share in the blessings of sexual companionship.

In summary, the Bible does not unequivocally condemn homosexuality nor unequivocally command heterosexuality.

Reconsidering Natural Law Teachings

Official Roman Catholic concern about the morality of same gender sex takes a decidedly more natural law approach. Biblical passages are still cited, but, since Roman Catholic moral theology has always depended more heavily on a nonsectarian methodology, it cannot presume its moral teachings are universally valid unless they are confirmed by anthropological (sociology, psychology, biology, and philosophy) considerations.

It has become more difficult to appeal to the notion that same-gender sex is not procreative and, therefore, cannot be a morally integral act since the Church permits heterosexuals who are sterile to marry and have sex. But, the Roman Catholic Church still uses this argument. Its stronger natural law argument, though, has to do with the lack of "complementariness" in same gender sex.[46]

The argument goes something like this: human sexuality is essentially constituted by gender complementariness. Sexual differentiation (males and females) is part of the created natural order and is essentially oriented to procreation. Even when sex cannot be procreative (in instances of sterility or pregnancy or postmenopausal sex), gender complementariness remains part of the truth of the human body and human sexuality. Same gender sex compromises this ("nuptial") truth of the body. It attempts to seek sexual mutuality with an object that cannot provide it. Hence the sexual pleasure associated with such an exchange lacks purposefulness and becomes merely self-indulgent. Moreover, in same gender sex, since the object of sexual pleasure is one's own gender, sexual love becomes a love for the self, not an "other." Since love is the Christian vocation, and since (according to this line of thinking) same gender sex is merely self-indulgent, same gender sex is sinful, contrary to the individual's well-being.

This line of thinking, however, fails to acknowledge that gender complementariness is not the only complementariness upon which genuine mutuality is built. If so, then any person of the opposite sex would constitute a suitable sexual companion for marriage. But few reasonable people reasoning reasonably would find this a reasonable proposition. Mutuality is built upon "personal" complementariness. Certainly for heterosexuals, this complementariness includes gender differences. Even for those who are gay and lesbian, not just any person of the same gender is sexually attractive. The unique features of the other person are what draw us into relationships of mutuality. For heterosexuals, mutuality includes gender differentiation, but for homosexuals, mutuality is grounded in gender sameness. The Church's attempt to describe heterosexual gender differentiation as universal and essentially normative of human nature is not confirmed by contemporary psychological or biological studies.

If same gender sex is really merely self-indulgent, then it would be personally disintegrating for those who engage in it. But this is where sociological evidence challenges the bias of the Church. Long-term successful gay and lesbian relationships confound the natural law theory that they lack the complementariness that would ground authentic covenantal love! How is it possible for gay men or lesbians to live in relationships of committed covenantal sexual love for ten, fifteen, twenty and thirty years and continue to be generous creative and contributing members of their communities (as teachers, health care professionals, counselors, priests, and social workers) if their love is merely or even predominantly self-indulgent? The Roman Catholic Church's appeal to phenomenological observation (its appeal to human nature as such) is not confirmed by the evidence.

Sexual intimacy as an experience of the embodied yearning and practice of mutuality is one of the conditions that enables human flourishing. Sexual intercourse alone does not ground the mutuality within which this flourishing occurs. It requires emotional intimacy, a reciprocal and soulful self-sharing. Integration of embodied yearnings (sexual desire) and emotional intimacy is central to a rich and graceful sexual relationship.

For those whose sexual feelings are predominantly homoerotic, the possibility of establishing a flourishing, graceful, and poetically rich relationship of mutuality with a person of the opposite sex is seriously impeded. Since there is ample evidence that successful, graceful, loving, and poetically rich relationships between persons of the same gender occur, cultural attempts to discourage them limit the options of homosexual people to constitute satisfying and ennobling sexual relationships. And from all evidence, this limitation is experienced as a harm, as an impoverishment.

Now, if there were significantly grave cultural reasons for limiting sexual identity to heterosexual or heterosexual marital, one might be able to justify limitations for some out of concern for the whole. But the arguments for social well-being are not persuasive. These usually take the form of claiming that the affirmation of gay and lesbian sexual identity (including gay and lesbian committed relationships) is harmful to heterosexual marriage which is said to be the basis of social stability and well-being.

Such a fear is based on several false assumptions. These include the fear that adolescents will choose to become gay and lesbian rather than heterosexual, that gay and lesbian families make heterosexual ones less desirable or stable, and that children raised in gay and lesbian families lack the parenting influence of both genders. Behind these stated concerns is a deeper one. Western societies have been grounded in a heterosexual and patriarchal cultural paradigm. The meaning we give to sexuality, family, parenting, and social relationships have all been related to heterosexual and patriarchal systems of meaning. The affirmation of gay and lesbian identity destroys sexism (patriarchal bias) and heterosexism (heterosexual bias). Giving up this cultural center is difficult and scary because it forces us to step into a new paradigm, a new system of sexual meaning, one with which we have little familiarity.

From all evidence at hand, adolescents are not likely to choose to become homosexual any more than they choose to become heterosexual. Heterosexual families are not weakened by gay ones but directly and indirectly strengthened. Strategies and resources for mutuality and fidelity in gay relationships can be sources of strength for heterosexual couples, as many have recounted. Providing honorable ways for gay men and lesbians to form committed sexual relationships with people of the same gender reduces the number of heterosexual marriages weakened by the presence of a spouse who has predominantly homoerotic feelings. Children raised in gay families show no increased propensity for gender confusion, sexual identity confusion, or difficulty establishing and sustaining successful sexual relationships than those raised in conventional heterosexual ones.[47]

Society is not weakened by shedding sexism and heterosexism, but it does change, and the change can feel disorienting for those who were privileged by the previous paradigm. But disorientation and loss of privilege should not be equated with immorality or moral confusion.

Given these considerations, let us now explore some of the challenges that gay men and lesbians face in developing a rich poetic sexual identity.

A Unique Ethic for Gay Men and Lesbians?

Is there a distinctive sexual ethic for gay men and lesbians? If the hetero-sexual-reproductive-household-management-centered ethic of traditional Christianity is valid, then it would seem that gay men and lesbians would need a unique morality. If, however, a reformed Christian sexual morality is centered on a poetics of intimacy and covenantal love, this would seem applicable to heterosexuals and homosexuals alike. But this contrast and comparison is too facile. Even if both heterosexuals and homosexuals are called to a poetics of sexual intimacy, the conditions and context within which they author their sexual lives is quite different. While these conditions are probably culturally and historically con-tingent, not universal or essential, they are, nevertheless, real and require attention. I want to highlight some of the unique conditions and, hence, unique features of gay and lesbian sexual morality.

Coming Out. One of the first conditions within which gay men and lesbians must author their sexual lives is a heterosexist culture. Although attitudes are changing, prevalent cultural messages still impress upon young people the idea that heterosexuality is statistically and morally normative. Most children are raised in heterosexual families, read heterosexual stories in school, watch television with heterosexual scripts, and are inundated with advertising that assumes a heterosexually-centered culture. Those who participate in organized religion are often taught that homosexuality is a sin. And, when jokes are made at school or around the neighborhood about dykes and fags, there are few who challenge their appropriateness. Most young people are encouraged to date members of the opposite sex and, even as younger children, are playfully encouraged to assume heterosexual roles with their playmates and anticipate heterosexual dreams for the future. Gender specific behavior is expected in terms of play, dress, and school.

Heterosexist culture does not refer to the fact that heterosexuality is statistically normative, that the largest number of people in society are heterosexual. Nor does it refer to the fact that heterosexuality is good, that it is a blessing and should be celebrated as such. Heterosexism refers to the belief that the only normal way to live out one's life is heterosexually. Patricia Beattie Jung and Ralph Smith define heterosexism as "a reasoned system of bias regarding sexual orientation. It denotes prejudice in favor of heterosexual people and connotes prejudice against bisexual and, especially, homosexual people."[48] They go on to indicate that heterocentrism "lies at the heart of this system of prejudice. Heterocentrism leads to the conviction that heterosexuality is *the* normative form of human sexuality. It is the measure by which all other sexual orientations are judged. All sexual authority, value, and power are centered in heterosexuality."[49] It refers to efforts in society to block the affirmation and celebration of sexual diversity. And in this sense, it is inimical to the cultivation of a rich poetics of intimacy for gay men and lesbians. Heterosexism includes all of the ways that persons of different sexual orientation are discriminated against in the various in-stitutions and rituals of society.

One of the greatest ethical challenges for gay men and lesbians is to reverse internalized heterosexism. One of the most crippling things for any human being is lack of self-esteem. This undermines the ability to form healthy relationships and/or to be successful at work and in the community. Many gay men and lesbians have internalized negative cultural messages about their sexuality. They dislike, distrust, and are uneasy with themselves. Internalized heterosexism cripples young gay men and lesbians. They may find it more difficult to initiate healthy relationships. They may suffer from a lack of self-esteem, making it difficult to succeed in academic or professional pursuits. Sensing they don't fit in, many young gay people feel marginalized from peers and family. Depending on how deep the internalized self-hate is, this can lead to self-abusive behavior which may even include suicide. Gay teens are at much greater risk for suicide than their heterosexual peers.

The reversal of internalized heterosexism is largely a matter of "coming out." It is difficult to understand how important coming out is unless one has experienced the self-hate and fear associated with being a gay man or lesbian in a heterosexist culture. There are several steps in the "coming out" process. They typically include: identifying one's sexual feelings as different from cultural norms, identifying internalized negative cultural messages, identifying information that challenges those messages, a decision to accept and affirm one's sexual feelings as good, and a decision not to accept cultural shaming messages. The final step usually requires disclosing to one's family and friends and co-workers that one is gay or lesbian. The self-disclosure of oneself as a gay man or lesbian theoretically shouldn't be necessary except in a heterosexist culture. In a nonheterosexist culture, no one would make assumptions about what other people's sexual orientation is. But since we live in a heterosexist culture, the gay man or lesbian who doesn't disclose his/her orientation is usually assumed to be "straight."

The identification of one's sexual feelings as different from cultural norms is most difficult. A heterosexist culture tends to eclipse evidence of sexual diversity. This is one of the ways it enforces heterosexuality. Many young gay men or lesbians talk about how they felt isolated and alone, as if no one else felt the way they did. Gay isolation is changing to the extent that more and more gay men and lesbians are "out." Gay characters in various television, music and movie media help young gay people identify others like themselves. Gay men and lesbians who live their lives openly in various professions, neighborhoods, and churches help young gay men and lesbians identify their own feelings, putting a name and a face on it.

The dangers of coming out must be compared with the harms of remaining closeted. While it is clear that for some coming out will mean loss of employment, expulsion from home, threat to physical well-being, and social ostracization, the alternative involves an interior dissonance and self-aversion that is crippling. Failure to honestly affirm one's own sexual feelings involves an accompanying disassociation from other feelings and emotions, some of which are foundational for authentic and flourishing interpersonal relationships. Disassociation from one's feelings and emotions can also lead to obsessive-compulsive behavior where individuals have more and more difficulty making choices about how they will respond to given situations.

Remaining closeted also contributes to the perpetuation of unjust stereotypes about gay people and can even encourage or mislead others who may have romantic feelings for a closeted gay person.

There are aspects of the "coming out" process that may appear to undermine the cultivation of sexual virtue. One is the heavy emphasis in gay culture, particularly gay male culture, on the male body and its sexual and visual representation. Although heterosexual culture includes pornography and sexually explicit entertainment and escort services, gay culture includes this in a more pervasive manner.

In the so-called gay ghettos and commercial districts of large urban American centers, sexually explicit publications, videos, and entertainment are common. On the surface, this would appear to corrupt the development of sexual virtue. These expressions focus on superficial and singular dimensions of sexuality, not on a rich poetic and multi-layered sense of sexuality.

But other dynamics are at work, some of which may serve the development of the poetics of intimacy for gay men. Growing up in a heterosexist culture, gay boys and girls were taught to feel shame and alienation over their homoerotic feelings. Since in most other respects gay adolescents are similar to heterosexual ones, sexual attraction becomes a distinguishing feature of gay male identity. Homoerotic feelings are what make gay men or lesbians different from others. But if these are a source of shame and alienation, the only way they can make peace with them and reverse internalized heterosexism is to reclaim the sacredness and goodness of their homoerotic feelings. I believe much of the fascination and compulsion around homoerotic literature, pictures, videos and entertainment is the need for gay men and women to make peace with that part of themselves that has been the source of shame and self-hate. They need to feel joy and delight and pleasure while looking at people of the same gender. They need to feel okay about images of gay sex. They need to reverse the revulsion they have been taught to feel toward these images, since imagination is an important part of one's ability to make moral decisions and to author one's life.

But since gay men and women have been taught to distrust their homoerotic feelings and not integrate them with their desire for companionship and the sharing of intimacy, the process of making peace with the more sexually explicit aspect of their sexual identity can become addictive. In other words, gay men and women bring with them a tendency of disassociating sexual feelings from relational matters, a tendency they were encouraged to cultivate in a heterosexist society. But if they have developed a pattern of disassociating sexual feelings from relational issues, it is likely they will carry these forward even when they make peace with the sexual feelings. They begin to feel better about their physical attraction to each other but have already established a pattern of distancing sexual feelings from deeper relational abilities.

Thus, a particular poetics of intimacy for gay men and lesbians needs to be developed, one that takes seriously both the internalized shame for homoeroticism and the disassociation of those desires from relational needs. As a consequence, resistance to intimacy may be more common in gay men and lesbians. This is not an intrinsic feature of gay sexuality. It is, rather, a symptom of deeply alienating biases in a heterosexist culture.

Dating/Meeting Other Gay People. One of the unfortunate stereotypes about gay people is that they engage in clandestine anonymous sexual encounters in dangerous places. Many large cities have notorious "cruising areas" where (usually) men meet for sex. Clandestine anonymous sex is not idiosyncratic to gay men, but it may have been more pervasive than in the heterosexual population. Clandestine anonymous sex is more a symptom of heterosexism than an inherent characteristic of homosexuality. Since heterosexist culture has shamed gay men and lesbians from openly pursuing romantic attachments in otherwise public/social institutions, sexual encounters had to be sought in hidden ways. Since openly gay and lesbian relationships were not affirmed, few gay men or lesbians could risk developing an ongoing stable relationship. "Someone might begin to wonder about them if a certain person was always around." All of this may undermine the acquisition of abilities to form sustainable interpersonal intimacy.

Much of the impetus for clandestine and anonymous sex came from repressive laws which criminalized same gender sex and permitted employers, landlords, and social service agencies to discriminate based on sexual orientation. There are still laws in many states that make sexual intimacy between two men or two women a crime. It is still legal to evict tenants based on sexual orientation in many states. There are only a few states which prohibit discrimination in employment. Nevertheless, the social and political landscape for gay men and lesbians has changed considerably. Many large American cities boast openly gay and lesbian elected officials, city and state commissioners, and antidiscrimination ordinances. Several hundred large American corporations have instituted domestic partnership benefits for gay and lesbian employees. Hence, the need to hide one's orientation, to pursue sexual relationships in secret or in anonymous encounters is diminishing.

A recent flurry of articles in gay publications notes a shift in social practices of gay men and lesbians. The prevalence and popularity of bathhouse encounters, circuit parties with heavy drug and alcohol consumption, and anonymous sex are waning as gay men and lesbians take themselves more seriously, as their heterosexual peers affirm them and their relationships, and as they come to understand the self-destructiveness of this behavior. These forms of behavior are beginning to be noted for what they really were, symptoms of personal and social alienation, not some inherent characteristic of a so-called "gay spirit." Douglas Sadownick puts it thusly:

> These authors raise a hue and cry against the many gay men who unknowingly collude with a venal, technocratic system that exploits our emptiness and pain so that we readily buy into industries that promote booze, quick sex and physical beauty. The acquisition of muscles, fame, money, and sex acts becomes the goal, distracting from the goal of becoming a genuine individual by facing one's genuine feelings— especially the negative ones.[50]

If gay men and lesbians are at risk of internalizing self-hate and pursuing practices that are not healthy, then they must root out those false internalized images and forge a new ethic.

How does this relate to the ethics of dating? Dating is a crucial process of developing the capacity for commitments to sexual covenantal mutuality. Dating is where the poetics of intimacy is learned and perfected. It is where narratives of interpersonal intimacy are initiated, the grounds upon which more formal commitments to lifelong covenantal mutuality are made.

The same kinds of ethical imperatives are present in gay and lesbian dating as in heterosexual dating. But as noted earlier, the context is different. For adolescents and young adults in high school who live at home, gay dating always carries with it the risk of peer and parental rejection. If educational, ecclesial and parental institutions want to push teens into dangerous superficial clandestine anonymous sex, they should continue the harsh rhetoric against homosexuality. This, of course, will lead to increased risk of teen suicide and transmission of HIV and other sexually transmitted diseases, not to mention risks of sexual violence. The higher than average risk of suicide among gay teens has been documented in several studies. A recent study in Canada suggests that sexual abstinence adds to that risk. Comparing young men ages eighteen to twenty-seven, 2.8 percent of active heterosexuals attempted suicide or deliberate self-harm compared to 9.4 percent of active homosexuals. But 17.7 percent of heterosexuals and 46.1 percent of homosexuals who were sexually abstinent attempted suicide or deliberate self-harm.[51] The shaming mechanisms that sever young people from the sources of intimacy and healthy psychosexual development and identity formation are harmful. This is an important instance of how the Church's teaching that the only moral option for gay people is that they spend the rest of their lives as celibates is unjust and inhumane.

A gay man or lesbian must learn to affirm and love himself/herself enough not to become inappropriately vulnerable in dating situations.[52] Too many gay people internalize negative messages about themselves and believe they do not deserve respect, love, or happiness. Vulnerability is an important condition for intimacy and mutuality, but it must be appropriate vulnerability. Casual and anonymous sexual encounters carry with them increased physical dangers.

Sexual intimacy is wonderful, but if it is not accompanied by opportunities for emotional intimacy it risks becoming disassociative and addictive. Since heterosexist culture fosters a disassociation of gay people's exterior selves from their interior selves, gay men and lesbians are at greater risk for disassociative behavior. Gay men and lesbians must learn to recognize that the seductiveness of physical recreational sex is in part accentuated by internalized heterosexism and is not necessarily in their best interests!

For some men and women who find themselves caught in a cycle of superficial recreational sex, only counseling can help them recognize and reverse internal aversions to intimacy. As with heterosexuals, sometimes these aversions stem from traumatic sexual or physical abuse as children.

A poetics of sexual intimacy should include the discipline of joining the emotional self with physical sexual urges. This may mean that sexual intimacy is best delayed until one has had time to develop a deeper emotional narrative with a prospective sexual partner. This should not be construed to suggest that sexual intimacy is wrong when it is not preceded by emotional intimacy, but simply that it is riskier.

Commitment and "Marriage." Gay men and lesbians have begun efforts in Europe, North America and other select nations to gain the right to legally validate their relationships as do heterosexual couples. These efforts have provoked a cultural war of unprecedented intensity. Some gay activists have argued that the effort to gain parity with heterosexuals in the institution of marriage only makes efforts to gain other more basic civil rights more difficult. In many political jurisdictions throughout the world, same gender sex is still a crime and gay men and lesbians have no protection from job, housing and social service discrimination based on sexual orientation. The effort to push "gay marriage" only exacerbates an already reluctant heterosexist culture to "dig in its heals."

Andrew Sullivan notes that the institution of marriage has always been of supreme symbolic importance. "It is the institution where public citizenship most dramatically intersects with private self-definition. It is where people have historically drawn the line."[53] Just as with the legalization of interracial marriages in the United States in 1968, when seventy-two percent of Americans disapproved of it and now only thirty percent disapprove, so too with the idea of gay marriage. Sullivan notes that eighty-four percent of Americans favor protecting homosexuals from discrimination in employment, eighty percent support protection in housing, sixty-one percent favor inheritance rights for gay spouses, and forty-eight percent favor social security benefits. But fifty-eight percent disapprove of same-sex marriage.[54] Sullivan states:

> . . . Americans rightly intuit, as they intuited with interracial marriage, that granting homosexuals entrance into this institution is tantamount to complete acceptance of homosexuality by American society. No other measure would signal approval in such a stark and unambiguous way. And many heterosexual Americans are not yet ready to go quite that far. They are prepared to tolerate, yes, even, in some ways, approve. But they are not yet ready to say that their heterosexual relationships are equivalent to homosexual ones; that their loves and gay loves are worth the same respect. [55]

Denmark and Sweden have given gay men and lesbians the right to legal marriage. Many municipalities in Europe and in the United States have granted provisions for registration of domestic partnerships or civil unions (which include same gender couples). Nearly two hundred large American companies have begun giving the same benefits to same gender couples as to heterosexual ones. San Francisco requires that all companies who do business with the city not discriminate on the basis of sexual orientation. This includes the provision that same gender couples receive the same benefits as heterosexual ones. This forced an interesting showdown between the Roman Catholic Archdiocese of San Francisco, who receives over five million dollars in social services contracts (Catholic Charities), and the city. A compromise was reached whereby Catholic Charities would grant benefits (largely insurance ones) to a person of one's choice in one's household.

Sullivan's anthology illustrates the ambivalence that many feel over this issue. Some argue that marriage is so rooted in patriarchal and heterosexist ideology that it is inherently destructive of the humanity of those who enter into it. They argue that gay men and lesbians should avoid marriage. Sullivan is one of many who see marriage as a civilizing institution, one that helps give healthy shape and form to sexual instincts.

Sullivan identifies the fears many conservatives have about affirming same-sex marriages. He states:

> They mean by "a homosexual life" one in which emotional commitments are fleeting, promiscuous sex is common, disease is rampant, social ostracism is common, and standards of public decency, propriety, and self-restraint are flaunted. They mean a way of life that deliberately subverts gender norms in order to unsettle the virtues that make family life possible, ridicules heterosexual life, and commits itself to an ethic of hedonism, loneliness, and deceit.[56]

Sullivan argues that there are very few incentives in society for homosexuals to live virtuous lives. "… there's little social or familial support, no institution to encourage fidelity or monogamy, precious little religious or moral outreach to guide homosexuals into more virtuous living."[57] Sullivan believes that conservatives fear that removing social biases against homosexuals would unravel society as we know it. But, it is not at all clear why this is the case.

> Those homosexuals who have no choice at all to be homosexual, whom conservatives do not want to be in a heterosexual family in the first place, are clearly no threat to the heterosexual family. Why would accepting that such people exist, encouraging them to live virtuous lives, incorporating their difference into society as a whole necessarily devalue the traditional family? It is not a zero-sum game. Because they

have no choice but to be homosexual, they are not choosing that option over heterosexual marriage; and so they are not sending any social signals that heterosexual family life should be denigrated.[58]

The question of same-sex marriage is part of a larger ethical question: do sexual relationships, heterosexual or homosexual, flourish best in monogamous committed situations? Many early gay activists had argued that a distinctive feature of gay relationships was their freedom from having to ascribe to the idea that sexual relationships were monogamous, that sexuality involved exclusivity. But recent trends in the gay community suggest that many homosexual couples value commitment and monogamy. If "open relationships" are typical of gay sexuality, why is this not being borne out statistically?

Is monogamy primarily related to property and parenting issues typically associated with traditional forms of heterosexuality, or is it one of the forms within which sexual intimacy flourishes best? This is an interesting historical question. In many respects, heterosexual marriage had flourished as a property and reproductive institution, with romantic affection being incidental. It is only recently that heterosexual marriage has actually been constituted around notions of romance and affection. As noted earlier, this makes the institution more vulnerable to dissolution. It is more difficult to sustain an institution centered around emotional expectations.

The fragility and vulnerability of sexually and emotionally intimate relationships may actually be an indicator of their value. When two people become emotionally intimate, they invariably surface deeper interpersonal psychological issues that long for healing and resolution. In relationships that center around more superficial or socially prescribed activities and forms, these deeper psychological issues don't necessarily surface.

The struggle associated with emotionally intimate relationships requires a commitment to exclusivity as the context or condition within which these interpersonal issues will be worked out. There is too much temptation to avoid them by seeking physical and emotional intimacy in situations that appear safer and less conflictual. Of course, ultimately they are not, but they appear so and need to be exposed for the illusion they are. An "open" sexual relationship is not "free" from the repressiveness of heterosexual marriage. Yes, historically, heterosexual marriage treated women as sexual property. But the form of heterosexual marriage is changing. Commitment in heterosexual marriage is ideally a commitment around sexual covenantal mutuality. Far from being repressive, it is a relationship that provides the opportunity to learn to love and be loved with greater integrity and trust.

Jung and Smith identify a number of characteristics around which same-sex relationships flourish. They are indebted to Margaret Farley's groundbreaking article, "An Ethic for Same-Sex Relations."[59] They highlight the importance of fidelity. They state:

> We believe that a mutual promise of lifelong commitment remains morally important for sexual relation—whether gay, lesbian, bisexual, or straight. Why? Because all human beings must *learn* how to love each other. Such schooling takes time, effort, and patience. The mutual promise and gift of fidelity—of a love that will be steadfast and enduring—bears witness to the patient healing Presence of God in our lives. ... Fidelity remains important because it facilitates love. Our efforts at loving require commitment because, although made for love, we are not born great lovers. We must learn how to love those whom we wake up next to and sometimes feel stuck with. Great loves do not hinge on the maintenance of romantic illusions. Instead they become increasingly intimate and truthful. This is true for all great loves—whether gay or straight. Such loving takes our full attention.[60]

Jung and Smith's observations, however, may mask another issue that is highlighted in Carter Heyward's ethic of sexual relationships.

For Heyward eros, as embodied yearning for mutuality, is one of our most intense experiences of God as the ground or matrix of our interrelatedness.[61] Heyward raises concerns about how eros is suppressed in contemporary social life, thus eclipsing our capacity to form various kinds of relationships of justice and mutuality. Heyward wants to encourage a sexual ethic that cultivates our connectiveness in erotic energy. Sexual exclusivity could be understood as a way of suppressing this erotic energy, thus cutting us off from the source of our capacity to move toward one another with greater justice and mutuality. The issue here is not one of either/or. Heyward envisions a way of understanding sexual relationships that are both committed (faithful) and open to other relationships which are grounded in erotic energy.[62]

Heyward admits that, for most people, the best way to honor sexually intimate relationships is with sexual fidelity, meaning not engaging in genital sexual intimacy with others.[63] But this does not exclude the possibility of friendships that include erotic energy and/or physical affection of some sort. A generation or two ago, few married couples would have entertained the idea of opposite sex friendships that complemented their primary relationship. Today, this is more common particularly as heterosexuals work in sexually integrated work places. And within the gay and lesbian community, friendships typically include persons of the same gender which often include various levels of sexual energy.

Gay and lesbian relationships may actually be in a position to model a new type of sexual fidelity for society as a whole. Not primarily grounded in property or reproductive responsibilities, they must develop and sustain commitments based on mutuality and covenantal love. Often this is done without supportive institutions. Long-term same-sex relationships may be a resource of immense proportion for understanding the dynamics of flourishing and enriching sexual intimacy. Unlike heterosexual counterparts which may have sustained commitments around parenting and/or household management, homosexual couples have sustained themselves around other values. At a time when heterosexual marriages seem threatened and more unstable precisely because the former values around which they were sustained cease to be compelling, they may look to homosexual couples for wisdom and insight!

This realization is what drives the move to recognize and celebrate same-sex marriages or unions at civil and ecclesial levels. Many heterosexuals now know same-sex couples in their families, at work and in their churches. These same-sex couples embody many of the ideals of covenantal love. The failure to recognize them as such is an injustice and prejudice that becomes increasingly obvious to those who know them. As noted by many authors, civil and ecclesial prejudice against same-sex couples only encourages the promiscuity and superficiality that conservatives bemoan about homosexual relationships. It is amazing that with so much bias in place same-sex relationships flourish as they do!

Since Christianity is centered around an ethic of covenantal love and justice, there is nothing that should restrict it from affirming and cele-brating same-sex unions or marriages. Some argue that marriage is by definition a heterosexual reproductive institution. If so, perhaps it is best to call same-sex relationships unions. But if the refusal to apply the term "marriage" to same-sex couples is in virtue of a prejudice about their inferiority, such a move is unacceptable. Same-sex covenantal mutuality is of the same quality and genuineness as heterosexual covenantal mutuality, and it should be celebrated as such.

> Beloved, let us love one another, because love is of God; everyone who loves is begotten by God and knows God. Whoever is without love does not know God, for God is love. . . God is love, and whoever remains in love remains in God and God in them. (1 John 4:7-8 and 16) (New American Bible version)

The unwillingness to celebrate and affirm evidence of covenantal mutuality in gay couples is in essence an unwillingness to celebrate God's grace and presence; it is a form of blasphemy in that it purports to speak for God while denying profound evidence of God's "decision" to grace gay and lesbian relationships with successful and empowering love!

Traditional Christian moral norms requiring sexual abstinence for gay men and lesbians cause harm in a number of ways. First, they increase the likelihood that gay men and lesbians will despair, risking increased incidence of suicide or compulsive anonymous sexual behavior that is physically and psychologically harmful. This is accentuated by the related bias against gay men and lesbians that ensues from such an ethic. Second, if certain individuals succeed in practicing lifelong sexual abstinence, they risk serious aversion to intimacy, which in turn risks making their relationships with family, friends, and associates unnecessarily superficial and cold. And third, sexual abstinence itself deprives gay men and lesbians of the enriching and maturing graces of sexual mutuality.

Only if there were other compelling dangers that prohibiting sexual intimacy for gays and lesbians might avert would such norms potentially be justifiable. The ones that are usually identified are fear that young people will be "recruited" or become sexually confused, fear that heterosexual marriage will be destroyed, and that children raised in gay and lesbian families will be impoverished or harmed. As noted in several sections of this book, none of these dangers are, in fact, real. In the absence of real and probable dangers, denying gay men and lesbians the grace of sexual intimacy is wrong and hurtful. It is not a witness to the love, compassion, and inclusivity of the gospel.

A Queer Poetics. Gay men and lesbians have fewer examples of flour-ishing poetic sexual relationships than heterosexuals. They are forced to be more imaginative about how to sustain and cultivate sexual intimacy in their lives. Many have taken the term "queer," traditionally a derogatory reference, and claimed it as an affirmation of the blessings that accompany poetic imagination in a heterosexist culture. Gay men and lesbians cannot simply adopt socially sanctioned forms of sexual intimacy; they must create new cultural forms. Thus, they may appear "queer" or different.

Two men sitting together at a romantic dinner table, two women celebrating their union with fellow congregants at a local parish, two men pushing a baby stroller through an urban park, or two women attending a parent/teacher conference for their mutual son are "queer" images in a heterosexist environment. They will appear increasingly less "queer" as culture changes. Contemporary gay men and lesbians are in the process of inventing new traditions and transforming old ones in order to sustain their love and their families.

Christian sexual morality, if it is to nurture poetic intimacy for all, must be willing to be imaginative with gay men and lesbians. Such a process would reflect the deep historical roots of Christianity's own queerness as a new religious tradition in the Jewish, Greek and Roman world. Jesus' prophetic character stemmed, in part, from his ability to help others imagine new ways of being in relationship with one another, ways that transcended many of the artificial boundaries of ritualistic purity, xenophobia, and addiction to self-mastery.

Contemporary gay men and lesbians must come to appreciate that they live in a poetically innovative time. With that comes a responsibility to give expression to the poetic voice within. Prophetic creativity always comes with a price. Those who feel secure in the established expressions of society and church will often look upon the contemporary prophet/poet as either deranged or dangerous. It is difficult to sustain poetic imagination and poetic intimacy when the prophets are being attacked as deviant, as threats to social and ecclesial well-being. But if one can keep things in perspective, courage and imagination are possible. Resources are being developed to nurture and sustain such a prophetic imagination both within the more well-defined gay and lesbian community and in institutions which, heretofore, had been heterosexist such as businesses, political entities, and religious institutions.

Gay men and lesbians have the same need for sexual companionship as heterosexuals. Gay men and lesbians, when free from social prejudice and discrimination, are able to achieve the same degree of well-being and graceful sexual intimacy as heterosexuals. Gay and lesbian relationships are not any more inherently selfish than heterosexual ones nor do they threaten heterosexual marriage. Celebrating gay and lesbian commitments will not increase the overall statistical presence of homosexuality nor will their parenting children do so either.

Given the scientific and sociological data, the continued vilification of gay men and lesbians and their sexuality is simply irresponsible. It will be a sad historical commentary on Christianity if it is unable to imagine a model of sexual morality that is able to embrace, celebrate, and nurture love and mutuality between gay men and lesbians. A poetic approach to sexual virtue provides the resources and conceptual framework for doing so. It acknowledges a variety of ways that adults can constitute psychologically healthy sexual identities and it celebrates many forms of poetic love.

Notes

[1]   Andrew Sullivan, "Introduction," in *Same Sex Marriage: Pro and Con.* ed. Andrew Sullivan (New York: Vintage Books, 1997) p. xxii and xxiii

[2]   *The Sexuality Debate in North American Churches, 1988–1995: Controversies, Unresolved Issues, Future Prospects.* ed. John J. Carey (Lewiston: Edwin Mellon Press, 1995).

[3]   Vote taken during the 1997 National Convention in Philadelphia.

[4]   *Christianity, Social Tolerance and Homosexuality*, Univ. of Chicago Press, 1980 and *Same-Sex Unions in Premodern Europe*, Villard Books, 1994.

[5]   Ibid., *Same-Sex Unions*, p.55.

[6]   Boswell, *Same-Sex*, p. 59; Plato, *Symposium* 180A.

[7]   Boswell, *Same-Sex*, p. 60; Aristotle, *Politics* 2.96-7 (1247A).

[8]   Boswell, *Same-Sex*, pp. 65–74; cf. Plutarch, *Erotikos* 760B.

[9]   Boswell, *Christianity*, p. 62, footnote 4.

[10] Boswell, *Christianity*, pp. 54–55.

[11] Boswell, *Christianity*, p. 59.

[12] Boswell, *Christianity*, p. 86.

[13] Boswell, *Christianity*, p. 87.

[14] Boswell, *Christianity*, p. 171.

[15] Ibid., pp. 171–184.

[16] Ibid., pp. 177 and 210–213.

[17] Ibid., pp. 190–194 and 218–226.

[18] Ibid., pp. 269–302.

[19] Cited by Simon LeVay, *Queer Science: The Use and Abuse of Research Into Homosexuality* (Cambridge, Massachusetts: MIT Press, 1996) 12–13.

[20] Ibid., p.13.

[21] Cited by Vern L. Bullough, *Science in the Bedroom: A History of Sex Research* (New York: Basic Books, 1994) 267.

[22] LeVay, Op.cit., pp. 67–85.

[23] Patricia Beattie Jung and Ralph F. Smith, *Heterosexism: An Ethical Challenge* (New York: SUNY Press, 1993).

[24] Ibid., pp. 48–51.

[25] Ibid., pp. 51–54.

[26] Ibid., p.56.

[27] Victor Paul Furnish, "Homosexual Practices in Biblical Perspective," in *The Sexuality Debate in North American Churches*, ed. John J. Carey, Op. cit., p. 268. This article is an abridged version of one presented to The Committee to Study Homosexuality of the United Methodist Church, 1990, revised in 1991 and 1992.

[28] Ibid., p. 269.

[29] Ibid., pp. 269–272.

[30] Michael J. Hartwig, "Galileo, Gene Researchers and the Ethics of Homosexuality," in *Theology and Sexuality* 1:1 (Sept. 1994) pp106–111.

[31] Furnish, Op. cit., p. 254.

32 Furnish, Op. cit., p. 255 and *The Personal Study Edition of the New American Bible* (New York: Oxford Univ. Press, 1995) p. 397 of the New Testament Section, note 7.

33 Mark Johnson, *Sodomy* (Chicago: Univ. of Chicago Press: 1997).

34 Furnish, Op. cit., p. 256.

35 Boswell, *Christianity*, Op. cit., p. 101.

36 Ibid., pp. 104–105.

37 Ibid., p. 106.

38 Furnish, Op. cit. p. 267.

39 Boswell, *Christianity*, Op. cit., p. 107.

40 Furnish, Op. cit., pp. 262–263.

41 Jung and Smith, Op. cit. p. 80.

42 Jung and Smith, Op. cit., p. 81.

43 Furnish, Op. cit., pp. 257–258.

44 Ibid., p. 258.

45 Ibid., p. 259 (references to Gerhard von Rad, *Genesis: A commentary. Revised Edition* (Philadelphia: Westminster, 1972).

46 "Patoral Care of Homosexual Persons," 1986, Congregation for the Doctrine of the Faith, Vatican. Refer also to new guidelines issued by the U.S. National Conference of Catholic Bishops on Same-sex unions, 1997.

47 Bozett, Frederick W. *Gay and Lesbian Parents*. New York: Prager, 1987 and Hartwig, *Parenting*, Op. cit.

48 Jung and Smith, Op. cit., p. 13.

49 Ibid., p. 14.

50 Douglas Sadownik, "Outrageous Behavior," in *Frontiers*, June 13, 1997, pp. 37ff. He cites Gabriel Rotello, Michelangelo Signorile, Bill Mann, Larry Kramer, Walt Odets, Ian Young and Daniel Harris in this article.

51 "Suicide Watch," *The Advocate*, November 12, 1996, pp. 41ff, citing a Canadian study by Christopher Bagley and Pierre Tremblay, Faculty of Social Work, University of Calgary.

[52] Refer again to Karen Lebacqz's concept of appropriate vulnerability, Op.cit.

[53] Andrew Sullivan, "Introduction," in *Same-Sex Marriage: Pro and Con*. ed. A. Sullivan (New York: Vintage, 1997) p. xxi.

[54] Ibid., p. xxi and xxii. References to Gallup polls.

[55] Ibid., p. xxii.

[56] Andrew Sullivan, excerpt from *Virtually Normal: An Argument About Homosexuality*, 1995, cited in *Same-Sex Marriage: Pro and Con*, Op. cit., p. 148.

[57] Ibid., p. 149.

[58] Ibid., pp. 152–153.

[59] Margaret Farley, "An Ethic of Same Sex Relations," in *A Challenge to Love*. ed. Robert Nugent (New York: Crossroad Publishing, 1989).

[60] Jung and Smith, Op. cit., pp. 183–184.

[61] Heyward, Op. cit, p. 99.

[62] Ibid., pp. 119–155

[63] Ibid., 119–155.

❖ Chapter Eight

The Poetics of Intimacy for People With Mental and Developmental Disabilities

Traditional Attitudes and Contemporary Shifts

Traditional Christian sexual morality held that the only morally acceptable context for sexual intimacy was within heterosexual marriage and for reproductive purposes. People with mental illness and mental retardation were thought to lack the requisite personal resources to initiate and sustain marriage or to parent eventual offspring. Moreover, it was thought that mentally retarded and mentally ill parents would produce mentally retarded and mentally ill children. Thus, they were either strongly discouraged or strictly forbidden from engaging in sexual intimacy or marriage.

As the household-management-and-reproductively-centered model of marriage gives way to models centered around covenantal love and intimacy, as new evidence points to the importance of sexual intimacy for human flourishing whether within or without marriage, as our information about developmental disabilities ("developmental disabilities" is the preferred way to refer to what used to be called mental retardation) and mental illness change, and as effective contraceptives exist which permit sexual intimacy without risk of untimely or undesired pregnancy, the question of how we ought to think about the poetics of intimacy for people with developmental disabilities and mental illness presents new challenges and opportunities.

Myths about people with developmental disabilities and mental illness have been shattered by contemporary psychological and sociological studies. Efforts in psychosocial rehabilitation have enabled us to witness dramatic and impressive evidence of the ability of people with developmental disabilities and mental illness to assume more autonomy and responsibility for their lives. When free from infant-alizing or overly restrictive institutionalized environments, many grow to enjoy the richness of self-determination, work, relationships and community life.

Nevertheless, the topic of sexual intimacy for those with developmental disabilities and mental illness is still a sensitive and controversial one. It is rare to find the topic addressed openly or extensively in scholarly journals or in human service agencies. Parents, teachers and community leaders often express apprehension and anxiety about the sexual lives of those with mental illness or developmental disabilities.

I believe one of the reasons for such apprehension and reticence is that alternative models of sexual morality (other than the traditional heterosexual-marital-and-reproductively-centered one) are not well known, understood or applied. Although advocates for people with developmental disabilities and mental illness have pushed for respect of their right to make choices about sexual relationships, the public is still limited by a model of sexuality that is tied to marriage and reproduction. Since marriage and parenting often seem unrealistic, out of reach, or even harmful, and since many do not have well thought-out alternatives, sexuality is gingerly sidestepped, intentially downplayed, or aggressively discouraged. The belief that long-term or lifelong sexual abstinence is not harmful accompanies traditional attitudes about sexual morality, so we assume that if people with developmental disabilities or mental illness practice long-term or lifelong sexual abstinence, no harm is caused and many harms avoided.

Consistent with the thesis of this book, I would like to propose that sexuality be discussed within the context of a poetics of intimacy. I would like to explore the challenges and opportunities of thinking about a poetics of intimacy for people with developmental disabilities and mental illness. I would like to make a basic claim against which future considerations will be developed: people with developmental disabilities and people with mental illness often have similar needs for sexual intimacy as those individuals without disabilities or illnesses. Long-term or lifelong sexual abstinence will be experienced by many of these individuals to be burdensome and undermining of their emotional and physical well-being. Unless the risks or burdens associated with sexual intimacy in particular cases outweigh the risks and burdens of long-term and lifelong sexual abstinence, it should be presumed that sexual intimacy is a good and that individuals' efforts to initiate and sustain sexual relationships should be supported and enabled in accord with their wishes and desires.

Just as we consider autonomy, health, education, nutrition, housing and work integral to personal well-being for individuals with developmental disabilities and/or mental illness, we should develop a similar appreciation for the importance of interpersonal intimacy and sexual pleasure in their overall sense of well-being and personal growth. This is not a dispensable luxury or a superficial activity. Sexual intimacy is an integral facet of personal, physical and spiritual well-being. It is *prima facie* unjust and immoral for us to deprive people who have develop-mental disabilities or mental illness from opportunities to develop intimate relationships (including those that are sexually intimate). Even where there is potential risk or harm, we do not have a right to suppress people's right for making intimate choices. If the presence of potential risk or harm were sufficient reason alone to override someone's autonomy, we would have to override many otherwise competent adults' decisions about intimate relationships in order to be consistent. We don't override such decision because we believe that even when some choices include risks or harms, there is a certain amount of dignity (even well-being) associated with having the opportunity to be self-determining. Indeed, we grow through making mistakes and could never become responsible without having the chance to make decisions however risky or harmful they might be.

We must make a commitment to support people in the process of acquiring the abilities and virtues which will enable them to make well-informed decisions as well as initiate and sustain flourishing and graceful relationships. Only in situations where an individual is so disabled as to render him/her incompetent and/or unable to ever acquire the skills and virtues for navigating intimate relationships do we have a right (perhaps an obligation) to make substituted judgments. In situations where there is risk of catastrophic harm to self or others, overriding an autonomously made decision might be justified as well.

Definitions

Developmental disability. Defining developmental disability, formerly called mental retardation, is controversial. Previous paradigms focused on measuring intelligence and classifying degrees of mental retardation. Contemporary models focus more on identifying different types of adaptive behavior for which some individuals experience greater or lesser disability. The American Association on Mental Retardation defines mental retardation as:

> ... substantial limitations in present functioning. It is characterized by significantly subaverage intellectual functioning, existing concurrently with related limitations in two or more of the following applicable adaptive skill areas: communication, self-care, home living, social skills, community use, self-direction, health and safety, functional academics, leisure and work. Mental retardation manifests before age eighteen.[1]

Such a definition requires us to move beyond assessing mental retardation solely with reference to intelligence and identify multiple and overlapping areas of personal function and intelligences. It also challenges us to address the kinds of supports needed to help individuals achieve higher function.

For people with developmental disabilities, many adaptive skills can be learned and supported through special programs and interventions. Contemporary focus is on supporting adults with developmental disabilities to achieve the greatest degree of independence and socially adaptive skills possible. This includes a shift away from institutionalization and toward community living. Documented evidence of the success of psychosocial rehabilitation in enabling individuals to develop abilities and derive happiness and satisfaction from exercising them should spur us forward in becoming better at rehabilitation including the support of abilities for initiating and sustaining intimate relationships.

Mental illness. Mental illness refers to a broad range of diagnosed conditions which cause individuals to suffer mental and/or psychosocial disability. People who are diagnosed with mental illness includes those who suffer from depression, bi-polar disorder (formerly called manic depressive), disassociative disorders, addiction, schizophrenia and schizophrenic related symptoms, characterological disorders, borderline personality disorder, and other illnesses.

Mental illness often manifests itself during young adulthood. Sometimes mental illness arises out of psychological or physical trauma. It can also develop in association with physical pathologies or injuries.

Some mental illnesses are episodic; others chronic. Some symptoms are able to be controlled or managed through medication; others elude therapy. Some symptoms can be managed or reduced through psychoanalytic therapy; others require psychotropic medication.

Disabilities associated with mental illness fall along a continuum and can be exacerbated or reduced by native intelligence, personal resources, and external stressors or enablers.

The Poetics of Intimacy and Developmental Disabilities

Since mental retardation or developmental disability stems from childhood, many of the skills which would enable people to initiate and sustain intimate relationships have not been developed. To whatever extent individuals with developmental disabilities have been infantalized (treated as incapable of developing certain abilities), their lack of basic relationship skills will probably have been intensified.

Psychosocial rehabilitation science believes that many disabilities can be addressed and overcome with suitable education and rehabilitation. Theoretically, this includes disabilities/abilities for intimate relationships.

Some individuals are mildly or moderately disabled; others severely. Psychosocial rehabilitation science recognizes variations in an individual's ability to acquire certain abilities. Nevertheless, recognizing limits does not justify a *carte blanche* dismissal of the right people have to be self-determining to the extent possible.

One's human dignity includes the right to opportunities for self-determination, for the exercise of autonomy. Earlier models of care for people with developmental disabilities emphasized paternalism and beneficence at the expense of autonomy. This invariably eclipsed the sense of well-being that accompanies opportunities for self-determination, it led to the imposition of unnecessary restrictions on freedom of movement and expression, to the proliferation of institutions where many individuals suffered physical and sexual abuse, and to a gross underdevelopment of many potentialities.

At the federal, state and local levels, reforms have been instituted. The model of psychosocial rehabilitation, which emphasizes the effort to support individuals in the development and acquisition of latent abilities, has been coupled with legislation which requires that people with developmental disabilities live in the least restrictive environment possible. The moral emphasis has shifted from a beneficent/paternalistic one to one where respect for autonomy has primary weight.

This has important ramifications for the sexual lives of people with developmental disabilities. Rather than focusing on the prevention of risks and harms, the new approach requires us to find ways to enable individuals to develop the abilities with which they could initiate and sustain sexually intimate relationships that are psychologically and physically healthy. Let's consider a few examples.

John is a moderately functioning twenty-year old individual with developmental disabilities. He has a job at a local supermarket and participates in a day support program in a large city. He lives with his parents. John has become fond of Sally, also a moderately functioning twenty-two year old person with developmental disabilities. At social events sponsored by the day program, they tend to hang out together.

John begins to express interest in visiting Sally at the group home where she lives. John's parents are initially supportive until they find out that John and Sally spend time alone in Sally's room. They are afraid that John does not know how to manage an intimate relationship, and they are afraid that either John will hurt Sally, that Sally's parents will sue them over John's possible indiscretions, or that John will be emotionally hurt when the relationship ends.

It is possible that John lacks some of the requisite skills to carry on an intimate relationship with Sally. But it is wrong to prevent John and Sally from having the kind of relationship where such skills could be learned. Such a strategy would leave them indefinitely unable to initiate and sustain such a relationship. John and Sally need supportive adults who can help them process and learn from the experiences they are bound to have in their relationship.

As noted in other sections of the book, virtues for initiating and sustaining relationships of sexual intimacy which are poetic rather than institutional and reproductive are more complex than the virtue of sexual self-control. While some of these virtues can be taught, others develop by struggling with the trials that accompany intimate relationships. Thus, when parents or social workers prevent John and Sally from having these kinds of relationships, their disabilities remain.

John and Sally are both legal adults and have the legal right to the least restrictive environment possible. This should include the right to form relationships with as few restrictions as possible.

Sally's group home supervisor has been schooled in a psychosocial rehabilitation model of care and is committed to supporting Sally in her efforts to develop and acquire abilities such as those associated with intimate relationships. But the agency which sponsors the group home is reluctant to encourage workshops on sexual relationships. They fear negative public reaction. Sally would like to offer workshops in relationship skills to the members of the home, but she had not been given permission to do so. She feels this leaves many of the consumers of services ill equipped to make good decisions.

Sally's parents, however, are supportive of Sally's new relationship and encourage her to speak with the group home supervisor. In turn, they encourage the group home supervisor to elicit sharing from Sally. Sally's parents have talked with her about sex. They use developmentally appropriate language to explain the graces and risks/challenges of an intimate relationship.

Sally and John have the potential to develop the abilities necessary for making good decisions about intimate relationships, to honor each other's vulnerability, and to express mutuality poetically. However, these abilities must be cultivated and developed. Infantalizing forms of parental or human service care deprive them of one of the vital human graces, intimate love.

Sally and John may or may not ever be capable of formalizing their love in marriage, nor may they ever be capable of parenting, but this does not mean they are incapable of or unsuitable for sexual intimacy. Legally and, at least from the perspective of the ethic outlined in this book, sexual intimacy is not tied necessarily or merely to heterosexual-marital-and-reproductively-centered relationships. Thus, Sally and John should have a right to access the graces of mutuality in the form that best suits their personal dispositions.

Risks for pregnancy or disease warrant serious consideration. Sally and John need adequate information about contraception and safe sex. Unless they are under a conservatorship, the decision about contraception is ultimately theirs. Risk of untimely pregnancy is alone insufficient to prevent them from intimate time together. If this were so, we should be consistent and forbid other adults from forming intimate relationships. We assume that otherwise competent adults have abilities to make good decisions, to anticipate risks and prevent them, and to assume responsibility for their own well-being. Sally and John are developmentally disabled and undoubtedly have disabilities in these areas. But our obligation is not primarily that of assuming responsibility for John and Sally's decisions, but to support their acquisition of the abilities for good decision making (in this case, decision making about sexuality).

Since the sexual moral model out of which many have operated excludes the goodness of sexual intimacy outside of marriage, many have assumed that people like Sally and John just shouldn't have sexual intimacy since it is assumed they will never possess the abilities to initiate and sustain marriage. Moreover, since it is assumed by many that long-term and lifelong sexual abstinence is not harmful, there is little imperative to work hard to help Sally and John acquire the abilities they need to navigate the complexities of a sexually intimate relationship even outside of marriage. These paternalistic and beneficent attitudes prevent some kinds of harm, but they perpetuate other types. These other types of harms need to be included in the moral calculus!

Let's consider another example. Maria and Max are participants in a day program at a human service agency. Max lives in a group home. Maria lives with her parents. Max and Maria have grown fond of each other. They are both high functioning people with developmental disabilities.

Max and Maria have sustained an affectionate relationship for over a year. Max wants Maria to move in with him at the group home. He presents this idea to the group home manager who tells him that it is against policy to permit live-in relationships. The reason given is that the agency believes that live-in relationships should only be permitted in situations where individuals are capable of living on their own.

Max then asks if he can get an apartment on his own. His social workers and parents respond to the request with the sentiment that they do not believe he has the skills, yet, to manage his own apartment. It is thought that eventually he might learn those, but he still has a lot of work to do.

This may be an example of a case where policy restrictions interfere with Max's legal and moral rights. Since Max lacks some of the skills necessary for independent living, he might also lack some of the skills necessary for sustaining healthy committed sexual relationship. But it is not clear how the current policy serves the acquisition of those skills. It might be interesting to speculate whether Max's social workers and parents also consider Max's interest in living with Maria to be a wish rather than a need or good integral to Max's and Maria's well-being. The bias against the importance of sexual intimacy may undermine an aggressive and committed effort to support Max and Maria in developing new abilities.

Another example involves Joe and Pearl. Joe is a moderate to high functioning individual. Pearl is a moderate to lower functioning individual. Joe has had a lot of experience in relationships. Pearl has had very little. Joe and Pearl meet at a social hosted by the agency from which they obtain various types of support, including housing.

Pearl falls in love with Joe. Joe, however, has a tendency to be rather aggressive sexually. At first, Pearl doesn't mind, but eventually this bothers her, and she expresses her concern to her social worker.

The social worker, Ken, faces several challenges. On the one hand, he doesn't want to revert to paternalism, forbidding Joe from being with Pearl. Ken knows that the situation is a good opportunity for Pearl and Joe to develop new virtues for poetic intimacy. These lessons most probably would include teaching Pearl how to be firm with Joe in telling him what she does or doesn't want him to do sexually. She needs to learn the skills for protecting her own physical and emotional vulnerability.

Ken has to find ways to address Joe's attitudes, dispositions and practices. Can Joe be taught to be more sensitive, more respectful of Pearl's vulnerabilities? If this is possible, good. If not, should Ken intervene? Currently, Pearl doesn't have the necessary skills to resist Joe's advances. From an ethical point of view, she has a right to a safe environment and this probably means that social workers and human service providers need to intervene. But, again the bias of care should be toward that of helping Pearl acquire the skills to intervene for herself, otherwise she will remain disabled in this area.

The model of psychosocial rehabilitation with its bias toward enabling individuals to acquire skills necessary for assuming more responsibility for their lives includes more short term risks, but these are outweighed by the acquisition of abilities that reduce dependency and risks in the future. Moreover, as this model of support and care becomes more common, care for adolescents will include anticipation of adult self-determination. This should make it more imperative that social and relationship skills be learned earlier when risks are less serious and where parental supervision and oversight is morally appropriate.

The bias toward self-determination does not mean that others (providers of support services) do not have an obligation to prevent harm to people with developmental disabilities. People who have low functioning ability and/or who have limited capacity for developing basic abilities have a right to a safe and humane environment and need more support and supervision. This presents even more formidable challenges in the area of sexuality. Does an individual with little or no ability to navigate the complexities of sexual relationships and with little or no potential for acquiring such abilities have a right to sexual intimacy and its concomitant goods, particularly those associated with sexual pleasure and intimate touch? In such instances, risks often outweigh benefits and ordinarily must be prevented.

It has been assumed that sexual intimacy involves mutuality. Two individuals share sexual intimacy as an expression of a free gift of self. Gross inequalities of power usually render free consent either impossible or disingenuous. A person who is very low functioning (no matter his/her chronological age) presumably cannot give genuine consent. Giving substituted consent for such an individual to have sex would seem to be negligent since the individual doesn't have the basic abilities to protect his/her physical and emotional vulnerability.

The Poetics of Intimacy for People with Mental Illness

"Thirty-five to forty percent of people hospitalized for psychiatric disorders are discharged to live with spouses[2] and [that] more than half a million people with mental illness live with spouses."[3] Depression, bipolar disorder, schizophrenia, and other illnesses occur among married heterosexual partners, gay and lesbian couples, and among both heterosexual and homosexual couples who are dating. For the moment, we will consider the challenges and opportunities facing married or committed couples.

There are few studies which document the challenges couples face when one or both companions are diagnosed with a mental illness. A major study in 1987[4] identifies a number of problems couples face such as "difficulties concealing worries from their depressed partner, increased arguing, reduced displays of affection by the depressed partner, and sexual problems, including complete lack of sexual relationship."[5] Problems are exacerbated by the financial difficulties with which people with mental illness struggle and the social isolation such couples face.[6] Edie Mannion documents not only the burdens couples face but the resilience or abilities that develop in response to mental health challenges.

For example, while marriages affected by mental illness show higher than average rates of divorce and separation,[7] and while mental illness often strikes during critical stages of coupled life (courtship, new marriage, child rearing), spouses or companions of those diagnosed with mental illness talk about the development of new abilities or perspectives that enhanced their overall sense of personal and coupled well-being. These include improved personal qualities, enhanced coping effective-ness, better perspective, personal growth, a sense of contribution, and gratification.[8] Within the perspective of a poetics of intimacy, these developments confirm how intimate relationships have the capacity to be personally transformative, even when such relationships are not "ideal" or conventional.

Mannion cites evidence that spouses or companions of those diagnosed with mental illness report that had they known about the challenges beforehand, they would probably not have married. However, once married, they felt an obligation to accompany their spouse through the challenges of mental illness. Clearly, these relationships shift from romance-based to companionate-centered relationships.[9] This is confirmation that sexually intimate relationships have diverse poetic voices and that such diversity can even be part of established relationships. Indeed, the ability of people to cope with new challenges is, in part, a poetic one. Poetic sensibility includes the ability to imagine or reconceptualize the form of a relationship.

Conversely, Mannion reports some positive outcomes of divorce and separation for both partners including continued friendship and support after divorce and increased resilience and self-sufficiency of the mentally ill partner who must assume more responsibility for his/her life.[10]

The morality of divorce and separation is related to some of the same issues discussed earlier in chapter six, namely whether commitment is sustainable, whether the parties hold each other to the commitment, and whether competing obligations are more serious and urgent (one of those being an obligation to one's own well-being). In situations where mental illness is severe or where either spouse or companion does not have the requisite personal resources to sustain relationship given the challenges, there cannot be, in theory, a morally binding obligation. One or both spouses/companions may come to the conclusion that their personal well-being (or that of others to whom they are responsible: children, other relatives, etc.) is in jeopardy given the challenges of the situation. They may come to the conclusion that these other obligations take precedence.

More commonly, the diagnosis of mental illness for one of the parties of a committed relationship challenges the couple to re-imagine or rethink the relationship, and this is where a poetics of intimacy may be more helpful than conventional moral categories. Couples who have already begun to think of their relationship poetically, to consider the different seasons, dynamics, and contours of committed life together, already have the fundamental resources for contextualizing the moods, seasons, and episodes of mental illness. Let's consider some examples.

Katrina and Steve met at a large university on the East Coast. Katrina was working in financial aid; Steve was majoring in management of information systems. Steve was a in his third year at the university. Steve's prospects for work were quite good. He worked part-time at a financial securities firm. After dating for a year, they married. Shortly after graduation, Steve began to develop symptoms associated with schizophrenia and, shortly thereafter, suffered a major psychotic attack. He was diagnosed with schizophrenia and put on psychotropic medicine. After several months in the hospital, Steve was released to return home with Katrina.

Steve's illness was manageable with medicine, and he was able to return to work. However, episodically, his symptoms would worsen, requiring medical interventions and some hospital visits. Steve's medication included several side effects including decreased sexual libido and inability to maintain an erection during intercourse. He also felt frequent irritability and agitation which interfered with his ability to relax and be intimate with Katrina.

Although Katrina had never anticipated a marriage with such challenges, she had a lot of affection for Steve and was committed to working through the emotional ups and downs of life with Steve's illness. Through assistance from a reproductive-technology specialist, they successfully conceived a baby and subsequently, their relationship gradually took on a more companionate and institutional form.

Another couple, Linda and Mark, faced formidable challenges when, after several years of marriage, Linda confronted Mark with what she perceived to be a serious drinking problem. She threatened to leave if he didn't get some help. Mark was fortunate to have found a psychologist who diagnosed an underlying depressive disorder. Marks' abuse of alcohol was an attempt to mask the depression. Of course, it made it worse. With proper clinical treatment of the depression, Mark was able to get his drinking under control and saved his marriage.

Robert and Juan are two men who live in a supported housing program. They have both been diagnosed with schizophrenia. They suffer severe recurrent symptoms and require extensive medication to manage their illness. Both have been unable to hold jobs and receive disability payments from Social Security. Robert and Juan were friends and used to go with each other to social functions sponsored by the agency which manages their supported housing. They used to sit with each other and point out girls they'd like to met. Each would help the other garner enough courage to get up and ask some of the women to dance. Neither was particularly successful at sustaining relationships with women.

Robert liked sharing his feelings with Juan. He never really considered himself gay, but he found himself attracted to Juan more and more. Juan was quite handsome and, having come from Puerto Rico, more accustomed to affection, even between men. One evening, after a social, Juan invited Robert to his room for a visit. Juan put on some nice music and they both eased back just to enjoy the serenity of the evening. Juan got up to retrieve some pictures his family had sent him. When he sat next to Robert to show them to him, Robert felt himself become uncontrollably affectionate for Juan, reached over his leg, and began to stroke him.

Juan was put off at first, but then relaxed. He let Robert express his affection. For both it was an awkward moment. A long silence ensued. Eventually, Juan indicated to Robert that he was tired and that Robert had better leave.

Juan and Robert began to find excuses to spend time in each other's rooms where they would invariably become sexually intimate. They did not talk about what was happening with each other or with case workers.

Both feared the reaction of housemates who were accustomed to making jokes about "queers and faggots" and bragging about how they would beat anyone up they thought was gay.

These examples suggest that people diagnosed with mental illness experience sexuality along the same continuum as those who have never been so diagnosed. They experience similar challenges and promises associated with sexuality and sexual relationships.

In addition to similar challenges and promises, they face exacerbating ones such as cyclical or episodic recurrence of psychotic symptoms, mood disorders which affect relational stability, side effects of medication, and socially stigmatizing attitudes which leave couples and individuals more isolated.

Psychosocial rehabilitation practitioners can be limited by their own models of sexual virtue. If they can only imagine a sexually satisfying or sexually healthy relationship along either traditional heterosexual-marital-and-reproductively centered models or heterosexual romance-centered ones, then companionate, nonmarital or nonheterosexual relationships may not be supported as they should. Or, if they do not believe that sexual abstinence is personally harmful, they might encourage sexual abstinence as preferable to the risks or the complexity associated with sexual relationships involving people the mental illness. This is unfortunate for it leaves such individuals ill-served and ill-equipped to find grace and meaning in their own humanity and in their relationships.

Conclusions

People with developmental disabilities and those diagnosed with mental illness face challenges in reclaiming their humanity in a society which regretfully and far-too-often regards them as less-than-fully-human. Sexuality and intimacy are important and vital resources for personal well-being.

In this arguably brief treatment of sexuality and developmental disabilities and mental illness, it is important to highlight that resistance to both recognizing the right of people with developmental disabilities and mental illness to pursue and form sexual relationships stems, in part, from ignorance about the value of sexuality and intimacy in people's lives. Thus, we must do more to elicit personal narratives about sexuality and how it enables people to grow, to experience supportive and satisfying companionship/mutuality, to maintain greater emotional and psychological balance, and to obtain important and healthy touch and physical intimacy.

Second, without a poetic model of sexuality, psychosocial rehabilitation practitioners, social workers and educators will invariably let their own bias toward a heterosexual-marital-and-reproductively-centered model of sexuality influence decisions about the potential certain individuals have for satisfying and meaningful sexual lives.

Third, while some contemporary rights-based approaches to sexuality would affirm the right of people with developmental and mental disabilities to consent to sexual relationships, they often lack a vision for the kind of abilities and virtues that could sustain sexually intimate relationships. Hence, a poetics of intimacy is vital for complementing a rights-based or consent-based approach to sexual morality. Such an approach should inform rehabilitative counseling and curriculum content development.

Fourth, the design of support services for people with developmental disabilities and mental illness needs to do more to honor the relationships that individuals form, even if they do not correspond to human service providers' models of ideal sexual relationships. Obviously, this must, in turn, take into account the right of other individuals in these programs to a safe environment, free from sexual harassment or sexually intimidating activity.

Notes

[1] American Association on Mental Retardation, 1992. *Mental Retardation: Definition, classification, and systems supports* (9th edition). Washington, DC.

[2] Edie Mannion, "Resilience and Burden in Spouses of People with Mental Illness," *Psychiatric Rehabilitation Journal* Fall 1996, 20:2, pp. 13–23, p. 14 from K. Minkoff, "A Map of Chronic Mental Patients. In J.A. Talbott (Ed.), *The Chronic Mental Patient*, (pp. 11–37). Washington, DC: American Psychiatric Association.

[3] Ibid., citation of H.H. Goldman, "Mental Illness and Family Burden: A Public Health Perspective." *Hospital and Community Psychiatry*, 33, 557–560.

4   G. Fadden, P. Begginton, and L. Kuipers, "Caring and Its Burdens: A Study of the Spouses of Depressed Patients," *British Journal of Psychiatry*, 151, 660–667.

5   Mannion, Op. cit., p. 14.

6   Ibid., pp. 14–15.

7   Ibid., p. 15.

8   Ibid., pp. 16–18.

9   Wallerstein and Blakeslee, Op. cit.

10   Mannion, Op. cit., pp. 16–18.

❖ Chapter Nine

Conclusions: A Gospel (Good News) Sexual Ethic

The marvelous message of Christianity, that God is present with and in our humanity, has implications for how we think about human sexuality. Although death relativizes the ultimate importance of our present earthly embodied existence, motivating us to think about an other-worldly existence after death, the Christian incarnation (God taking on human existence in Jesus) calls us to celebrate the fact that we do not need to leave our bodies or our current earthly material lives in order to encounter God.

Jesus, as both fully human and fully divine, is an example of human excellence, an excellence built not on the escape from human nature in order to share in God's being, but an excellence in which God's grace/presence enables us to live out our humanity in all of its rich capacity.

Jesus showed us that cultivating intimacy with God is not primarily a matter of religious asceticism, particularly an asceticism of withdrawal (although we all need solitude periodically). Cultivating intimacy with God requires living intimately with others and with ourselves.

One of the premises of this book is that sexuality is our embodied capacity for intimacy. Sexuality is the body's way of yearning for intimacy (or mutuality, as most poignantly developed by Carter

Heyward). Sexuality is our embodied capacity to be self-disclosive, to actually communicate on an intimate level with others.

While there are many types of intimate relationships and various levels of intimacy, sexually intimate relationships are those which have the greatest capacity to root out personal mystifications (self-concepts built upon what we thought we had to be like in order to be loved), enabling us to love with greater integrity and authenticity.

Since Christianity teaches that the greatest mark of human excellence is love, and if love has to do with relationships where each party is loved as he/she is and not in response to how we or others want them to be, then rooting out personal mystifications is an important process for realizing the Christian ideal. I can't love others with integrity or be loved by others with integrity if my love is motivated by personal mystifications which I either project onto myself or onto others.

If sexually intimate relationships are those which have the greatest capacity to move our love toward a more genuine and authentic form, then long-term or lifelong sexual abstinence poses a serious risk to Christian life. Not only does it deprive individuals of a rich context for personal growth in the virtue around which Christian life is centered (love), but it also deprives them of other natural human blessings such as touch, companionship, mutuality, and support.

As noted in other areas of the text, some individuals have access to extraordinary resources or circumstances where they are able to grow in personal authenticity, love with greater integrity, and be intimate with self and others in ways that are nonsexual or nongenital.

Also as noted, there are individuals for whom sexually intimate relationships may represent other risks or harms much more serious than those posed by their absence. For these individuals, temporary, long-term and lifelong sexual abstinence may be preferable.

But for most people, sexually intimate relationships remain a vital resource for personal transformation, for love, for touch, and for social bonding. If Christian morality seeks to foster human flourishing, well-being or excellence, then mandatory or imposed long-term and/or lifelong sexual abstinence is immoral because it deprives individuals of a resource without which most cannot achieve the flourishing, well-being or excellence to which they are called.

Traditional Christian sexual morality expects the divorced, gay men and lesbians, single adults, and many individuals with various types of disabilities, to practice long-term or lifelong sexual abstinence. These expectations were developed at a time when the model of human nature was more essentialistic and dualistic and when the model of marriage was heterosexual-marital-patriarchal-household-management-and-repro-ductively-centered.

Our model of human nature is less essentialistic/dualistic and more metaphorical or poetic and our model of marriage and other committed sexual relationships is centered around covenantal mutuality and intimacy. Thus, not only is the control of sexual desire and pleasure not a primary constituent good of human excellence, but the kinds of virtues or abilities needed to sustain modern committed sexual relationships are more varied and complex.

Thus, we need a new approach to sexual ethics that corresponds to new models of human nature and committed sexual relationships. We need to help young adults become poets of intimacy. This cannot happen if the primary objective of sexuality education and sexual morality is abstinence before and outside of marriage.

As noted earlier, premature sexual involvement for adolescents poses serious risks for sexual trauma, emotional trauma, and disassociative approaches to sexuality and intimacy. However, a significant amount of premature adolescent sexual involvement stems from earlier childhood issues where children's physical boundaries were not respected, where children were abused, where children were seriously mystified or where they did not get sufficient good touch and love.

Young adults, those seventeen and older, need to establish successful narratives of poetic intimacy. Long-term sexual abstinence, particularly if built solely upon the virtue of sexual self-control, poses serious risks for leaving young adults ill-equipped to make informed choices about marriage/committed sexual relationships, and ill-prepared to become sufficiently vulnerable to sustain an intimacy-based model of marriage/committed sexual relationship.

There are significant risks associated with forcing the divorced to remain sexually abstinent for the rest of their lives. These include the loss of sustaining relationships of intimacy and touch as well as the loss of the ordinary context whereby these individuals might continue to grow to love with greater integrity and depth. Christianity does not serve these individuals by prohibiting remarriage nor has the ban of remarriage had any impact on decreasing the incidence of divorce. Contemporary divorce rates are less a consequence of decreased respect for marriage and more the symptom of a greater inherent fragility of intimacy-based marriages and quite possibly the consequence of an inadequate sexual ethic which has done little to enable young adults to acquire the kinds of sexual virtues that would sustain intimacy-based relationships.

Gay men and lesbians have the same need for committed sexual relationships as do heterosexual men and women. Since sociological evidence now overwhelmingly shows that gay men and lesbians are able to achieve the same kind of relational well-being and grace as heterosexuals, the continued Christian expectation that gay men and lesbians practice lifelong sexual abstinence is nothing more than culpable prejudice. It is analogous to the earlier Roman Catholic failure to take seriously clear and certain reason put forth by Galileo for a heliocentric or even non-centric universe. Human sexuality is not heterocentric or patriarchal. Human sexuality is biologically and culturally varied. People can and need to achieve sexual identity in different ways. The imposition of heterocentric and patriarchal models of sexual virtue on everyone is harmful and undermining of many people's personal and social well-being.

People with various kinds of diasabilities also have a need for intimacy, for touch and for companionship. While some individuals may lack basic capacities to sustain committed sexual relationships and/or marriage, this should not disqualify them from establishing other kinds of sexually intimate relationships which may be more poetically suitable to their lives. Human service providers need to adopt a poetic approach to sexual morality as a way of rethinking the validity of different kinds of relationships, as a way of reforming sexuality education components of services, and as a way of developing rehabilitative and supportive services that take such relationships into consideration.

In summary, anthropological and cultural shifts have precipitated a profound revolution or paradigm shift in human sexuality. During times of such change, we often do what we can to upgrade previous models and ethical norms to accommodate changes, but at some point the new paradigm requires more than superficial changes. We must begin to think about sexuality not from a heterocentric, patriarchal, household-management or reproductively-centered perspective. We must begin to think about sexuality from the perspective of a poetics of intimacy. We must ask how we can best support the human project of learning how to love and be loved with greater depth and integrity in accord with the poetic character of our personal, relational, social and spiritual lives.

Anything less falls short of enabling human excellence in our age and does not merit being associated with Christianity whose mission is to proclaim good news to human beings!

Since there is a reciprocal relationship between Christian anthropology, Christian theology and Christian ethics, new models of sexual virtue are grounded in new models of God and new models of relationship with God. We have used the idea of a perfect, self-possessed and unchanging being, God, to motivate our own efforts for perfection, self-possession and the suppression of unsettledness. Relationship with such a being requires asceticism, containment of sexual desire and emotions, and a single-heartedness which is not compatible with the complexity of intimate human relationships. This is why the ascetical celibate has been held up in the traditional Christian thought as a moral paradigm.

A return to Biblical metaphorical language about God helps complement rationalistic models prevalent in Greek philosophy (which so heavily influenced early Christian theology). Process theology and new efforts by physicists to think about God in scientific cosmological frameworks may also help to develop models of God which are more relational and dynamic. These, in turn, might help us embrace more relational and dynamic models of human excellence.

Thus, if truth is viewed as less static and absolute and more relational, dynamic and evolving, the moral ideals which motivated sexual abstinence will have less metaphysical or theological appeal and basis. The use of sexual abstinence to achieve control over the ever deepening and transcending being that we are, the use of sexual abstinence to avoid the complexity and unsettledness of relational life, the use of sexual abstinence to achieve single-hearted devotion to an absolute, detached and perfect Being are, at root, futile and misplaced. All of these efforts eclipse the poetic or metaphorical character of our humanity, of our relationships and ultimately of the ground of being, God.

A poetics of intimacy is not only an approach to enriching our own capacity to love with greater integrity and depth, it is also the lens through which we grow to see the world and God in their poetic richness. In this sense, human sexuality is a type of mystagogy, teaching us and inviting us to participate intimately in the being and wonder of God.

❖ Bibliography

Aarons, Leroy. *Prayers for Bobby: A Mother's Coming to Terms with the Suicide of Her Gay Son.* San Francisco: HarperSanFrancisco, 1995.

Allen, Joseph. *Love and Conflict: A Covenantal Model of Christian Ethics.* Nashville: Abingdon Press, 1984.

"Always Our Children," National Conference of Catholic Bishops, October, 1997.

Augustine. *Against Julian.*

———. *De fide et operibus.*

Barnard, K.E. and Brazelton, T. B. (eds.) *Touch: The Foundation of Experience.* Madison: International Universities Press, 1990.

Baum, Gregory. *Religion and Alienation.* New York: Paulist Press, 1975.

Bagley, Christopher and Tremblay, Pierre, "Suicide Watch," in *The Advocate,* Nov. 12, 1996, Faculty of Social Work, Univ. of Calgary.

Basil the Great. *Epistola* 199 ("ad Amphilochium").

Boswell, John. *Christianity, Social Tolerance, and Homosexuality.* Chicago: Univ. of Chicago Press, 1980.

———. *Same-Sex Unions in Premodern Europe.* New York: Villard Books, 1994.

Bozett, Frederick W. *Gay and Lesbian Parents.* New York: Prager, 1987.

Bradshaw, John. *Creating Love.* New York: Bantam, 1992.

Brown, Peter. *The Body and Society: Men, Women, and Sexual Renunciation in Early Christianity.* New York: Columbia Univ. Press, 1988.

Buber, Martin. *I and Thou.* trans. Ronald Smith. New York: Collier, 1986.

Bullough, Vern L. *Science in the Bedroom: A History of Sex Research.* New York: Basic Books, 1994.

Calvin, John. *Commentary on Genesis.*

———. *Divine Institutes.*

Carey, John J. (ed.) *The Sexuality Debate in North American Churches: 1988-1995: Controversies, Unresolved Issues, Future Prospects.* Lewiston: Edwin Mellon Press, 1995.

Carr, David. *Time, Narrative, and History.* Bloomington: Indiana University Press, 1986.

Clement of Alexandria. *Christ the Educator.*

Countryman, William. *Dirt, Greed, and Sex: Sexual Ethics in the New Testament and Their Implications for Today.* Philadelphia: Fortress Press, 1988.

Crosby, Michael. *Celibacy: Means of Control or Mandate of the Heart.* Notre Dame: Ave Maria Press, 1996.

———. *The Dysfunctional Church.* Notre Dame: Ave Maria Press, 1991.

Crossan, Dominic. *Jesus: A Revolutionary Biography.* San Francisco: Harper SanFrancisco, 1994.

Damian, Peter. *De Celibatu Sacerdotum.*

Davis, Walter. *Inwardness and Existence: Subjectivity in/and Hegel, Heidegger, Freud, and Marx.* Madison: Univ. of Wisconsin Press, 1991.

Demasio, Antonio. *Descartes' Error: Emotion, Reason and the Human Brain.* New York: Grosset/Putnam, 1994.

deWall, Frans. *Good Natured.* Cambridge, MA: Harvard Univer. Press, 1996.

"Divorce, Marriage, and the Church," The Report of a Commission Appointed by the Archbishop of Cantebury. London: SPCK, 1972.

Ellison, Marvin M. *Erotic Justice: A Liberating Ethic of Sexuality.* Louise-ville, KY: Westminster John Knox Press, 1996.

Fadden, G, Begginton, P, and Kuipers, L. "Caring and Its Burdens: A Study of the Spouses of Depressed Patients," *British Journal of Psychiatry*, 151, 660-667.

Fanslow, Cathleen A., "Touch and the Elderly," in *Touch: The Foundation of Human Experience* ed. K. E. Barnard and T. B. Brazelton. Madison: International Universities Press, 1990.

Farley, Margaret. *Personal Commitments: Beginning, Keeping, Changing.* San Francisco: Harper Collins, 1986.

———. "An Ethic of Same Sex Relations," *A Challenge to Love*, ed. Robert Nugent. New York; Crossroad Pub., 1989.

Farley, Wendy. *Eros for the Other: Retaining Truth in a Pluralistic World.* Penn State Univ. Press, 1996.

Flaks, David K. et al., "Lesbians Choosing Motherhood: A Comparative Study of Lesbian and Heterosexual Parents and Their Children," *Developmental Psychology* 31:1, 1995.

Foucault, Michael. *History of Sexuality: Volume 2, The Use of Pleasure.* New York: Pantheon Books, 1978.

Fox, Matthew. *A Spirituality Named Compassion.* Minneapolis: Winston Press, 1979.

———. *Original Blessing.* Santa Fe: Bear, 1983.

———. *Whee, Wee, We: A Guide to a Sensual, Prophetic Spirituality.* Santa Fe: Bear, 1981.

Furnish, Victor Paul, "Homosexual Practices in Biblical Perspective," in *The SexualityDebate in North American Churches*, ed. J.J. Carey.

Gold, Michael. *Does God Belong in the Bedroom?* Philadelphia: Jewish Publication Society, 1992.

Goldmann, H.H. "Mental Illness and Family Burden: A Public Health Perspective," *Hospital and Community Psychiatry*, 33, 557-660.

Gove, W., Briggs-Style, C., and Hughes, M., "The Effect of Marriage on the Well-Being of Adults," *Journal of Family Issues* 11 (1) March 1990, pp. 4–35.

Gudorf, Christine. *Body, Sex, and Pleasure.* Cleveland: Pilgrim Press, 1994.

Guindon, Andre. *The Sexual Language.* Ottawa: Univ. of Ottawa Press, 1977.

———. *The Sexual Creators.* New York: University of America Press, 1986.

Hammer, Dean. and Peter Copeland. *The Science of Desire: The Search for the Gay Gene and the Biology of Behavior.* New York: Simon and Schuster, 1994

Hartwig, Michael, "Parenting Ethics and Reproductive Technologies," in *Journal of Social Philosophy* vol. 26:1, Spring, 1995.

———. "Galileo, Gene Researchers and the Ethics of Homosexuality," in *Theology and Sexuality*, 1:1, September, 1994.

Hatfield, Robert, "Touch and Sexuality," *Human Sexuality: An Encyclopedia*. ed. by Bullough, V., Bullough, B., and Stein, A. New York: Garland Pub., 1994.

Heidegger, Martin. *Being and Time*, trans. John McQuarrie and William Richardson. New York: 1962.

Hegel, G. F. *The Phenomenology of Spirit*, trans. A. V. Miller. New York : Oxford University Press, 1977.

Heyward, Carter. *Touching Our Strength: The Erotic as the Power and Love of God*. San Francisco: Harper Collins, 1989.

Hogan, Richar M. and LeVoir, John M. *Covenant of Love*. San Francisco: Ignatius Press, 1992.

Jerome. *Epistles*.

Jordan, Mark. *The Invention of Sodomy in Christian Theology*. Chicago: Univ. of Chicago Press, 1997.

Jung, Patricia Beattie and Smith, Ralph F. *Heterosexism: An Ethical Challenge*. New York: SUNY Press, 1993.

Keenan, James F., "Proposing Cardinal Virtues," *Theological Studies* 56 (1995) pp. 709–729.

Kopfensteiner, Thomas R., "The Metaphorical Structure of Normativity," *Theological Studies* 58 (1997) pp. 331–346.

Lamanna, Mary Ann and Agnes Riedmann. *Marriages and Families: Making Choices and Facing Change*. Belmont, CA: Wadsworth, 1994.

Laumann, E. O., Gagnon, J. H., Michael, R. T., and Michaels, S. *The Social Organization of Sexuality*. Chicago: Univ. of Chicago Press, 1994.

Lawler, Ronald, Boyle, Joseph, and May, William E. *Catholic Sexual Ethics: A Summary, Explanation, and Defense*. Huntington: Our Sunday Visitor Press, 1996.

Lebacqz, Karen, "Appropriate Vulnerability," *Sexuality and the Sacred*, ed. James Nelson and Sandra Longfellow. Louisville: Westminster/John Knox Press, 1994.

LeDoux, Joseph. *The Emotional Brain.* New York: Simon and Schuster, 1996.

LeVay, Simon. *Queer Science: The Use and Abuse of Research into Homosexuality.* Cambridge: MIT Press, 1996.

———. *The Sexual Brain.* Cambridge, MA: MIT Press, 1993.

Levinas, Emmanuel. *Totality and Infinity,* trans. Alphonso Lingis. Pittsburgh: Duquesne Univ. Press, 1969.

Lorde, Audre. *Sister Outsider: Essays and Speeches.* Trumansburg, NY: Crossing Press, 1984.

Luther, Martin. *Babylonian Captivity of the Church.*

Mackin, Theodore. *Divorce and Remarriage.* New York: Paulist Press, 1984.

Mannion, Edie. "Resilience and Burden in Spouses with Mental Illness," *Psychiatric Rehabilitation Journal.* 20:2 (Fall 1996) 13-23.

May, William F. "Code and Covenant or Philanthropy and Contract?" *Ethics in Medicine: Historical Perspectives and Contemporary Concerns.*

McAnarney, Elizabeth R., "Adolescents and Touch," *Touch:The Foundation of Experience.* eds.T. E. Barnard and T. B. Brazelton. Madison: Inter-national Universities Press, 1990. pp. 497–515.

McFague, Sallie. *Metaphorical Theology.* Philadelphia: Fortress Press, 1982.

———. *Models of God.* Philadelphia: Fortress Press, 1987.

McPherson Oliver, Mary Anne. *Conjugal Sprituality: The Primacy of Mutual Love in Christian Tradition.* Kansas City: Sheed and Ward, 1994.

Meeks, Wayne. *The Origins of Christian Morality.* New Haven: Yale Univ. Press, 1993.

Montagu, Ashley. *Touching: The Human Significance of the Skin.* New York: Harper and Row, 1986.

Moore, Thomas. *Soul Mates.* San Francisco: Harper Collins, 1994.

———. *The Soul of Sex.* New York: HarperCollins, 1998.

Murdoch, Iris. *The Sovereignty of the Good.* London: Routledge, Kegan, Paul, 1970.

Nelson, James. *Embodiment.* Minneapolis: Augsburg, 1978.

Ogden, Shubert. "The Reality of God," *Process Theology.* ed. E. H. Cousins. New York: Paulist Press, 1971.

Origen. *Select. in Ezech.*

Palmer, Helen. *The Enneagram in Love and Work: Understanding Your Intimate and Business Relationships.* New York: Harper Collins, 1995.

"Pastoral Care of Homosexual Persons," Congregation for the Doctrine of the Faith," Vatican, 1986.

Peck, Scott. *A World Waiting to be Born.* New York: Bantam Books, 1993.

Pearlin, L. and J. Johnson. "Marital Status, Life Strains and Depression," *American Sociology Review* 42:704-715.

Phipps, William E. *The Sexuality of Jesus.* Cleveland: Pilgrim Press, 1996.

Pinckaers, Servais. *The Sources of Christian Ethics,* trans. Sr. Mary Thomas Noble. Washington, D.C.: Catholic University of America Press, 1995.

Pope Gregory II. *Epistola* 14 ("ad Bonifacium").

Pope John Paul II. *"Familiaris Consortio."*

———. "Lessons from the Galileo Case," *Origins,* Nov. 12, 1992.

Rahner, Karl. *Foundations of Christian Faith: An Introduction to the Idea of Christianity,* trans. William V. Dych. New York: Seabury Press, 1978.

Ranke-Heinemann, Uta. *Eunuchs for the Kingdom of Heaven: Women, Sexuality,and the Catholic Church.* trans. Peter Heinegg. New York: Penguin Books, 1990.

Riley, Gregory J. *One Jesus, Many Christs: How Jesus Inspired Not One True Christianity But Many.* San Francisco: Harper Collins, 1998.

Sadownik, Douglas, "Outrageous Behavior," in *Frontiers,* June 13, 1997.

Schuster, Mark. "Impact of a High School Condom Availability Program on Sexual Attitudes and Behaviors." Alan Guttmacher Institute, 1998.

Sex Information and Education Council of the United States, "Guidelines for Comprehensive Sexuality Education," 1991.

Sears, James T., "Dilemmas and Possibilities of Sexuality Education" *Sexuality and the Curriculum,* ed. James T. Sears. New York: Teachers College Press, 1992.

Sipe, A. W. Richard. *Sex, Priests and Power: Anatomy of a Crisis.* New York: Brunner/Mazel, 1994.

———. *A Secret World: Sexuality and the Search for Celibacy.* New York: Brunner/Mazel, 1990.

Smith, Janet. *Humanae Vitae: A Generation Later.* Washington: Catholic University Press, 1991.

Solomon, Robert, "Sex and Perversion," in R. Baker and F. Elliston (eds.). *Philosophy and Sex.* Buffalo: Prometheus, 1975.

Spong, John Shelby. *Liberating the Gospels.* San Francisco: HarperSan Francisco, 1996.

Stark, Rodney. *The Rise of Christianity.* San Francisco: Harper Collins, 1997.

Sullivan, Andrew, "Introduction," *Same Sex Marriage: Pro and Con.* ed. Andrew Sullivan. New York: Vintage Books, 1997.

———. *Love Undetectable: Notes on Friendship, Sex and Survival.* New York: Knoff, 1998.

———. *Virtually Normal: An Argument About Homosexuality.* New York: Alfred A. Knopf, 1995.

Tertullian. *Adversus Marcionem.*

Thomas Aquinas. *Summa Theologica*, IIaIIae.

"The Truth and Meaning of Human Sexuality," Vatican Commission on the Family.

Vacek, Edward Collins. *Love, Human and Divine: The Heart of Christian Ethics.* Washington, D.C., Georgetown University Press, 1994.

Vendler, Helen. *Poems, Poets, Poetry: An Introduction and Anthology.* Boston: Bedford Books, 1997.

Verbrugge, Lois M., "Marital Status and Health," *Journal of Marriage and the Family* 41: 267–285.

Wallerstein, Judith and Blakeslee, Sandra. *The Good Marriage.*

Wojtyla, Karol. *The Acting Person*, trans. Andrzej Potocki, *Analecta Husserliana*, vol. 10. Boston: D. Reidel Pub., 1979.

———. *Love and Responsibility*, trans. H. T. Willets. New York: Farrar, Straus, Giroux, 1981.

Wrenn, Lawrence G., "Marriage—Indissoluble or Fragile?" in *Divorce and Remarriage in the Catholic Church*, ed. L.G. Wrenn. New York: Paulist Press, 1973.

❖ Index